T0244104

THE ARMISTICE DAY KILLING

THE ARMISTICE DAY KILLING

THE DEATH OF
TOMMY BALL
AND THE LIFE OF THE MAN WHO SHOT HIM

COLIN BROWN

First published by Pitch Publishing, 2022

Pitch Publishing
9 Donnington Park,
85 Birdham Road,
Chichester,
West Sussex,
PO20 7AJ
www.pitchpublishing.co.uk
info@pitchpublishing.co.uk

ISBN 978 1 80150 107 1

Typesetting and origination by Pitch Publishing

Printed and bound in Great Britain by TJ Books Ltd

Contents

In memory of my late father Bert Brown, a Nechells lad from Cook Street, who attended his first match at Villa Park as a tenth birthday present in December 1922 and who passed away in 2017 at the age of 104. Up to the time of his death, he was probably the last surviving person to have seen Tommy Ball play.

Acknowledgements

I AM grateful for the text and narrative vetting voluntarily undertaken by personal contacts.

My friend and neighbour, long-serving CID officer Steve Jones, was able to offer appropriate guidance and correction on policing procedures. On the legal side, my fellow tai chi camp follower, criminal barrister Matthew Dunford, gave clarity on several matters of fact, while family solicitor Graham Ettinger offered wise counsel on aspects relating to libel.

The football angles were checked by my close friend of over 50 years, former work colleague, flat-mate and next-door neighbour in the Doug Ellis Lower, Christopher Turner. My son-in-law, Damian Barrett, who has on several occasions seen forward action 'under the flag' with the Royal Marines in Central Asia and the Middle East, offered well-informed opinion on ballistics.

I am similarly indebted to the several professionals and volunteers who willingly undertook specialist research at my request, and their names are recorded at the conclusion of the book.

The not insignificant task of checking my grammar and formatting was undertaken by good friends Andy and Liz Morton. Any errors will have been inserted by me during final text revisions.

It is important to record the encouragement given at the outset by my *Heroes and Villains* editor Dave Woodhall, and that consistently given by Perry Barr resident Dot Ryan, with whom Dave unknowingly put me in touch. Dot has subsequently spent many hours keeping Tommy Ball's grave in good order.

I was lucky to have a publisher in Jane Camillin who kept faith in me over an extended run-in period and offered necessary patience to a rookie publishing for the first time, and I thank Duncan Olner whose cover design was a formidable reading of my mind.

Several persons kindly granted permission for the publication of photographs, and I am grateful to Christopher Turner, Nick Brown, Kat Barrett, Dot Ryan, members of the extended Stagg family and to Vanessa Smith of the Strategic Property Unit at Staffordshire County Council.

Vintage Aston Villa photographs were acquired from the Albert Wilkes Archive at Colorsport, which was highly appropriate as 1920s sports photographer Wilkes was a former Villa and England centre-half. My thanks to Andy Cowie who painstakingly searched the company archives, and to Simon Inglis for kindly pointing me in the right direction.

Heartfelt thanks are due to my late wife Christine, who encouraged me to become involved with this work and who enthusiastically joined me on my initial research-led trip to County Durham. Appreciation is also due to fourth-generation Aston Villa enthusiasts Nick Brown and Kat Barrett who have given unstinting support through often difficult times.

Finally, I have never had any intention of benefitting financially from this venture and am more than happy to ensure any author royalties forthcoming are directed towards the charity Acorns Children's Hospice. Acorns has a long history of partnership with the Aston Villa club, and I am delighted to receive their endorsement and thank their supporter services officer Andrea Murphy for her good offices in expediting the present arrangement. I would encourage everyone turning up to watch matches at Villa Park to give generously to the charity's regular street collectors.

Introduction

MOST SERIOUS football enthusiasts, whether Aston Villa fans or not, are broadly aware of the story of Thomas Edger 'Tommy' Ball, a former coal miner, born in 1900 and signed from colliery football by Aston Villa in February 1920.

Ball holds the dubious distinction of being, in November 1923, the only active British professional football player deemed in law to have been murdered. Many will have visited his grave in St John's churchyard in Perry Barr on Birmingham's northern edge and many more will have read internet accounts of the killing or come across it as a footnote within various books covering Villa's history.

Few will know much, let alone care, about Ball's convicted killer, a middle-aged former soldier and policeman named George Stagg. Fewer still will have an awareness of the controversies that surrounded Stagg's conviction and imprisonment.

The known factual outline is straightforward enough. On the evening of Armistice Day, 11 November 1923, Ball went out from his rented home in Perry Barr, then a largely rural area to the immediate north of Aston, for an evening drink with his wife Beatrice. Sometime after his return, and in circumstances and for reasons never fully established, he was shot dead by Stagg who was his next-door neighbour and landlord.

Though it was never in doubt that Stagg fired the fatal shot, no one knows for certain what happened, or why it happened. Apart from Stagg himself, the only other person who may have witnessed the shooting was his wife Mary. As was her legal right as spouse of an accused person, Mary, for reasons that were unclear at the time, declined to appear in court.

In February 1924, following no fewer than five legal hearings in little over three months, Stagg was convicted of murder at the Stafford Winter Assize. Despite a plea for 'mercy' from the jury, he was sentenced to be hanged.

A month later, the sentence was sensationally commuted by the country's first Labour Party home secretary to life imprisonment. Following a few years in Parkhurst Prison, Stagg was committed to Broadmoor Hospital as insane and died in 1966 in Highcroft Hospital, a mental institution in Erdington, which stood barely a 15-minute drive from the Aston Villa club's stadium.

The combination of professional sport, death by shooting, courtroom drama and high politics has in recent years re-emerged as attractive to feature writers, essayists and football historians discovering the story. There is no shortage of internet leads to follow up, though most new accounts, many doubtless subject to editorial word-count limitations, have not been investigative but have drawn heavily on what has been written before. This has inevitably meant that in places historical fact and long-established folk speculation have become entwined.

Initially, my sole aim in taking an investigative approach was to present as accurate a picture of the affair as the surviving evidence allowed: I had no greater ambition than to feature it as a one-off essay within my then regular submissions to the *Heroes and Villains* street-sale fanzine. It soon outgrew that aim, and, as I became drawn into the personalities within the drama, I decided to take a fresh interpretative look at the case in its entirety and to correct the narrative wherever I felt it had been previously misrepresented or misunderstood.

The 'sharp end' of this aim has been to use the evidence with which I have worked to offer an informed personal interpretation of the events of 11 November 1923.

As I began to sift the evidence, a secondary aim presented itself. Rather than following the traditional pattern of concentrating on the loss to Aston Villa of a good player who might have gone on to represent England, I decided to look more closely at the many other persons involved. Within this aim, I thought it worth making a more searching appraisal of Ball's killer, about whom a surprising amount of contemporary material survives. Consequently, the enlarged scope of my work took the book from being simply 'the death of Tommy Ball' to a hopefully more rounded and balanced view of the tragedy.

My third aim has been to take a critically enquiring look at the legalities surrounding the case history and at the interlocking contemporary political situation that determined Stagg's fate. Given the natural sympathies for Ball and his widow that the story presents, and which all readers will certainly share, most people at the time, and perhaps to the present day, would probably have considered Stagg's 1924 death sentence to have been only right and proper. My research, however, has thrown up concerns as to whether the judicial process was handled with the even-handedness that any accused person, in any age, has the right to expect.

I have been made very aware of the cloud that the tragedy still casts over many lives. Although it would be spurious to mask the identities of those alive in 1923, out of respect for sensibilities

I have refrained from identifying living descendants. In the interests of accuracy, I have included house numbers of properties pertinent to the narrative.

I feel certain there is more to be uncovered, including, potentially, any recorded oral statements that may have been made by Stagg to authorities during his time in prison or in mental institutions. If such evidence exists, it remains elusive owing to legal time limits over record disclosure. In addition, there will certainly be family stories from all sides which, should they come to light, might substantially alter narrative and interpretation. I fully welcome that.

Perhaps this book will prompt the emergence of those stories. Should there be demand for a reprint, anyone contacting me via my publisher can be assured that any new information that justifies reappraisal, expansion or alteration of the present text will be represented.

Colin Brown, January 2022

Part 1

Tommy Ball – From Coal Dust to Stardust

Spotted

We can perhaps imagine the excitement in the Ball household on the morning of Saturday, 17 January 1920 when the knock of the Aston Villa scout on the door at 48 Reservoir Street, Wardley Colliery, Gateshead, was awaited. The expected visitor was coming with the forms to finalise the transfer of the Balls' second-youngest son, Tommy, from a colliery football side in Gateshead to the country's most successful professional club in the relatively short history of the association football game.

Joseph Ball, a Durham-born miner of Irish descent, and his wife Euphemia had only recently moved to Wardley, but had brought up nine children, seven boys and two girls, born between 1883 and 1904, in the County Durham pit village of Usworth. The village lies some eight miles to the north of Chester-le-Street and was one of a concentration of Durham coalfield pit villages wedged between Newcastle upon Tyne and Gateshead to the west and Sunderland on the east coast.

Aston Villa fans reading this may smile wryly to learn that several previous chroniclers, doubtless confusing the name with the club's extremely brief 1998 signing from Everton FC, have chosen to refer to the village as Unsworth.

The aspiring footballer, Thomas Edger Ball, was born on 11 February 1900 at 7 High Row, Usworth Colliery. His eldest brother, Joseph, was later killed in the Great War and Tommy's other older brothers, David, John, James and Hubert, all lads in their 20s and 30s working in the mines, only Tommy and younger brother, Norman, remained at home. Daughters Elizabeth and another Euphemia, had also married and moved on, and by 1921 only Tommy's younger brother, Norman, and himself inevitably a collier, was still at home.

With its two bedrooms and maybe a box room, High Row would have presented considerable comfort difficulties for such a large family. Limited sleeping, washing and toilet facilities would certainly have offset the value of sharing a home with a supportive kinship group. Nor was there an abundance of cash around, and career prospects, at least for the menfolk, were generally limited to employment in one of the local pits, a career that especially, for underground workers, carried with it an ever-present risk of injury or death.

Sometime before 1911, the family had eased their overcrowding with what may have been a dream move into a house containing eight rooms, so providing that essential additional sleeping space. This was just five minutes around the corner at 36 Douglas Terrace and close to their eldest son and his family at number 45. This was not far for daughter-in-law Sarah to run to in tears while clutching her black-edged telegram in February 1916.

High Row, which still exists, and the now demolished Douglas Terrace home were then 'tied' houses belonging to Usworth Colliery, and such dwellings were a common 'win-win' for the pit bosses who owned them. The workers virtually lived on the job and the many male, and some female, children formed a production line of ready labour, while a percentage of their wages went straight back to the colliery owner in the form of rent.

To offset the amount of rent each might have to contribute for separate houses, many fathers would want to keep their youngsters in the family home for as long as possible, even when married, while a great many pit workers would stay in their jobs into their late 60s or 70s for fear of eviction once retired. Colliery widows were always vulnerable to destitution and a trip to the workhouse, especially those younger women, such as Tommy's sister-in-law Sarah Ball, whose husbands had been killed underground or in the war and who, like her, still had a houseful of bairns to look after.

It has always been assumed that the Balls lived in Usworth at the time of Tommy's move to Aston Villa, but the newly released census for 1921 shows that at some point after 1911, with diminishing numbers at home, they had moved into a presumably much smaller tied cottage attached to a colliery in near-neighbouring Gateshead. The move, I would guess around 1915, was probably made possible after Joseph's work transfer to Wardley Colliery and it is known that Tommy began to make his name playing for that pit's football team before moving on to the neighbouring Felling Colliery side.

When the opportunity for the move to Aston came, it would have created something of a sensation in the Usworth area. To be asked to join a team some distance away, though not rare, did not happen every day and, with due respect to both Sunderland and Newcastle United who were both giants of the game, for the buying team to be the country's premier pre-war side would have been beyond most people's wildest dreams.

For historians of the game, Tommy was not the only player with Usworth connections to end up at Aston Villa. In 1937, the club signed Ronnie Starling who had previously worked in the village pit and had been picked up by Hull City in 1925 after he had moved to nearby Washington Colliery. Ronnie was 11 and living in Pelaw, next door to Wardley, when Tommy went to Villa and would certainly have known about the move and pondered the glamour and riches that lay in the world beyond the pit villages.

The Colour of Money

As Tommy, when on the point of signing for Aston Villa, was not quite 21 years of age, he was still below his legal 'majority' and it was his father's responsibility to undertake negotiations and approve the contract. Preliminary discussions had doubtless taken place between Aston Villa's representative and Mr Ball senior in the company of Felling Colliery FC club officials. Tommy's guaranteed wages and bonuses would have been established and the small matter of a fee to the Felling club, who held Tommy's professional registration, would have been agreed.

Thereafter, a few unofficial loose ends to 'look after' the Ball family would have remained to be tied up before the contract was signed. Despite wanting the best for their lad, the Balls would have been acutely aware of how much money Mrs Ball would lose in weekly housekeeping once another breadwinner had left home. I would guess, therefore, that Joseph Ball's signature would have come at a price.

Such negotiations were probably 'bread and butter' to a club like Villa, whose astute club secretary, and long-standing team manager, Mr George Ramsay, would have given clearance for any additional unrecorded monies which would secure Joseph's assent.

To give an idea of the sort of money Villa had access to, their 'gate' income for the 1920/21 season, as illustrated within the pages of *Aston Villa: The First 150 Years* by Farrelly, Abbott and Russell, was just over £39,000. Even when wages, bonuses and taxes were deducted from that figure, the Villa club, with a bank balance in April 1921 of £23.898, or £1,196.999 in 2022 figures, was doing very well indeed. Ramsay would not have let a few bob a week to help with Mrs Ball's housekeeping stand in his way.

In addition, although players were not allowed by league rules to take a 'cut' of the fee paid to the selling club, it is inconceivable that buying clubs did not offer personal inducements to persuade players to move, especially when it meant a young man having to relocate some distance away from the security of his family. For certain, a few notes would have been slipped into Tommy's pocket, perhaps to get a new shirt, tie, hat and suit and have a bit of ready pocket money to start off his life in the Midlands. The club would also have been paying the costs of his lodgings.

A Newcastle United Link?

Tommy is said to have moved to the Felling Colliery side after shining with the Wardley Colliery team. I am open to correction, but employment at a given pit does not seem to have been an absolute qualification for selection for that pit's team and as Wardley and Felling were neighbouring collieries, it is possible that football transfers from Wardley to the more senior neighbouring side were common.

There is a story that Tommy moved from one or the other of the colliery sides to Newcastle United, and it has become a commonly repeated error to say that Tommy was signed by Aston Villa from Newcastle United rather than from Felling Colliery. In welcoming him to the club *The Villa News and Record*, Villa's match programme, for 7 February 1920 is quite specific in saying he was signed from the Felling club and I am indebted to former editor Rob Bishop for providing original text with this information.

In fact, there is no evidence that Tommy ever played for Newcastle. That club's very obliging official historian, the prominent football writer Paul Joannou, was kind enough to check both the club's surviving player ledgers and their Football League registration records and found no mention of Tommy Ball anywhere.

Why the legend persisted is a mystery, but I suspect it was a result of easy 'Chinese whispers' journalism on the part of reporters who covered the trials of Tommy's killer in 1923 and 1924. Paul does correctly emphasise that in those days many professional teams' players began their careers as trialists and then amateurs in a club's, often extensive, lower sides. Aston Villa, for instance, were regularly fielding six junior sides beneath first-team and reserve-team levels well into the 1960s. It would have been quite possible that Tommy had put on Newcastle's black and white shirt as a trialist or occasional amateur player, though, with no known surviving record, this cannot be proven. If any newspaper or photographic evidence to support such an appearance by Tommy does exist, both Paul and I would be keen to know.

A Windfall for Felling

As a great many professional players of the time came from humble social backgrounds, and many had been spotted playing for works football teams, it was not unusual for working lads from the Northumberland and Durham coalfields to be picked up by professional clubs. Felling Colliery FC gave its young players a decent chance of moving upwards as it was rather better than an ordinary works team and played in the highly competitive Northern

Football Alliance, which had been founded in 1890. With its better clubs not far beneath Football League level, the Alliance was considered a fertile breeding ground for ambitious players.

It would not be an overstatement to describe the wider area as a hotbed of the game and a lot of lads, supported by their parents, would have seen football as their way out of the pit or the shipyards: the most usual lucky ticket was if one of the area's First Division outfits, either Newcastle United or Sunderland, showed an interest. Otherwise, it could have been one of the several other north-eastern sides who were then playing, or aspiring to play, in the Football League. South Shields, for instance, was a mid-table Second Division team in 1920, while ambitious clubs Darlington, Hartlepool, Durham City and Ashington each joined the newly formed Third Division North in 1922. Predictably, scouts from clubs further afield also turned up at matches in the area and the growing strength of the Felling Colliery side, which went on to take the Alliance title in 1922, attracted considerable interest.

In the years just after the Great War, and following a complete lack of competitive football since April 1915, most professional clubs were busily rebuilding their playing strengths. In the spring and summer of 1919, for example, the Aston Villa club had trawled the country to sign nearly a dozen young hopefuls in readiness for the forthcoming season when league and cup football were to begin again. Being aware that professional clubs needed to fill their books with new talent, many of the more 'savvy' and affluent junior clubs hedged against their better players being lost to one of the league clubs by shelling out a few shillings per week to tie their leading lights to a small professional contract.

A lad's signature thus represented a potential hard-cash bonus should a small club be lucky enough to negotiate a fee to transfer the player to an outfit further up the pecking order.

At some point, maybe in late 1919, Tommy was playing well enough to be included in such a group and, with parental permission, Felling obtained Tommy's signature. It proved to be a shrewd move. It would not have made Tommy a full-time player as he and other young hopefuls would hold down the 'day job' Monday to Saturday lunchtime and then get paid a couple of shillings on what, for others, would be Saturday afternoon off. It was a classic football scenario which enabled ambitious young men to move through the ranks.

Following this model, Felling Colliery FC's treasurer must have thought Christmas had come a little late as on 30 January 1920, almost two weeks after Tommy signed for Villa, the colliery club continued its good business by selling Gateshead-born centre-forward Dicky Johnson to Liverpool, where he had moderate success in scoring 28 goals in 77 appearances over a five-year stay. As an interesting footnote, on 25 November 1922 Tommy Ball made an appearance for Villa at centre-half in the 0-1 home defeat to Liverpool and found himself directly marking his former Felling team-mate. For the record, Johnson failed to score, but the 'banter' would have been worth listening to.

While the fee they paid for Ball's services is not known, history tells us that once he had his eyes set on a player, Villa's Mr Ramsay rarely came out of negotiations without getting his man, even if it meant finding a few pounds over the odds. At around this time transfer fees for the leading players were just nudging £3,000, so the fee authorised for a young untried lad playing with a non-league side would probably have been measured in, at most, the very low hundreds of pounds.

Although that level of outlay would have been a mere trifle for a club with Villa's budget, it is worth noting that in 1920 £1 was equivalent to just over £34 a century later. Even a modest fee of

£100, quite probably doubled when Dicky Johnson's transfer fee was added, would have kept the colliery club solvent for several months, if not seasons. It almost certainly enabled them to rebuild their team for their successful push to the Alliance championship the following season.

Not that Tommy would have needed much inducement to sign for the Villa. The phrase 'the world at his feet' has often been used to describe Tommy's ascent to stardom, and in the exciting days of January 1921 the prospect of earning good and regular money playing in front of large crowds alongside and against international players, and in the world's most famous football ground, must have seemed exactly like that.

For Joseph and Effy Ball, the famed 'brown envelope' that doubtless found its way into their house would have been manna from heaven.

An Escape from Jeopardy?

The Balls' exciting stroke of good luck was, however, to have a wicked irony. For one of their youngest children to have the prospect of what, on the face of it, was a career which was not life-threatening would be a massive contrast to the daily worries about the dangers of mining faced by Mr Ball himself and by his five working sons.

Pit life was, of course, exceptionally dangerous and fatalities within the Durham and Northumberland coal fields were commonplace until well past 1945. By the time its closure in 1974, over 200 men and boys had died in accidents at the Usworth pit alone, and by the same date 50 had been killed at Wardley and 190 at Felling.

The Ball family knew the dangers better than most as the pit had taken the life of Tommy's grandfather, John Ball, who was killed in 1885 at the age of 68 in an underground gas explosion in Usworth Colliery along with 41 others. The obelisk memorial erected by their fellow workers in tribute to Tommy's grandfather and the men who died with him can be found in the grounds of the Usworth parish church of Holy Trinity, Donwell, which lies just to the east of the A194. To emphasise the dangers, only a few steps from the memorial is the grave of Jared Ball. As far as I can ascertain, he was not related to Tommy but was of similar age and, working as a surface pony driver, was crushed between coal tubs at Springwell Colliery, Gateshead, in May 1913 aged 14.

Tommy's move into the apparently safe environment of professional sport would certainly have gone some way towards offsetting his parents' lasting grief for their eldest boy, Joseph Junior, who had been killed in action in France in February 1916 at the age of 33.

As an historical curiosity, though born and bred in Usworth, Joseph had served in the Tyneside Irish Brigade, which recruited heavily into the many local families of Irish descent and comprised four battalions, initially just over 3,200 men in total. The battalions were later subsumed within the Northumberland Fusiliers and, four months after Joseph's death, the regiment took considerable casualties during the infamous 'first day on The Somme' on 1 July 1916. Joseph Junior left behind a 30-year-old widow and three daughters aged nine, eight and six, so perhaps the sweetener paid by Villa to the Balls included some recognition of the family's commitments to their daughter-in-law and to the bairns – one certainly hopes so.

Joseph and Euphemia could never have imagined that his move to Aston to play sport would cost them the life of a second son killed by gunshot.

Tommy's Heritage

Apart from the Irish connection through the Ball family, there was Scottish lineage as Euphemia's paternal family, the Edgers, were originally from Kelso before her father moved to Byker in Newcastle where she was born and married. I mention this because, although the common assumption has been that Tommy was destined to play for England, football historians have never appeared to consider that he was equally qualified by descent to play for Scotland or for Ireland.

The Scottish connection also brings me to a common error in the telling of the story which involves the spelling of Tommy's second given name. This was Edger, after his mam's maiden name, but incorrectly shown in many accounts as Edgar. The initial error may have come, somewhat unforgivably, from incorrect typesetting in the Aston Villa match programme's obituary notice within its 24 November 1923 edition and thence passed on via the popular press to posterity.

Observers seeing Tommy's grave may therefore be excused for thinking the mason who inscribed Edger on its surround had made an embarrassing mistake. He was, however, evidently better informed than either Villa's programme editor or the West Bromwich registrar who chose to record the name incorrectly on Tommy's death certificate. It is not quite a dismissible offence, but, as many readers will know, modern registrars are ever fearful of allowing that sort of mistake to creep into a legal document for which they have the responsibility of signing off.

While we are commenting on inaccuracies it is worth noting that following his death, *The Scotsman* of 19 February 1924 was amongst several papers referring to Tommy as a 'native' of Newcastle upon Tyne. That his mother was native of the city by birth is correct, but Tommy was not. The mistake possibly came about because the Felling Colliery club for whom he played was situated within Gateshead and thus incorrectly seen by casual observers outside the North-east as part of Newcastle. A bit like accusing a native of West Bromwich of being a Brummie!

Usworth, where Tommy was born, has never been part of Newcastle and nowadays is formally located within Washington, thus being part of the city of Sunderland. Indeed, the local motor works, constructed on the old Second World War RAF Usworth site, is invariably referred to by news outlets as Nissan's 'Sunderland factory'. It is perhaps not stretching a point to say many Usworth residents, now and then, may not have looked west to Newcastle for their regional identification or for their footballing loyalties.

Maybe Tommy supported Newcastle United – he may certainly have been keen to play for them – but it is just as likely that his favours and ambitions centred on Sunderland FC, in those days virtually the equal of Aston Villa in reputation and historical deed. The clue to Tommy's loyalties probably lies in the fact that Sunderland FC was one of only two non-Midlands clubs represented at his funeral either by personage or by floral tribute, the other being Middlesbrough FC, though Tommy was certainly not from Teesside.

Assuming Tommy's supporting loyalties may have lain with Sunderland, there is some irony in the fact that it was Aston Villa who, by beating Sunderland 1-0 in the FA Cup Final in 1913, prevented the Wearside club from achieving the first 'cup and league double' of the 20th century. Equally, by drawing a league match a week later and, would you believe, at Villa Park, Sunderland effectively secured the league title, and, in their turn, denied Villa the 'double'. What a time for football supporters, with the season going into its final two weeks with either Villa or Sunderland able to win both major trophies and having to play each other in both competitions to decide things. Imagine what Sky would have made of that!

I write, of course, in the certain knowledge that many modern football fans will find it a little difficult to imagine that immediately before the Great War these clubs were, to use modern media parlance, the 'big two' of English football.

Growing Up

Tommy would have had the advantage of having received a relatively good education for a working-class lad of the time. Up to the age of 11, and like his brothers, he would have attended Usworth Colliery School, which had been built in 1863 and lies a short walk from High Row. Though the pit is long gone, with a sentimental and proud nod to the past, the school still thrives today under its original name.

Usworth children had been lucky as the school was one of several in the area built by philanthropic money. In Usworth's case, it opened seven years before the introduction of compulsory elementary schooling and had been funded by the local pit's then owner. Sir George Elliot was a Newcastle-born former miner who had made a bit of money and, evidently for good reason, was known locally as 'Bonnie Geordie'.

Thereafter, Tommy would probably have spent a year at Usworth Central School, which was built in the wake of the 1870 Education Act by Durham County Council. The Act had established basic compulsory education for all children up to the age of 12 and Tommy, having stayed in school probably until at least his 12th birthday and possibly a little beyond, would have been both numerate and literate. This was still something of a novelty when many of the adults in labouring families in the early 1900s, without the advantage of schooling, were signing their names with a cross. This was true of Tommy's mam Euphemia when registering his birth and also his father when signing off the 1921 census return.

Around the age of 13 we might presume that Tommy would have been in pit service. This career was hardly a choice but virtually inevitable as the Balls had been pitmen for several generations and it was usual for a serving man's son to follow on when the time came. As Durham coalfield pit employment records for the time are virtually non-existent, it is not possible to say, categorically, where Tommy or any of his immediate family worked, but their occupation of one of Bonnie Geordie's tied properties strongly suggests that Joseph Ball, at least, worked in Usworth colliery before eventually moving to another pit cottage, and presumably employment to go with it, at Wardley. There is a clear likelihood that Tommy would have also gone to the Wardley pit for whose football team he played.

I have, to this point, used the shorthand 'coal miners' to describe the dominant local occupation, but, interestingly, Tommy's father and older brothers are recorded on 1911 census returns not as coal miners but as 'stone miners', most likely bringing up ironstone. None of the local pits appeared to have specialised in this, though it is quite likely that many pits took advantage of ironstone seams found while working the area.

Wherever he spent his working life, it is possible that Tommy initially saw service underground doing 'lads' jobs' like operating the tunnel ventilation doors, pushing the tubs of freshly hewn coal or rock, or leading pit ponies through the tunnels. Approaching his 20s, he may well have graduated to face work and, under normal circumstances, freedom from accidents permitting, another 40 or so years of this would have been in front of him. But he now had his escape route.

Industrial Birmingham, and notably its Aston district, was a tough, overcrowded place with no shortage of poverty. Looked at from the dirt and death of the north-eastern coalfields, however, the prospect of going there to be paid to play football in front of large crowds, with the seemingly realistic prospect of winning medals and newspaper headlines, must have seemed a ticket to paradise.

The Promised Land

Allowing a day or two for Tommy's registration to be lodged with the Football League and for his 'digs' to be sorted out, we can reasonably presume the grand adventure would have begun sometime around 22 January. This allowed a week or so for Tommy to settle in before making his Aston Villa debut for the reserves away from home on 31 January against Rochdale's first team in the Central League.

Tommy would have turned up, smartly dressed, at Newcastle Railway Station to make the nervous cross-country journey to Birmingham New Street. There, a club official would have met him and taken him, probably on a number three tram, to the terminus depot in Witton, a short walk from 11 Woodall Road, in those days a smartish terraced lodging house virtually over the road from the Villa Park ground. It is worth considering how much of a fish out of water Tommy may have felt himself to be when he arrived at New Street. From the broad Brummie accents on the station platform and those on his first tram ride, to the street children's voices around Woodall Road, he would have felt himself to be almost in a foreign land. The grid pattern of the terraced streets of the immediate area would, however, have had the comforting familiarity of similar roads in Usworth and in Gateshead.

It was good practice for Villa to place a new boy so near to their ground. At five minutes walking distance away from Villa Park, it was handily placed for daily training. In those days the notion of dedicated training grounds did not exist, so daily journeys to the ground for training were necessary: the present out-of-town Bodymoor Heath complex was not opened until 1971.

I once took a non-Villa-supporting work friend to see a match at Villa Park. As a keen amateur player his immediate reaction was 'I would give my right arm to play here'. I bet Tommy felt the same way when he walked over for his first day in his new workplace. With its beautiful barrel-vaulted main stand in Witton Lane, which remained a feature until 1963, it was the world's premier football stadium and was constructed to hold around 60,000 spectators: in the first season of competitive post-war football, the club welcomed over 40,000 on nine occasions. It was heady stuff for a young hopeful.

Meeting the Gaffers

Tommy's first day at the club would have involved a formal welcome from the man who sanctioned his signing. In those days clubs did not use the terms 'manager' or 'head coach' and, as with many clubs, the Villa sides were theoretically selected into the 1930s by the club's committee. In Tommy's time, and for many years beforehand, the reality was that the team was selected on the committee's behalf by the nearest thing to a manager any club at the time had. This was the legendary figure of club secretary, former captain and probably de facto match programme editor George Burrell Ramsay.

Scotsman Ramsay had been at the club in many roles since joining as a player in 1876 and had run the senior side for over 30 years before the war. In that time, Ramsay had won six Football

League titles and five FA Cups, including the mythical 'double' in 1897, and was to bag another FA Cup win three months after signing Tommy in 1920. Ramsay would have wanted to check very quickly that he was getting his money's worth with Tommy and would have left the newcomer in no doubt as to what was expected both on and off the field.

Since the early 1890s, Ramsay had worked in partnership with the equally legendary 'trainer' Joe Grierson, though whether a trainer decided tactics, was responsible for fitness or was simply the 'sponge man', or a combination of all three, would vary from club to club. Whatever his precise role at Aston Villa, there could be little doubting that the autocratic style reportedly employed by Grierson had helped maintain the high levels of on- and off-field discipline which had contributed to the club's success. Approaching the age of 60 when war finally brought an end to organised football, Grierson decided it would be the right time to retire.

In deciding who would succeed Grierson on the resumption of competition in 1919, Ramsay had gone for a local Aston-born man, and former star full-back in the team, Alfred 'Freddie' Miles, who was to be a key figure in this story. It has always gone down well with the crowd to have a 'Villa man' in key position at the club and he looked to be a very safe pair of hands: one imagines that he might have been expected to replicate Grierson's famously glacial relationship with the players. Miles was probably hopeful of eventually taking over day-to-day team management duties when the ageing Ramsay finally decided to retire to the committee room.

When he took over from Grierson, Miles was, in effect, being promoted from the dressing room and this has always brought challenges to those similarly advanced within team sport. He was doubtless easily able to impress any new boy, though he would have had a bigger challenge in establishing his authority over the household names with whom he had once changed, played alongside and shared jokes. Certainly, in team photographs, Miles always looked suitably stern and could, if necessary, pull a bit of 'show us your medals' rank, having played in the 1905 FA Cup-winning team and been a key man in the 1910 league championship side.

Miles had also played very successfully in Tommy's left-full-back position, so would have known exactly what he and Ramsay wanted from the new man, but he could not possibly have envisaged the posthumous service he was to provide. It was to be his character reference on Tommy's behalf, given from the witness stand at the Stafford Assize, that challenged George Stagg's assertion that Tommy Ball had been attacking him while under the influence of drink.

Meeting the Lads

After the welcoming handshake, Miles would have weighed and measured the new man, then moved him into the dressing room to prepare for a training session. This probably began with another handshake, this time from club captain Andy Ducat, a man of national sporting renown, being one of the old-style breed of sportsmen who played professional football during the winter months and county cricket in the summer. In south Londoner Ducat's case, the cricket he played was for Surrey.

Ducat had already played international football for England on six occasions, and six months after Tommy's arrival he was to gain his solitary international cricket cap playing in that summer's third test match against the touring Australians. To offer a sporting curiosity, Ducat's first innings for England saw him caught behind while an edge of his bat was sheared off by the ball and the fragment simultaneously flew on to the bails of his wicket and dislodged them.

No doubt like all sports dressing rooms, the one Tommy went into at Villa Park reeked of embrocation, feet, nervous armpits and other unsavoury smells, while competing accents would have made it sound like the Tower of Babel but with added swearing. Like all newcomers to an almost closed shop, Tommy would have needed to watch his step: no changing in someone else's favourite spot or using a wall peg with established ownership. And certainly no inappropriate joining in of the established players' 'banter', which, for his benefit, would most likely have deliberately excluded him by centring on shared past footballing glories and war service. Ability, longevity and trophies would be the tickets to that privilege.

Tommy would probably have been a bit uncomfortable if any of the chat flying around concerned the club's pre-war rivalry with Sunderland, though winger Charlie Wallace, who was from the town, might have offered a friendly word in a familiar accent. Apart from Wallace's comforting dialect, Tommy would recognise the distinctive Northumberland accents of the Stephenson brothers, Clem', Jimmy and George, who were from Seaton Delaval, and of 'Jack' Thompson from nearby Cramlington.

The remainder of the squad were from across the country, some signed after the war and still to make their mark and some with the medals and stories to show participation in previous deeds in the shirt. There was certainly plenty of past glory on which the established players could dwell, as in the four seasons prior to the Great War, and the one which overlapped it, Villa had won the First Division title once and been placed second in the four other years. For good measure they had also won the FA

Cup in 1905 and 1913 and reached the semi-final in 1914. By the time he was changed into training kit, Tommy would have been fully aware of the difference between this dressing room and that at Felling Colliery.

In all, six of the 1913 FA Cup-winning team were still at the club and may have been present in the dressing room, namely Tommy Weston, Jimmy Harrop, Jimmy Leach, Charlie Wallace, Sam Hardy and Clem' Stephenson, while Ducat and Frank Moss may well have played but for injury. In addition, Wallace, Weston, Moss and Jimmy Stephenson had seen ground action in France, youngster Dicky York had flown over the battlefields as a pilot, while Clem' Stephenson and Sam Hardy had served at sea.

Of the assembled group, Hardy and Clem' Stephenson arguably had the highest national profiles. Former Durham City player Stephenson was a star forward about whom Tommy would have heard a lot in dressing room and pit talk back home. As inside-forward support to the legendary assaulter of goalkeepers Harry Hampton, he had scored 55 goals for Villa in the five seasons before the war. Sam Hardy, beyond any doubt, belonged to the 'living legend' category, being universally reckoned the greatest goalkeeper the country had ever produced.

Tommy's possible mentor, Charlie Wallace, had just squeezed into the 1910 championship side, making one appearance, as had man's man Frank Moss, back from war with the visible knee scars from his wounding at the third battle of Ypres. Another local Aston man, Moss brought with him tough, post-convalescence, man-management experience as an army PTI and had 'future team captain' written all over him.

Moss was not the only hard man in the squad, as the position of dressing-room alpha male would almost certainly have been held by the country's most notorious centre-half, the irascible and widely feared South Yorkshireman Frank Barson. A century later, Barson still holds an esteemed place in Villa folklore, and has been the subject of numerous colourful anecdotes, many of which were probably true.

Tommy, with little common ground and not a lot to boast about, could be excused for feeling a little uncomfortable and may have expected to get a lukewarm welcome from Tommy Weston, the man who had been the established pre-war left-back and the player whose place in the team he might hope to threaten. As it was a typical sports dressing room, several of the senior men would certainly have been 'winding up' Weston by making pointed reference to the arrival of a fit-looking younger man who played in his position.

To balance things a little, the several hopefuls signed by Villa during the summer and autumn of 1919 would have been just as eager to impress Tommy, though a bit less able to walk the walk. Tommy's early pals may have been drawn from the likes of newish signings like Hubert Bourne, Walter Boyman, Jack Hampson, Jim Lee, 'Jack' Thompson, Andy Young, George Blackburn, Billy Walker and Clem' Stephenson's younger brother, George.

Blackburn, a tough-tackling defensive wing-half-back, was to go on to form a notable partnership with Ball and the pair can be seen as forerunners of the later twin centre-back pattern. 'Jack' Thompson, however, who had just enjoyed a run in the first team as left-full-back, may have been someone else who was not too pleased to see another player in that position turning up. The simple fact that Tommy had been brought down from the North-east was probably a hint to Thompson that he was not seen as a long-term prospect. Duly enough, Villa let him go in August 1921 following 28 appearances for the senior side.

Former youth-team player and future star Dicky York was also around and beginning to make his name on the right wing, while rookie forward Billy Walker had broken into the first team only a week before Tommy's dad signed forms and had scored both goals in the home FA Cup win against Queens Park Rangers. As all Aston Villa supporters will tell you, these goals were the first of a club record 244.

York, Walker and Blackburn were to be pall-bearers at Tommy's funeral.

Another 20-year-old had turned up in the same week as Tommy and, though he would also have been changing nervously, the lad did have the advantage of sharing military experience with some of the older players. It was Tommy's first meeting with his soon-to-be playing partner at full-back in the forthcoming reserve match at Rochdale. The 'barrel-chested' 6ft 2in-tall Tommy Smart would go on to make 452 first-team appearances and win five England caps. Whether Ball, with his distinctive accent, and Smart, who was pure black country, could initially understand what the other was saying is open to question. That Smart settled down almost immediately to form a strong full-back partnership with the veteran Weston may have in part been helped by the fact that, as both men came from Halesowen, bonding and communication in the vernacular were unlikely to have been problems.

As Ball and Smart had signed in the same week, the club had done good business, so backing up *The Villa News and Record's* immodest claim that the directors 'are leaving no stone unturned to secure fresh talent'. There is some truth in this, for although Villa could have reasonably been expected to spot talent like Smart in the West Midlands it was a bit more of a feather in the cap to spot it in a colliery team on Tyneside.

Learning the Ropes

It has often been said incorrectly that Tommy had been signed as a centre-half. Some have even said he had been signed as a replacement for Frank Barson, though the eventual date of the latter's transfer, well over two years later in August 1922, and in unexpected circumstances, does not support this view. Neither does the fact that until Barson left Tommy's senior appearances were dotted around the midfield and defence; he certainly deputised for Barson on several occasions but only settled at centre-half once the great man had moved on and left the vacancy.

In its 7 February 1920 edition, *The Villa News and Record*, the club's match programme, welcomed Tommy to his first home match vs Everton reserves in a Central League game which Villa were to win 3-0, and the text clearly states that Tommy was signed as a left-back. The inference I draw is that it was the veteran defender Tommy Weston, now turning 30, whose place Ramsay thought might soon become available.

Tommy was described in the programme as standing 5ft 10.5in and 'tips the beam' at nearly 12 stones, which was considered 'quite a useful build'. They may well have added that with six or seven years of working life in a colliery behind him he would be a strong and fit young man.

It soon became apparent that if Ramsay's initial idea had been to groom Ball as Weston's successor things were not going to go according to plan as during his first three seasons Tommy was identified by the press as a utility player. *The Sheffield Daily Telegraph*, for instance, described him, somewhat condescendingly, as an 'emergency man' who played with 'varying degrees of success', a view supported by Birmingham's *The Daily Gazette*.

Tommy would have been upset not to have enjoyed a better start to his Aston Villa career and the first disappointment would have been not gaining selection for the match in which he had surely been dreaming of playing. He may have thought his home roots would have counted in his favour for a run-out when Villa were due to entertain Sunderland in the third round of the FA Cup a week after the match with Everton's reserves. He was doomed to disappointment. Ramsay and Miles would have been well aware of Tommy's roots, but this was the FA Cup: the competition meant a lot to Villa and there was no room for unnecessary sentiment as far as selection was concerned.

Had Ball been chosen it would also have meant a very inexperienced, and risky, full-back pairing with Tommy Smart, the other new lad, who, having made his debut the previous Saturday against the Everton senior side, had already been elevated to the first team. It was the safe and sensible choice, therefore, to continue to select Weston in the number three shirt. Smart's swift rise in the pecking order was a contrast that must have been keenly felt by Ball, especially as Smart held his place thereafter and, playing alongside Weston, went on to step into Villa folklore by gaining a winner's medal three months later in the 1920 FA Cup Final against Huddersfield Town.

By contrast with Smart, our Tommy had to be content with only a single senior selection during his first season, playing out of position at right-half on 7 April in a 3-6 home hammering by Bolton Wanderers. The match, played on a workday Wednesday afternoon, unsurprisingly attracted a small crowd of only 25,000 and Villa, coming off the back of a heavy Easter programme and only 17 days away from the FA Cup Final, put out an inexperienced team. With significant understatement *The Birmingham Gazette* described the match as 'an unwelcome experience', though the diehards who were able to attend were treated to a bit of a thriller with six goals within the first half hour giving the home side a 2-4 deficit to turn round. The Villa team, which contained several reserves, was unfortunate enough to come up against a virtuoso display from Bolton's Welsh international forward Ted Vizard.

In fairness to Tommy, the step up in just two months from facing colliery forwards on their half day off to dealing with an established full-time professional, international player was considerable. *The Birmingham Gazette*'s considered opinion was that 'Ball worked strenuously to check the raids of Vizard but he was outclassed by the forward'. Unfortunately for Tommy, he had been given the runaround in front of a critically knowledgeable crowd and, as ever at Villa Park, the fans would not have been short of generous advice on how he might improve. The whole experience would have been a salutary lesson and he would have come off the pitch knowing that any lingering ambition of being selected to play in the cup final on 24 April had gone. In fact, Ramsay sensibly wrapped him in the proverbial cotton wool until the following September when an injury to Barson gave him another chance.

As ill luck would have it, Tommy's long-awaited second senior appearance, on 15 September, was away at his nemesis Bolton Wanderers. Deputising for Barson at centre-half, he endured another hammering, this time 0-5, so in his first two senior appearances, both against Bolton, the defence had shipped 11 goals. It was not an auspicious beginning, but by the end of the season injuries meant he had made 13 appearances in three different positions, so his feet had moved just a little further under the table.

The 1921/22 campaign saw Tommy, still without an established 'best' position, used as a utility reserve, mainly to cover defensive midfield injuries to first-pick starters Barson or Blackburn. His selections were most notable for a frantic period between 10 and 31 December when he turned out on six occasions, including four matches in Christmas week. No chance of getting home for a welcome couple of days with the family, but with the bonus money from four December wins and a draw he would have had the comfortable wherewithal to send his mam a few bob to help out with the Christmas dinner table.

Whether 11 appearances during the season counted as progress is debatable and Tommy's 'out-of-position' selections in midfield may have made him feel a little more insecure. With Weston getting no younger, however, he might still have hoped to move into the side in due course in his original position. When Weston was dropped following a home match against Birmingham on 11 March, it was not Tommy who was drafted in but local lad Percy Jones. As if this was not bad enough, it would have been a major setback both for Tommy and for Percy when, in April 1922, Villa brought in Tommy Mort, a specialist left-back from Rochdale, as a direct replacement for Weston.

We can assume that Ramsay considered Ball to be useful enough to have around the place but considered he would not make the grade in the longer term in what had been his preferred position. You will have noticed, of course, that the principal requirement to play full-back at Villa did seem to have been the good luck to be christened 'Tommy'.

As it happened, Mort turned out to be an inspired signing and went on to play 368 games over the following 12 seasons. To Villa fans of the time, the names 'Mort and Smart' as a full-back pairing rolled off the tongue as naturally as did 'bread and butter'; their efforts at the back led them to being affectionately known on the terraces as 'death and glory', and in 1924 they were selected to play together for England. If Frank Barson had not left the club in September 1922, thereby creating a vacancy at centre-half, it is debatable whether Ball's Villa career would have withstood Mort's signing. We shall come to that in due course.

A Good Match

If things were not going according to plan on the football field, Tommy's private life had taken a considerable upturn with his courtship of local girl Beatrice Richards.

Beatrice, otherwise 'Beatie' or 'Belle', had been born at 198 Bracebridge Street in the New Town Row area of Aston on 14 May 1902. She was the second of four daughters, Maud, Lilian and Alice being her siblings, of 43-year-old pork butcher William Richards and his 42-year-old wife Elizabeth.

The couple wed on 7 May 1922 at the now Grade 2 Listed Holy Trinity Church in Birchfield, which lay within the West Bromwich local authority area and on the edge of the cluster of terraced streets in which Tommy lodged, and not far from Beatrice's home in nearby Aston Lane. There is little doubt that each partner married well and that their respective families were more than happy with the match.

Tommy's new father-in-law, William Richards, was a self-made man. On Beatrice's 1902 birth certificate he was strangely listed as a rather humble-sounding 'Mineral Water Maker's Carter', a 'barrow boy' if you prefer, selling refreshments on the streets. Curiously, the previous year's census has him as a 'journeyman butcher' which makes far more sense as it was in the butchery trade that he made his mark. A 'journeyman' tended to move around post-apprenticeship getting experience in the trade wherever opportunities became available. Richards evidently made speedy progress through the trade as by 1905 he had set himself up in business. By 1911, he was running his own shop at 322 New Town Row, a good trading address in a then heavily populated area of Aston. To quote his well-designed, though wordy, business flier, he was trading as 'Richards, W [Aston] Ltd [founded 1905] Pork Butcher, Lard Refiner, Sausage Manufacturer, Pie Maker'.

Richards had done well, and in quick time. At some point after the Great War, he moved his business to nearby 200 High Street, which was conveniently situated on the corner with Bracebridge Street, minutes away from the family home. Since Kelly's Directory for the 1920s and 1930s lists him as trading variously at numbers 200 and 202 High Street, we may safely presume that at some stage he doubled his counter space and storage with the purchase of the neighbouring property. The shop is certainly represented in *Birmingham Forum* online photographs as being double-fronted and it had upstairs staff accommodation accessed from the street. This was where Beatrice lived briefly following her husband's death and it is highly likely that the newly-weds lodged there for the seven months until they were able to move next door to George Stagg in Perry Barr.

Bracebridge Street lay at the centre of a densely populated area on the main tram route from the Birmingham city centre into Aston. It was a modest, yet famous, street of factories and two- and three-storeyed terraced housing, many converted into shops on the ground floor. The fame came from the street being the site of the internationally renowned Norton Motorcycle Works which had opened there in 1898.

The houses and shops are long gone and the area is now redeveloped as a brownfield business park as a result, in most part, of the 1972 construction of the Aston Expressway which runs traffic out of the Birmingham city centre virtually past Villa Park into the northern suburbs or on to the M6 motorway. It is a far cry from the day in 1954 when Queen Elizabeth II paid a visit to the Norton factory. I remember that day vividly as I and my classmates were marched the few minutes from St Saviours School in Alum Rock Road to watch the Queen's motorcade pass along Washwood Heath Road.

The Richards business is still recalled online in the *Birmingham Forum* by correspondents who went into the shop as children, and memories include the apparently regular escape attempts made by piglets being delivered to the shop. One view on the website was that there was a slaughterhouse attached to the shop – another says not. A further observation, that the animals were killed 'out the back', might satisfy both points of view. Whatever the truth, and unfortunately for the piglets, the alluring smell in the shop of pork pies being baked remains well remembered.

At some point after 1911, as befitted a man entering the ranks of Birmingham's lower-middle classes, Richards upgraded the family domestically with a move to the more desirable address of 226 Aston Lane, Witton. It was, again, a terraced dwelling but probably had an extra bedroom and a back garden. This was then located on the edge of West Bromwich almost at the point where it joined Aston. It was only minutes away from Villa Park, though even closer to Woodall Road where Tommy was lodging.

How Tommy and Beatrice met is a matter of conjecture but, for certain, the young Villa players who lodged in the area would have mingled with everyone else on a daily basis and been well known. They were no doubt as attractive then to the young ladies as the rising football stars of any age have always been.

For a courting couple Aston was a lively place with a thriving night-time economy and there was ample scope in the area for young men and women to enjoy each other's company. Maybe the couple would visit one of Aston's seven cinemas and possibly they went to the Aston Hippodrome, a nationally famous music hall, though well before its later days as a – how shall we put it? – burlesque theatre. There were also half a dozen dance or concert halls and over 60 public houses.

Many of the pubs had the local trademark street-corner main door, but it was best for Villa players not to be spotted by anyone who might tell Mr Rinder, the Villa chairman, that you liked a glass of beer. With Villa's young players living amongst the community, social media, had it existed, would have had a field day keeping the world informed on how they spent their generous wages and on whom.

Tommy and Beatrice chose a Sunday as their marriage day, which, for some reason, I think of as being particularly romantic, and the date was thoughtfully selected as league football had finished the week before. Temporarily free of contractual playing or training commitments, Tommy could concentrate for a few weeks on his new responsibilities as a married man. No doubt his team-mates, similarly liberated, were more than happy to gather after the nuptials for a guilt-free celebratory glass or two of Ansells and perhaps a chat with Mr Richards about the prospects of getting a halfpenny off a pound of sausages.

Interestingly, although the bride's father signed as witness to the match, Tommy's dad, Joseph, did not, so raising the question as to whether he and Effie attended. As Tommy's witness was his younger sibling, Norman, then barely 18 years of age, my suggestion is that he had forged a closer relationship with the brother nearest to him in age than with his surviving elder brothers, then aged 34, 32, 30 and 25 years. Whether any or all of them, or either of his sisters, attended is an open question, but the cost of travel and accommodation for such a large group would have been steep and it may not have been easy to get five brothers and their father out of work at the same time.

Although it has been invariably repeated by chroniclers that Joseph Ball 'died young' leaving his wife to bring up the children, he must still have been alive at the time of the wedding because the word 'deceased' was not placed on the marriage certificate behind his name as the groom's father. Further research has established that far from 'dying young' he passed away in 1937 at an address in Chester-le-Street, outliving Effy by 13 years. The recent census confirms they were still together in 1921, so the long-established notion that Tommy had been brought up by a single mum is clearly incorrect.

As suggested beforehand, the match looked a good one for all parties. Tommy's family could be proud of how well their lad was doing in life. With a prestigious well-paid job, weekly coverage in the national press, a wedding attended by nationally known sports stars, an attractive wife and a prosperous father-in-law, it was a far cry from the prospects in Usworth and somewhere near the utopia that the Balls had hoped their son had left home to find.

For Tommy, it was certainly a move up the social ladder as his nouveau riche father-in-law was becoming a prominent local personage who knew how to make a bit of money. Access to that level of social mobility was certainly not available to many pit workers of the time.

Having a footballer as a son-in-law would not have been to Richards's disadvantage either and through Tommy's Villa connections there were doubtless business contacts to be made. Nowadays, he would probably have his eye on the lucrative prematch pie contract.

'Doing All Right'

Richards would also have been delighted to welcome into the family a man whose prospects for adequately looking after one of his four daughters appeared sound. Tommy was being paid £7 a week, or £6 in the close season, so was bringing in nearly £400 a year as his basic wage, which equates to just over £18,000 in 2022 money. The weekly wage for a footballer had dropped by a pound since the end of the war and Tommy would maybe have earned a couple of shillings under the maximum anyway, owing to a sliding scale based on senior appearances that was used by most clubs at the time. It would still, however, have represented a significant level of earning for a young man from his social background.

In addition, Tommy was on the considerable pay incentive of a £2 per match win bonus, or just over £108 in modern money, an unimaginable incentive if you were a Durham miner on piecework. By his death, Tommy had picked up this bonus on 39 occasions and Villa's subsequent league record over the following decade suggests that had he maintained his position in the team over that period he would probably have earned the win bonus another 120 times. At 2022 rates, this would have netted him around £12,000 gross in bonus payments alone, and then throw in an extra £1 above basic for drawn matches.

In addition to these earnings, on retirement from the game there might well have been a secure managerial position waiting for him at his father-in-law's enterprise.

To emphasise Tommy's privileged financial status, we should bear in mind that footballers at the top level avoided the endemic post-war unemployment, which affected all sectors of the economy throughout the 1920s and into the 1930s. Tommy's £7 a week was at least three times the average weekly wage for a white-collar colliery clerk back at Usworth or Wardley and approaching double that which a faceworker could expect. He would also have imagined that his chosen career had come without the daily threat of accident or worse.

Tommy's brothers may have looked on his good fortune with a mixture of pride and envy as the low wage then paid to miners was proving to be a major bone of political contention. From 1921, the government, as part of its cost-cutting strategy, relinquished the temporary control over miners' wages it had assumed during the war, so returning unregulated employment responsibilities to private owners. By and large, and to no one's surprise, the owners took full advantage of an opportunity to deflate wages to pre-war levels or lower. In national terms, this reduced the faceworkers' average weekly wage from a relatively good £6 per week in 1917 to £3.90 by 1925, or in 2022 value from just over £300 down to £195.

As a footballer, therefore, Tommy was in the fortunate position of being able to shield his wife and any eventual family from the uncertainties of wage levels that placed his da' and brothers in precarious circumstances. It may be of interest to note that, when he joined the army in 1914, Tommy's killer, as a policeman with ten years' service in the force, had been picking up less than the £2 a week Tommy would have earned as a win bonus. Only the 2 per cent of college-educated professional men in the country, such as teachers and solicitors, might, with luck, match Tommy's annual wage.

For Beatrice, Tommy offered athletic good looks and glamour and she was surely widely envied for having attracted a celebrity husband who might even become an international player. Nowadays, there are any number of glossy 'chatterbox mags' and online 'clickbaits' that feature similar couples happily showing off their disposable wealth or inventing long-running stories about relationship issues. In 1922, women had few legal rights and the shadow of the workhouse still loomed should a husband have died or fallen on hard times. Tommy's income and prospects were therefore a considerable advantage both to his young wife and to her father who, if things turned out badly, might expect to have to put his hand in his pocket to help out.

The Unanswered Questions

Whether the marriage was happy is another question. His killer, George Stagg, was to claim in his court deposition that Tommy was 'often drunk and knocked his wife about'. In truth, such behaviour, had it existed, would have been hard to disguise in adjoining, semi-detached houses such as those Stagg and Ball were to occupy. Should you believe what Stagg was later to say, Beatrice had confirmed to him, immediately after the shooting, that her husband 'kicks me about', a claim she later emphatically denied in court.

Though nothing has ever been proven, it may be borne in mind that both casual and habitual domestic violence against women were reputedly commonplace, even in 'happy' marriages. The reader may or may not be surprised to know that the then public reaction, from both sexes, was not always bound to be favourable to victims and any complaints made to the police over domestic violence were not necessarily likely to result in intervention, let alone prosecution.

There also emerged widespread though unproven rumours, which we shall come to, that Tommy and his neighbour's wife, Mary Ellen Stagg, 15 years his senior, had undertaken an illicit affair. Whether the word 'affair', as bandied around in those days, was meant to imply lingering looks or something a little more physical is hard to determine. If the latter, such behaviour would also have been difficult to cover up within the solitude of a pair of isolated semi-detached houses. My personal reflection is that nothing, other than handed-down hearsay, has emerged to substantiate the rumours.

A Home Together

As suggested earlier, it is possible that the newly-weds spent their early married days living 'above the shop' in High Street, Aston. If so, they were fortunate as modestly living in the 'front room' and a bedroom of a parents' or in-laws' house was the limit of the expectations of many newly-weds of that time, and young couples often considered themselves lucky to be offered such lodgings. As I well remember in my own family, such arrangements were commonplace into the second half of the century.

The couple made their first steps into independent living on 17 January 1923 by renting one of a pair of isolated semi-detached properties in the hamlet of Hamstead within the then rural Staffordshire area of Perry Barr. In those days this area lay within the larger administrative area of Great Barr and the overall civic jurisdiction of West Bromwich.

Perry Barr in 1923 was largely dominated by grassland, except at its more urbanised southern edge where it was contiguous with Aston and indistinguishable from it. With its many substantial out-of-town properties, it was, like nearby Sutton Coldfield, becoming a popular dormitory area for upwardly mobile Brummies. It was eventually to be partially incorporated into Birmingham, and therefore Warwickshire, by public vote in 1928.

At the 1921 census, just before the Balls moved in, the population of the area, even including its urban fringe with Aston, was recorded as being just over 2,400 persons occupying only 480 dwellings, many of them in isolated positions. By 1931, following a programme of planned urbanisation, the population had rocketed to around 20,000, just shy of its present figure, and the area began to take on its modern form.

The property the Balls rented, one of the pair of elderly houses known as Somerville Cottages, stood about a quarter of a mile down a road then known as Brick Kiln Lane, now renamed Beeches Road. This ran eastwards from the Walsall Road, now A34, at Tower Hill. It is not far north of the modern Alexandra Stadium, home of the renowned Birchfield Harriers and central arena of the 2022 Commonwealth Games. The line of the old Brick Kiln Lane now passes directly beneath the M6, a little to the east of Junction 7.

Although much green land still exists in the locality, largely as residue of the local Perry Hall estate's extensive parkland, it may come as a surprise to those who now live there, or pass through it, to learn it was described in court in 1924 as an 'isolated spot'. From Tower Hill it was about a two and a half mile bus ride courtesy of the Midland Motor Omnibus Company, or 'Midland Red' as it was universally known, south into Aston and another three miles or so into Birmingham city centre.

The ease of communication was certainly one of the reasons why the couple were pleased to move to Perry Barr. In the days before most people had motor cars, or football clubs travelled to away games by motor coach, the location was very handy for Tommy. He could easily get to training and home matches or travel into 'Brum' to meet his team-mates at New Street or Snow Hill stations for away fixtures, while occasionally the team might travel for an away game from Witton Station, which lies a five-minute walk from the ground. The location of the cottage would also have enabled Beatrice to easily visit her family in Aston Lane or to entertain them at her cottage.

Somerville Cottages were owned by former policeman George John Alan Stagg who lived with his family in the adjoining mirror-image house. It was not necessarily the last word in chic living and the cottages stood on a then unmade and unlit lane. As I shall explain later, I believe it likely that, when purchased by Stagg, the cottages had been 'tied' to the Perry Hall estate and probably released on to the market because of the expense of upkeep. If that was the case, the properties might not have been in the best of condition, but it was a first foot on the ladder for the newly-weds. Importantly, it was also a countryside location, a novel living experience for them both.

The exact position of the cottages is not clear from the 1890 Ordnance Survey map as this did not generally identify individual buildings by name unless they fulfilled a function other than to house people. From the building indicators on that map, as best I can tell, the cottages were on the left-hand side if heading east from the Walsall Road.

The most accurate indicator comes from the deposition of Police Superintendent William Mollart, who took crime-scene measurements on 15 November 1923. These established that the cottages lay 450 yards from the junction with the Walsall Road, thus probably between 15 or 20 properties downhill from where Beeches Road now meets Foden Road, and the Balls occupied the first of the pair. A Brick Kiln Lane still exists at the Witton end of Aston, but this is not the road in question.

Beyond the north-facing back gardens of the cottages stood open fields and one or two visible copses. The fields abutted the two backyards and gardens, which were bordered with privet hedging. Critical to the action on the evening of Tommy's death, each back garden had a wooden paling gate built into the side perimeter hedging, giving direct access both on to the fields and to pathways running down the sides of the houses on to Brick Kiln Lane.

Each cottage had a side and rear door and, as was usual, the rear door was the one commonly used and the families would access this from their hedge gate. There was no external lighting around the cottages nor on the road. With reference to future events, it is important to bear in mind that the only night-time illumination into the gardens would be thrown, probably weakly, from gas lighting within the back-facing rooms. As I live in a similar situation, I can attest to the fact that, even with indoor and garden electric lighting, anyone approaching my property from the back fields on a moonless night can do so in the certain knowledge that they will be virtually unseen until the moment they enter the garden.

The internal demarcation of the two back gardens was simply marked by the line of a demolished brick wall, probably at no more than one visible course in height, so there was nothing to prevent any animals, such as dogs or poultry held by either of the houses, from straying on to the other's land. We know from Beatrice Ball's court deposition that there was a pigsty somewhere in her garden where, for a time, the chickens owned by Ball were cooped. It is likely this had been provided for the couple by Beatrice's father, the butcher, hopeful perhaps of cheaply acquiring some locally sourced pork. Rearing pigs and chickens is not, perhaps, the sort of extramural activity that might appeal to today's young stars and their partners.

Both Stagg and the Balls had a dog and Stagg claimed to have his chained outside at night to warn of intruders, which you might think a sensible precaution.

An Elite Sporting Area

To relate the general locality to football, Aston Villa won the league and FA Cup 'double' in 1897 with a team popularly known as the 'Perry Barr Pets' after the location of their then home ground in Wellington Road, Perry Barr. This was to be found just beyond the border with Aston and, ever so slightly, into West Bromwich. It may offend the sensibilities of present Villa supporters but, when playing at Wellington Road, matches against 'the Baggies' were, in strict local government terms, West Bromwich derbies. No wonder the club rivalry was, and has remained, so intense. Older supporters still regard the matches against the Albion as the most important of local derbies, seeing Villa's rivalry with Birmingham City to be rather 'new school'.

That two of the greatest contemporary clubs in the country, both founder members of the Football League and regular trophy winners, had developed in such a relatively tiny geographical area seems a small wonder, though Tommy would have noted some similarity with the development of football in the Newcastle–Sunderland conurbation. An even closer geographical context also developed with the situation of 'same-city' clubs in Liverpool and in Nottingham.

To briefly digress, Aston Villa moved a few hundred metres down the road into the Aston township only in 1897 when they took up residency at the so-called 'Magnificent Meadow' of the Aston Lower Grounds, site of the modern Villa Park. This was part of a former pleasure gardens of considerable repute that had played host to attractions as diverse as international cricket and rugby union, ballooning and Buffalo Bill's Wild West Show. There was also a permanent ice-skating rink and Villa's pitch was laid on the site of a public boating lake that lay within the complex and which had, for many years, attracted relaxing workers and their families on their Sunday afternoons off.

It was another seven years before Aston's size and economic importance was rewarded with Urban District Council status and 14 years before Aston residents, and there were a substantial 75,000 of them at the time, voted by majority to be incorporated into Birmingham. The alternative, and long-held, local view was that in 1911 Aston was 'taken over' by the city. Whatever your view of matters politic, in 1911 Aston Villa played within the city of Birmingham for the first time.

To return to the subject in hand, the area's new status brought with it a need to alter matchday surveillance arrangements and Birmingham City Police duly took over street and ground patrols from the Staffordshire force. It is a matter of conjecture whether a Police Constable G.J.A. Stagg of the City Police 'D' Division, now working out of the Victoria Road police station in Aston, was ever on duty keeping order at the new stadium on a Saturday afternoon sometime between 1911 and 1914, but the chances were that he had taken his turn in so doing.

More intriguing is whether Stagg had patrolled pitchside when Freddie Miles, the man whose court testimony arguably sealed his fate, had played.

Breakthrough

No one could have foreseen the lucky break that gave Tommy his big chance, but when Frank Barson signed for Manchester United in August 1922 it really was a case of the right man being in the right place at the right time. The lateness of Barson's unexpected departure, reputedly following an acrimonious fallout with the board, caught Villa off guard and they entered the new season without an established replacement.

Barson, a notoriously difficult man to manage, had been in an on-and-off dispute with the Villa board since September 1920 when he had declined a directive to relocate from Yorkshire to Birmingham. He had once even refused to turn up for a First Division game and been suspended by the club for two weeks. The dispute had festered, and as plenty of other clubs were aware of the situation, Villa should perhaps not have been surprised when he took up an offer to play elsewhere.

The lateness of Barson's eventual departure, however, seemingly caught Villa off guard as they had publicly declared during the summer break that they had offered him a new contract and were confident of keeping him on their books. Indeed, Ramsay was quoted in the press as saying there was no truth in the rumour that Barson was contemplating signing for one or other of the wealthy Manchester clubs. Amazing how history repeats itself, isn't it?

Thus, Aston Villa entered the new season without an established replacement. Tommy Ball was clearly not the man earmarked for immediate succession as Ramsay tried both amateur centre-half William Barnie-Adshead, a qualified doctor and a Worcestershire cricketer, and our alpha-male future captain, wing-half-back Frank Moss.

After the side had lost three of the first four games, shipping ten goals in the process, Tommy got his chance for a very welcome 2-0 home victory on 9 September against Villa's great rivals from up the road. Shoring up the defence and being on the winning side against West Bromwich Albion would have certainly endeared him to the fans rather more than had his humbling experience against Bolton. Spare a thought for Barnie-Adshead who had been signed from university football only days before he was pressed into senior services, and had even scored a goal in a losing match vs Cardiff City, but who, after two losing appearances, was never selected again.

Selecting a reserve player like Tommy who had not yet settled into any position was probably a rather desperate last throw of the die by Ramsay, but to Tommy's great credit, it worked and thereafter the centre-half slot was his. He eventually made 74 senior appearances in the First Division plus three FA Cup matches; to the time of his death he was never dropped, only missing the odd game through injury.

Most Villa historians have emphasised the tragedy of Tommy's death by promulgating the view that he was on the verge of an England cap. Although this may well have transpired, and the England selectors of the day always appeared keen to include Villa men in their sides, it certainly cannot be proven. No one to my knowledge has pointed out that Tommy was, by descent, equally qualified to represent both Scotland and Ireland and it is quite reasonable to speculate that either of these countries might have attempted first pick.

Making an Impression?

As I have already noted, although he was clearly not without ability and no one doubted Tommy's tenacity and effort, reading between the lines it appears that a little bit of 'class' was missing. Doubtless the guile, tactics, pace, energy and physicality of the seasoned professional players he was up against took some getting used to. To support this view, Derrick Spinks in a 1990 article, said, 'Ball was never destined for great things on the pitch'.

Tony Matthews, a serial chronicler of former Villa players, praises with a couple of faint damns in calling Ball 'a determined player though a little rugged … [who was] rapidly gaining in polish'. This may be roughly translated as 'promising, but not yet there'.

The Birmingham Gazette's obituary appreciation of Tommy published on 20 November 1923 ran along similar lines, citing his early appearances as 'shaky' but noting 'week by week saw a steady but sound improvement in his work until he started the present season as one of the strongest centre half backs in the country'.

The paper credited him with being 'rugged and determined ... a pluckier player never stepped on the field' and noted that he often played through injury. It was *The Birmingham Gazette*'s prediction that Ball 'promised to go far' which may have given rise to the belief that he was destined to play for England. In all, I cannot help thinking the paper's appreciation reads uncomfortably like the morale-boosting, end-of-term report for a worthy, hard-working, though not especially gifted, school student.

The 17 November 1923 edition of *The Villa News and Record* also offered a fulsome, yet objectively critical, obituary summary of Ball's career. This included the estimation that 'though he had the makings of a footballer of more than average ability ... he gained brilliance through perseverance ... and had the pluck to plod to reach first-class form' and 'at first there seemed some doubt that he would be able to wear Barson's boots'. It added the endorsement that 'he was a man who meant to succeed, and by patience, diligence, determination and a careful regard to the advice of old players he improved to such an extent that he became a reliable, confident and very capable centre half back'.

At a time when there was no shortage of old players around the committee rooms of Villa Park to offer advice, the most important old player to heed would be George Ramsay. The tone used in the programme rather suggests that it was Ramsay who was writing, or at least approving, the obituary and, by the by, taking due credit for Tommy's progress. In fairness to him, Ramsay certainly knew as much about the game as any man living and, if he did write or approve the lines before they went into print, the somewhat measured appraisal of Tommy's progress and abilities must be taken at face value.

Tommy's First Division playing record is included in the appendices at the rear of this work and, when analysed, it shows the one heavy defeat at the back end of the 1919/20 season, then six defeats, six victories and one draw in 1920/21, the defeats being at the price of 33 goals conceded, or a hefty four per game. In 1921/22 Tommy played in five winning teams, one draw and five defeats. In 1922/23 he played in 35 games, winning 14, losing 11 and drawing ten in an improving season, while in the 1923/24 season, up to and including 10 November, he had won six out of 14 played, with six draws. That amounted in total to 31 winning games in the league, with 19 draws and 24 defeats, a respectable but not outstanding record, and you have to throw in two FA Cup wins in 1921/22 and a defeat in 1922/23.

But, as Paul Lester wrote, in autumn 1923 Ball's form was so good 'as to have established him as the most reliable player in the team'. Certainly, the conceding of only 40 goals in his 35 appearances in 1922/23 suggests that his presence, and regular central defensive partnership with George Blackburn, had been shutting the door on opposition forwards a little bit more than previously.

It should always be borne in mind that leaving home and living in rented accommodation in a new area while initially knowing no one could be culturally unsettling for a young man. To begin with Tommy may well have felt a bit lost and such a learning curve is regularly cited as a justification of the modern 'loan' system, which pushes young hopefuls into similar 'sink-or-swim' deep waters away from the comforts of family life. It was probably no coincidence that Tommy's upturn in form in 1922 followed his marriage when he began to enjoy a more confident and settled life.

Mr Ramsay's Insurance Policy

Ball's improving form did not, however, stop Villa going to Aberdeen in August 1923 to sign, as an amateur, the highly rated centre-half Dr Victor Milne, who had already chalked up 123 appearances in the highly competitive Scottish First Division and had twice been named as a reserve for the national team.

According to Goodyear and Matthews, it was Milne who was signed to replace Barson, and Matthews in his *Who's Who of Aston Villa* is specific in saying that Milne 'took over' the centre-half slot from Barson. Well, he did eventually but well over a year after Barson had left and only following Ball's death. Had Milne been earmarked as Barson's successor this could only have been the case if Ramsay had harboured limited faith in Ball's long-term prospects, and there may be some truth in that.

It was a view evidently shared by the *Dundee Evening Telegraph* of 22 August 1923, quoted by Farrelly, Abbott and Russell, which actually said 'they [i.e. Villa] believe he will fill Frank Barson's place satisfactorily.' A little presumptuous, I think, though it is quite possible that Ramsay had deliberately fed this information to the Scottish press. Make of that what you will. It was also interesting to see that the article claimed the good doctor was joining Villa 'as a professional' when every account one reads of Milne's career is quite specific in confirming his amateur status.

Taking account of Ramsay's carefully phrased obituary assessments of Tommy's ability, my conclusion is that Milne would have been brought in as insurance in case Tommy did not maintain his form. I am in good company in this respect as, in their book *Aston Villa, The Complete Record*, Rob Bishop and Frank Holt make the precise point that Milne was signed as cover for Tommy. Despite what the *Dundee Evening Telegraph* suggested, the previously cited Farrelly, Abbott and Russell masterpiece also endorses that view.

In later years, Milne was to confirm on film that Aberdeen had been paid £1,500 for his transfer or in excess of £75,000 in

2022 terms. This was not the sort of money clubs then shelled out on players who might have been brought in just to turn out for the reserves and make the odd senior appearance covering an injury; they had young hopefuls like Tommy Ball and Percy Jones for that sort of job. The carrot of an opportunity to develop his medical career in the midlands had also been dangled in front of Milne. By taking some trouble in doing the groundwork necessary to open doors for the ambitious Scotsman should he choose to come south, Mr Ramsay must have had good reasons for getting his man.

Whatever the reason Ramsay signed Milne, Tommy would have remembered the hard lesson learned when Tommy Mort had been brought in over his head as a full-back. He would have been only too aware of the new, well-rated, taller and significantly more experienced man with a reputation for being a prolific passer of the ball and doubtless worked on his game accordingly.

Milne deputised for the injured Ball on two occasions in September 1923 but otherwise did not get a look-in until the weekend following Tommy's death. In the way that things eventually worked out, however, Milne's signing looks in hindsight to have been a flash of inspiration on Ramsay's part and over the few years following Ball's death the club was to be very thankful they had him. The Scotsman had seen war action as a gunner on the Western Front and the presence on the books of a mature, experienced and talented centre-half, able to immediately fill a void in the team, was more than fortunate. As Milne was registered as an amateur thus drawing no wages, at least officially, it looked a good piece of business.

Had things turned out differently during the fateful 1923/24 season, Tommy rather than Vic Milne might well have played for Villa in the 1924 FA Cup Final against Newcastle United.

Had he supported either Sunderland or Newcastle a final-tie match against 'the Toon' would have been a dream come true, though for significantly differing reasons. He would, in fact, have probably made a return to the North-east on 12 January 1924 when Villa played away in the FA Cup first round to Ashington, then founder members of the new Third Division North.

Just a month after this game, the man who shot him was sentenced to death.

Part 2

George Stagg – From Bristol to Brum

A West Country Boy

George Stagg's background was similar in many respects to that of Tommy Ball. He had not been born or raised in Birmingham, he was of the working class, came from a family of several siblings and had looked beyond an urban labouring life for his financial security. In Ball's case, the security had been offered by football; in Stagg's case, it was the army.

He was born in October 1878 in the heavily populated St James parish of Bristol to parents who hailed from Somerset. George's father, also George, was born in 1845 in the prosperous market village of Axbridge and his wife, Sarah Tinknell, was born three years later in the more modest nearby hamlet of Mudgeley, near Wedmore, where the couple settled after marriage in 1867.

I have had cause to spend a lot of time in that area and once passed a sunlit couple of hours scouring the tombstones in St Mary's churchyard, Wedmore, to see who I could come across. Despite it once having been a common local name I didn't find any Staggs, but I did find some Tinknell resting places, including that of Simon, George's maternal grandfather.

Apart from George, the family eventually comprised three more boys, Tom, Simon and Isaac, and three girls, Betsy, Alice and Frances. Although there was also one infant death at some point, given the infant mortality rates of the times the family, like the Balls, probably counted themselves as particularly fortunate in having so many children who survived into adulthood.

Unlike the Balls, the Staggs were often itinerant in pursuit of George senior's work as a carpenter. Their first move was to Bristol around 1875 before returning to Mudgeley, where they were recorded in the 1881 census as lodging with Sarah's older sister and her two children. They then moved out of the area to Oxford where they appear in the 1891 census before finally moving, at some time before 1895, into Aston. In 1899, George's father was to pass away and his mother returned to Bristol to live in the Barton Hill area with three of her unmarried, grown-up children, Simon, Alice and Isaac.

Queen and Country

It was no doubt a tough and unpredictable life for all, but the army has traditionally been a means of escape from overcrowding and financial hardship and in 1895, at the age of 17, young George enlisted in the 1st Battalion Royal Warwickshire Regiment, now the Royal Regiment of Fusiliers. 'The Warwicks' were a renowned fighting regiment and had seen action during the 19th century doing their bit in Queen Victoria's so-called imperial 'small wars'.

George duly played his part in colonial campaigns by serving in the Sudan under General Kitchener. He was present fighting the Dervishes, the enemy frequently referred to by Corporal Jones of *Dad's Army* fame, at the battle of the Atbara in April 1898 and, in the following September, at the better-remembered battle of Omdurman.

Most descriptions of Stagg give this information, but in the interests of obtaining a fuller picture of the man, I have acquired evidence from the regimental archive that he was awarded both the Queen's Sudan Medal (QSM) and the Khedive's Sudan Medal (KSM). The latter was given by the then head of an Egyptian government grateful for the crushing of the so-called Mahdist insurrection on his southern border.

Collectors will be interested to know that George's Khedive medal was issued with both the 'Khartoum' clasp, indicating his presence at Omdurman, and with the scarcer 'Atbara' clasp. When a similar pair of medals belonging to a private soldier serving in the Rifle Brigade, though having only the single 'Khartoum' clasp, came on to the market in 2021 their auction estimate was given as £495.

Adding a premium for the rarer Atbara clasp, and a further premium for George Stagg's notoriety, should his pair suddenly emerge on the market, I would guess we would begin at around £1,000 for the set, quite probably a good deal more. Throw in Stagg's later Great War medals and his silver discharge badge, as we shall come to, and you have an uncommon and slightly more valuable collection.

I was tickled recently when watching a rerun of a *Dad's Army* episode in which Corporal Jones arrived on parade improperly dressed with his Sudan and Great War medals on his chest. He showed off both the QSM and the KSM, proclaiming proudly to a nonplussed Captain Mainwearing that he had an Atbara clasp.

Civvy Street

It is not clear precisely when Stagg left the army, but it was either 1902 or 1903. Having initially found work as a railway porter, he evidently decided to return to the uniformed, disciplined life and on 29 September 1904 joined Birmingham City Police as PC 127 working out of 'D' Division. This unit had responsibility for much of north-east Birmingham including parts of Stechford, Saltley, Bordesley Green and, eventually, Aston. Following the latter's incorporation into Birmingham in 1911, the Division used the Victoria Road police station which lay about a ten-minute walk from the Villa ground, hence my previous thought that he may well have taken his turn there on crowd duty on Saturday afternoons.

George's police career proceeded in a normal manner with annual incremental recognition for his length of service. Beginning at 'Fourth Grade' in 1904, he was paid 27 shillings a week, which at 2022 rates equates to around £168. By 1914, with ten years' service to his credit and promoted to Police Officer Grade One, he was earning one pound 16 shillings per week, or just under £225 at 2022 rates.

Though this was not remotely comparable with a top footballer's weekly wage, it was not at all bad for the standards of the time. Throw in the fact that the job was pensionable, then something of a novelty, and you might agree that George was doing all right for himself. He had even earned himself a recorded commendation in 1906 'for exercising his powers of observation and arresting a housebreaker'. For this public service, he was awarded a handsome gratuity of one guinea, worth one pound and one shilling or around £130 at 2022 values.

Following his marriage to local girl Mary Ellen Cannon on 9 September 1906, at the now demolished church of St James the Less in Ashted, the couple settled into rented terraced accommodation at 54 Whitacre Road, Bordesley Green, possibly occupying a bedroom with shared kitchen, as was a normal arrangement at the time. Between 1907 and 1910, they had three children, George Junior, Frances and Ellen ('Nell').

Although Bordesley was administratively well within Birmingham, it remained, as it had been from medieval times, part of the ecclesiastical parish of Aston and was spiritually administered from Aston Church. To the chagrin of many couples unwittingly wedded there on a matchday Saturday afternoon, the church sits virtually next door to Villa Park and there were always passing crowds to cheerfully wish the less-than-happy couple well. Or something like that.

Not everything, however, had been plain sailing for George. In March 1905, he had been reported to his superiors by a female occupant of a house in Aston for 'improperly calling her up' at 5.40am after her husband had left for work. Although it does not sound good, his service record simply notes 'explained' and the episode, whatever the reason for the occurrence, did not prevent his annual grade promotion.

A much later breach of discipline, recorded on 5 October 1914, had wider-reaching consequences. The record tells us that Stagg had been formally cautioned for 'speaking in an insolent manner' to his immediate superior, an Inspector John Walker, on 16 September while on 'protection duty' at Salford Circus. For keen observers of matchday traffic congestion, this is where the A5127 Lichfield Road slip onto Spaghetti Junction is today situated. I have no clues from the newspapers of any event on that day such as a public meeting, VIP visit or a disturbance of some kind. Given the date, I would guess there may have been a recruiting point within the vicinity which created some kind of stir.

Whatever it was, the caution was doubtless an unwelcome 'knuckle wrap', but it did not prevent the almost immediate award of George's annual wage increment with the career-landmark added financial entitlement for ten years of service. We must therefore conclude that his general conduct as a police officer had met with the full approval of his employer and that he could move on from the incident.

AWOL

A month later, on 16 November, Stagg incurred a further written admonishment in absentia due to his having been absent from duties without leave (AWOL) for two weeks.

We know of at least one thing he had done whilst absent because on 9 November he had turned up at Whittington Barracks near Lichfield, a few miles up the road into Staffordshire, to sign on for armed forces service and was attested under service number 3/8205. He was one of 570 officers of the city police to do so, 50 being subsequently killed in action. The difference was that most of the others had given notice of their intention to their employer. By the time George's absence from work was formally recorded, he was in northern Scotland undertaking basic military training and a month after that he was on the front line in France.

Communications were reinstated at some point, since on 16 January 1915 he was, without obvious fuss, 'allowed to resign' from the force. Whether George was given no option but to do this, or the police thought it not worth their while taking further disciplinary action while he was responding to the national emergency, is not known. The upshot was that George lost his pensionable job and Mary Stagg lost the not inconsiderable potential advantage of a compensation payout to widows of serving policemen killed in action.

Let us pause awhile on this. Going AWOL was a serious issue and Stagg, aged 36, which in those days was considered moving into middle age, had been in a secure pensionable job and had a wife and three children under the age of eight to support. Jeopardising financial security, not to mention putting himself at considerable personal risk, requires some level of explanation.

As it appears improbable that George was going to face further disciplinary action for stepping out of line at Salford Circus the decision was not, on the face of it, a knee-jerk reaction to his spat with Inspector Walker. As many readers will recognise, however, a falling-out with a workplace superior can make anyone's life a bit difficult and if this was the reason for George going AWOL, it could be seen as a classic case of his cutting off his nose to spite his face.

We should, perhaps, bear in mind the strange times he was living through. An impulse decision to forgo home comforts and steady paid work was not particularly unusual in 1914; a great many young, and not so young, men made the seemingly illogical decision to leave home, family and waged employment for the privilege of being shot at by the German army or navy. In Stagg's case, there may have been nothing more to it than another bloke who wanted to 'do his bit' and who did not see much further than that.

If we are to believe the press reports of 1923 and 1924, the decision may have come back to haunt him. Newspapers of that time contained the oft-repeated information that at some point after he had been invalided out of the army, late in 1915, George had unsuccessfully tried to rejoin the police service in Birmingham but was debarred, apparently owing to disability following his being wounded in action. *The Staffordshire Advertiser*'s court report from February 1924 goes further by suggesting he had never left the city force and was simply told he could not return because he was unfit for service. This is not untypical of the general misinformation surrounding George Stagg that the newspapers ran with as his record card clearly dates his formal resignation in 1915.

Intriguingly, Corinne Brazier, my contact at the West Midland Police Force, can find no archival record of any attempt to re-enlist. It would not surprise me if the press, often guessing at George's backstory, had invented the attempt to rejoin. There always remains the possibility that, at a time when there was considerable public interest in his background, someone 'on his side' had ensured that incorrect information made its way into the papers. This may be related to the fact that George's defence counsel at Stafford was keen to emphasise in court his client's good character and patriotism, and possibly added a bit of gloss to his backstory to cover up any awkward questions should the absenteeism that had led to his resignation from the force come to light in court.

Had the reported re-enlistment attempt been correct, which I doubt, there is a high probability that the AWOL issue would have closed the door on his picking up his police career when hostilities were over. The open-arms welcome back into the service enjoyed by his fellow police volunteers who had obtained formal permission to join up was probably always unlikely to be offered. Even had he been successful in rejoining it would have meant him being treated as a recruit and he would have, for the second time, begun at the bottom of the pay scale.

George's name is included on the Birmingham City Police 'Great European War' Roll of Honour board. This records those serving policemen who joined the armed forces and was for years mounted within the West Midlands Police headquarters building. I had originally thought it strange that, despite being included on that record, he is not included within the online WMP History Society list of casualties.

His 1915 resignation from the force provides the answer: as a serving officer, despite being AWOL at the time he enlisted in the army, he would qualify to be recorded on the police enlistment roll, but at the time of his wounding in March 1915 he was no longer in police employ and thus did not qualify for further mention in their records.

Your Country Needs You

Whatever the reason for him walking out on his police entitlements, George Stagg was hardly taking his leave to lie back on a bed of roses. As I have noted, he may have been one of the thousands who 'took the shilling' on an impulse and then, after the event, told their employer/parents/spouse/sweetheart what they had done. In George's case his wife did have a level of financial security as he still received, in perpetuity, the police pension entitlements he had already earned, and for the short duration of his active service I have no doubt that the income went directly to Mrs Stagg who would also have picked up part of his army wage.

Despite the prospect of cash in hand, Mary's reaction to the news of her husband's enlistment can only be guessed at, especially when she learned to where he had been posted.

For a man born in Bristol, raised in Somerset, settled in Birmingham, enlisted in Staffordshire and with previous military service in the Warwicks, it came as a surprise to me, and probably him, that he was deployed to Scotland. His new regiment, the Seaforth Highlanders, was hardly barracked round the corner but at Fort George, near Inverness in north-eastern Scotland. Why he did not join up at one of the Birmingham recruiting centres is another mystery as this might have taken him back into the familiar territory of the Warwicks.

Instead, he enlisted in Lichfield and perhaps, for some reason, he hoped to be placed in situ with the South Staffordshires just up the road; instead, only four days later, he arrived at Fort George to join his new regiment, known after its founder as 'the Mackenzies'.

At a time when conscription was non-existent, volunteers were needed, and lots of them. In August 1914, the British standing army of 950,000 was relatively small and critically underpowered compared to Germany's four and a half million men under arms. Moreover, it was still optimised for Victorian-era, short-term conflicts against native foes largely in Asia and in Africa.

Although its soldiers were famously well-trained professionals the army had run into trouble in the late 1890s and early 1900s against the Boers in South Africa when faced with a colonial war which, unusually, dragged on. The unexpected difficulty in subduing the Boers, coupled with high sickness levels and the growing anticipation of a likely European conflict, had caused considerable government concern that the army's size and structure would at some near point require drastic revision. Battling Boer mounted irregulars who specialised in hit-and-run raids and tactical ambushes on the High Veldt was, in any event, not good preparation for taking on the highly mechanised German fighting machine in battles on rain-sodden fronts likely to cover dozens of miles.

Unsurprisingly, deficiencies in contesting the British army's first European war for a hundred years became apparent as early as August 1914. After giving the advancing Germans a significant 'bloody nose' at Mons just over the French border into Belgium, the army, numerically, could not hope to hold the line and prevent the enemy from pouring into France. To reduce casualties and buy time for reinforcements to be shipped out, a morale-sapping

71

retreat into France was ordered. The government had to face the stark reality that unless they could persuade the Germans to fight the war entirely at sea where the British fleet appeared all-powerful, there was no way, under present circumstances, they were going to have the manpower to emerge victorious.

Football and War

The resultant recruiting drives of autumn 1914, fronted by the famous picture of General Kitchener, exceeded all expectations. Within the context of this book, it is worth noting that professional and amateur sports were seen by the authorities as fertile recruiting grounds, owing to the publicity to be generated by famous role models joining up and the possibility of setting up recruiting stations amongst large groups of spectators of military age.

Most regiments were eventually able to count former professional footballers amongst their ranks. The Middlesex Regiment even created a 'football pals' battalion which was to include Aston Villa player Tommy Barber, who had scored the winning goal in the 1913 FA Cup Final, and former player Billy Gerrish, who was to die in action on The Somme.

In the first instance, however, football came in for severe public criticism for lacking patriotism. The existing league campaign was not suspended but began as planned on 2 September, a full month after war had been declared, the season continuing until its planned close at the end of April 1915. By contrast, cricket, then well into its season, was suspended almost immediately and the forthcoming (amateur) rugby union season, in which all club matches were classified as friendlies, was cancelled.

Aston Villa moved to offset criticism by encouraging their players to undertake voluntary military training while the season was in progress and allowed the club's facilities to be used for army recruitment. This included the 'plum' fixture when Villa entertained Sunderland on 5 September and recruiting desks were set up around the ground. To get the spectators in the mood to sign up, a crowd of 20,000 was treated to marching military bands playing the national anthems of allied countries.

Aston Villa players also voluntarily donated money to the national emergency and chairman Rinder put on record his belief that the sport would be suspended in due course. As previously noted, five players who were to appear for Villa in the 1919 FA Cup Final had been under arms during the war, as had their later signing Dr Victor Milne.

Why Scotland?

The downside of successful recruitment initiatives was that large numbers of untrained men required fast and effective preparation for disciplined army life and thence for combat. Unsurprisingly, there were not enough experienced men under arms to act as officers, instructors or barrack room mentors for the numbers that joined up. There was therefore considerable effort put in by the army to re-recruit former soldiers to carry out such essential work and many 'old sweats' from the Boer and Sudan wars were enticed back into the colours.

On registering, Stagg would have been immediately identified as someone who could be sent into the conflict with minimal training and who might be useful in offering informal, yet informed, peer advice to his less experienced comrades and to set the requisite standards of barrack-room discipline. Even without promotion to non-commissioned officer status, an easily retrained and disciplined old timer like Stagg could prove useful in licking the younger men into shape and veterans of the war often commented on how influential such men had been to 'green' recruits.

As the Seaforths had been one of the regiments earmarked for fast deployment into France, this may have been the reason why a man with Stagg's record was immediately detailed to Inverness. He would have already been familiar with the regiment as their 1st Battalion, in which he was to serve, had fought alongside the Warwicks at Omdurman. Maybe when he was told he would go to Scotland he found some comfort in being directed to an outfit he knew something about.

At that time, soldiers were still required to wear on their tunics the ribbons of any medals won, so a visibly older and combat-experienced veteran like George would have stood out as a natural leader in his billet. Judging by his official regimental photograph, taken just prior to deployment to France, it would have taken a very brave man to challenge that informal authority. I have often wondered about Stagg's accent. As a teenage soldier with the Warwicks, his Somerset 'burr' would doubtless have attracted 'banter' from the older men, but I doubt whether any of the young lads in his Seaforth billet would have dared imitate any acquired Brummagem vowels. At least not to his face.

I had thought that getting up to Inverness would have been something of a trek, but I discovered that in the autumn of 1914 daily rail services were operating into the north of Scotland from Devonport and Portsmouth on the south coast to take naval ratings to the northern Scottish fleet bases. The service terminated at Invergordon, calling at Inverness en route, and was routed through Birmingham, picking up at Snow Hill Station. From the south coast, it was a 24-hour journey to Invergordon, so his journey to Inverness would have taken George something approaching 20 hours and I doubt there would have been a readily vacant seat for anyone getting on at Brum.

On arrival at Inverness, George was fast-tracked into 'F' company which prepared men for almost immediate deployment to France. After only two weeks of basic training, and at the age of 36, he was considered physically and mentally fit enough, and sufficiently competent in skill-at-arms, to be sent out for overseas service. On 18 December 1914, just a month after joining up, George arrived in France where he and other volunteers, including a couple of fellow 'fast-trackers' recruited from the London area at the same time, joined up with the Seaforth's 1st Battalion.

The battalion had begun the year based in India before being shipped back to Europe via the Suez Canal, landing in Marseilles and heading by train to northern France. The arrivals from India would all have been long-term enlisters with up to 20 years' service behind them. They were coming from the heat and humidity of Asian conditions, and most probably brought with them a healthy scepticism regarding the winter weather they could expect in north-eastern France as well as the new recruits about to be forced on them.

Into Action

By any standards Stagg's ability to prove himself fit for active service is impressive, though it was perhaps to his advantage that the infantry was still using the Lee Enfield bolt-action rifle he would have been familiar with from the 1890s.

The most proficient fully trained men could fire up to 30 aimed rounds a minute from such a weapon, 20 being an average performance. Even that average is some going and at Mons many of the forward units of the German army, advancing over the

Belgian coalfields and canals and faced with relatively small 'dug-in' numbers of highly trained riflemen armed with Lee Enfields, were convinced they were being strafed by machine gunners. The fact that Stagg had proved himself up to scratch as a marksman was presumably not lost on jurors in 1924.

It appears scarcely credible to the modern mind that a man could have seen action at two seemingly utterly contrasting theatres of war as the Sudan and the Western Front.

In the former, British troops faced generally poorly armed native irregulars, many having only swords or spears. Nevertheless, at close quarters they were a foe to be reckoned with: in poet Rudyard Kipling's words, 'You're a poor benighted 'eathen, but a first-class fighting man'. It is no surprise that Philip Warner in his *Army Life in the '90s* says the first rule of infantry engagement against native irregulars was simple: you had to shoot your man before he could get to you. I doubt whether George ever forgot that, nor when considering the events of 11 November 1923 should we, because it begins to make some sense of things.

In imperial conflict, British army tactics needed to be adapted to local conditions, but some aspects had remained constant over the previous century. At Omdurman, the infantry had formed ranks into squares, as they had done at Waterloo 80 years beforehand, and a regiment of lancers even employed a potentially suicidal open-field cavalry charge, a tactic that would have been recognisable to anyone who had fought either in Napoleonic battles or in the Crimea in the 1850s. The Western Front, however, was to offer no such opportunities; forming squares no longer featured in infantry training manuals and, to their general disappointment, cavalrymen often found themselves deployed only on scouting missions.

British casualties at Omdurman had been light, with only 47 men killed. Less than 20 years later, war in northern France was the scene of mechanised slaughter on an industrial scale. A connecting point, marking the end of the old 19th-century colonial tactics, was that hundreds of the Dervishes at Omdurman were wiped out by artillery fire and machine gunners before they could get close to the British. Another connection was that some of the British regiments dug and defended trenches against enemy attack. This was the future and George would certainly have recognised both tactical connections when he arrived on the Western Front.

Copping a Blighty One

At the battle of Neuve Chapelle, fought in the Pas de Calais area north of Lens between 13 March and 15 March 1915, George was severely wounded with a bullet passing through his left calf.

Despite over 13,000 British and Indian troops being killed or wounded in a carnage almost laughably classified by military historians as a 'small battle', some experimental tactics used were deemed to be reasonably successful. The use of 'creeping' battery fire from supporting heavy artillery aimed in front of attacking infantry to clear barbed wire and opposition troops out of their way became standard fare, though, as on the Somme the following year, not always well executed or successful: the less risky trial of issuing units with aerial photographs of the German trench patterns was subsequently deemed indispensable to ground actions.

Although his wound was a setback, it did mean that Stagg was fortuitously unable to be present at the later battle of Aubers Ridge in May 1915 when the first battalion of the Seaforths fought in an engagement so ill-conceived that a political crisis erupted at home concerning the under-availability of ammunition at the front. The battalion was badly mauled by machine-gun fire and what was left of it found itself transferred back through the Suez Canal to the Mesopotamian port of Basra, in modern Iraq, to confront the Turks.

Following his wounding, George would have been transferred through a pattern of medical centres beginning with an assessment close to the front line. This was followed by treatment at a field dressing station known as an 'ambulance', though this was a moveable tent rather than a motor vehicle, and then at a regional casualty clearing station. As the wound was serious enough to keep him away from the front, he would have been transferred to a base station near to one of the Channel ports and thence repatriated to Britain for the long railway journey to hospital in Scotland.

After several months' treatment, and recuperation with the Seaforth's home-based third battalion at Cromarty, George Stagg was honourably discharged from service on 10 September 1915. As his military pension is recorded as beginning on 11 October, he may well have had a case for being denied a month's payment.

Apart from bullet entry and exit scars which were noted on his 1924 Home Office medical assessment, the exact nature of George's leg injury is not known. His pension card entry was not well served by the hands of the various Ministry of Pensions clerks who contributed to it between 1915 and 1927. The handwriting that described the initial leg injury and the scribbles written over several years of periodic reassessment are, apart from one or two words, virtually illegible. As his 1924 prison medical report made no reference to skeletal damage, and I think we can assume it was more serious than a flesh wound, it was possibly the perforation of an artery, which was a common gunshot wound during the Great War.

A Dodgy Chest

To my surprise, not one but two disabilities are noted on the pension assessment. As said, the leg wound is illegibly recorded but a second issue, is surprisingly clearly shown as 'pleurisy'. This was new information having never, to my knowledge, surfaced previously in the public domain. It needs to be set alongside George's eventual 1924 prison medical report, which although it reveals that he declared time in hospital in 1917 while apparently suffering from tuberculosis, said nothing about pleurisy.

This is especially puzzling as a compulsory annual review was in force for all wounded veterans receiving a pension, so by his prison incarceration in 1923 he would, presumably, have been medically reassessed by the Ministry of Pensions on seven previous occasions. The prison authorities at Winson Green, where he was held pre-trial, and including the examining doctor, must have had access to this information but, for some unaccountable reason, it was not noted in his pre-trial report. One presumes that as pleurisy is a viral infection it may have cleared itself up well before the events of 1923 took place.

The 1924 prison report does, however, mention 'shortness of breath'; whether that represented the tuberculosis, which he had claimed, or the wartime pleurisy, or both, we do not know. To have had one respiratory medical problem would have been serious enough, but to have possibly suffered from two such illnesses was bad luck in the extreme. To confuse matters, the 1924 press reports went a bit further and suggested a 'heart complaint'. There is no mention anywhere else of such an issue, but like a lot of things about George Stagg, it is that which has no evidence to support it that has survived as fact.

To add to the medical confusion, the *Illustrated Police News* for 22 November 1923 featured the 'fact' that Stagg was 'said' to have been gassed at Neuve Chapelle. Not only is this not officially recorded on his war pension record, it is most unlikely to have occurred. The first instance of the Germans making tactical use of chlorine gas, at Ypres in April 1915, was after Stagg was out of the front line and possibly back in Scotland. Perhaps a reporter mistook his respiratory ailment(s) as the effects of exposure to gas or perhaps someone thought it might make better dramatic 'copy'. And copied it has been ever since.

Whatever chest complaint(s) he suffered from, if George did undergo hospitalisation in 1917 there was clearly an ongoing problem and this could, at least partially, explain why he initially found a return to civilian work difficult to come by or maintain. He may well have been suffering from chest problems before re-enlistment, but in autumn 1914 recruiting desks did not always turn away men who were carrying a non-visible medical condition, especially when they had the sort of service record that George could show. They were similarly cavalier with the enlistment of underage boys.

Then again, Stagg may have thought it could count against his enlistment and simply did not mention it. It is probably fair to say that any existing respiratory illness would have become quickly aggravated by winter conditions at the front. Given that in 1915 men from all over the army were being sent back to the front line when either physically or mentally unfit, certainly by modern standards, Stagg's overall condition must have been serious. Indeed, his pension card records him as being 80 per cent disabled, however that was calculated.

As suggested, with the post-war government's eye always on clawing back a bit of money, George's disability pension, as was customary, was periodically reassessed to determine whether the disability had been overcome. In the case, for example, of an amputee whose prosthetic limb(s) eventually enabled him to return to work, a saving could be made and the pension was duly withdrawn. As Stagg's disability record is only available up to 1927, we have no way of knowing whether the pension continued beyond that date, but given the value of his estate at death my guess is that it did.

Services Rendered

To add to his Sudan medals, George's Great War service earned him the British War Medal, the 1914/15 Star and the Victory Medal, the famous 'Pip, Squeak and Wilfred' general service collection. Although it was quite usual for Sudanese and Boer War veterans to rejoin in 1914, and many long-service career soldiers from those conflicts were still under arms at the outbreak of the war, it was rare for a man with such a collection to survive the conflict. To that extent he was an unusual specimen and probably seen by contemporaries as rather lucky to have 'copped a Blighty one', as they said of non–life-threatening injuries that finished a man's war for him.

It would certainly surprise me if his Great War and Sudan medals had not been in his wife's possession after Stagg's conviction in 1924, but whether they were retained long enough to be part of her or his estates after their deaths in the 1960s is an open question. From the 1920s Great War campaign medals have been extremely common in 'antique' shops and the like and were not always recognised by families as having emotional or hereditary value. Until recent times, sets were certainly not of any significant monetary value, and it would be quite usual for families to see no point in holding on to them even when the recipient was still alive.

Like my maternal grandfather, a Nechells Green volunteer in the Warwicks, many ex-servicemen of the Great War hardly ever took their medals out of their boxes. I now have these; the box, in decent condition, retains its original War Department handwritten Stella Street address. I have heard of some men who simply, and quite understandably, threw away the medals as a bad memory. After all, why should they want to keep mementos of their mates being killed? It is always possible, therefore, that Stagg's Great War and Sudan collection was disposed of as seemingly having no great value or interest to anyone, though, tantalisingly, it could remain forgotten somewhere in a family bottom drawer.

Nowadays, the growth of Great War information available on the internet and our recent centenary interest in that conflict have enhanced the emotional and monetary value of family war medals of all descriptions. As a caveat emptor, should you ever be offered what purport to be Stagg's Great War or Sudan medals, check the rim for his engraved name and correct regiment(s) before you part with a small fortune.

Because of his wound George was also awarded the 'discharge badge', formally known as the 'Silver War Badge'. This was designed for wounded or otherwise legitimately demobilised soldiers to wear on their right breast when in civilian dress, lest they be branded in the streets as service-avoiding cowards worthy only of the infamous 'white feather'. Around the rim the words 'For King and Empire. Services Rendered' were clearly displayed.

Add to this Stagg's apparent disavowal of drink and the fact that upon leaving the army, as he told the court at Stafford, he 'scraped and saved' to buy his two properties, you have a picture of an austere, driven, but not entirely unsympathetic man.

To round off his wartime experience, George lost Isaac, the nearest in age of his three brothers, killed in action in 1917 while serving with the Royal Field Artillery. His eldest sister, Betsy, who had previously emigrated to Canada, passed away in Moosejaw, Saskatchewan, nine days before the Armistice in November 1918, and his mother died in Devon the following year. For good measure, I believe his mother-in-law, Ellen Cannon, who had been lodging with him and Mary, died at some point in 1923. Should the mood have taken him, George Stagg certainly had plenty to be morose about.

'Scraping and Saving'

The 'scraping and saving' described by Stagg at his trial, though often misrepresented as 'scrimping and saving', was necessary if he was to make anything of his life from 1915 onwards. This was especially so if he had shortages of breath attributable to either or both of the possible chest conditions noted previously. It may also be that his leg wound, which had plainly been a serious one, caused him difficulty when walking, and these medical issues are worth remembering when we later trace his movements to search for a doctor immediately following his shooting of Tommy Ball.

From late 1918, when vast numbers of men were returning from the war and clamouring for jobs, George was at a clear disadvantage. Unless he could find a means of income other than labouring, irregular, low-paid work in the north Birmingham factories was probably the best he could do. Unfortunately, there appears to be no surviving record of where, and for how long, he was employed.

He was, however, fortunate enough to be in receipt of two pensions. His police pension entitlements up to March 1915 were his in perpetuity and he had a war wounds pension which continued to at least 1927 and most possibly beyond. As the latter provided for a man wounded in action and unable to work to be compensated according to the number of dependants he had and up to the wage level he had earned pre-war, he was, in overall terms, being paid at 1914 police rates with a pension on top. Any other employment, however brief, would have represented a financial bonus.

The relatively generous Great War pension was to be a source of some concern a couple of decades later when many men wounded in the Second World War found themselves to be in receipt of a lower war wounds pension than those still drawing one following 1914–18 injuries.

So, although not rolling in money, his public service meant that George was not on the breadline either. Throw in any casual work and possibly, up until October 1923, a contribution from his working-age son and maybe a bit of 'housekeeping' from his eldest girl who would have left school, I guess, in 1920. One way or another, in 1919, George had the wherewithal, and was ambitious enough, to move everyone 'upmarket' from Bordesley Green into a leafy part of Erdington, a couple of miles to the east of Aston, at 12 Oliver Road.

Doubtless the good housekeeping of his wife was also a positive factor. Mary, as a lifelong diabetic, had her own medical problems, so quite what the couple made of her pregnancy in late 1918 is open to conjecture. The arrival of a new child may have confirmed a brighter, happier future; on the other hand, already with two children under the age of 13, it was another mouth to feed at a time when every penny counted.

Cyril was born on 10 April 1919 and the couple had appeared to take in Mary's widowed mother Ellen Cannon, then in her 60s, making the need for additional accommodation more pressing. All things considered, George would already have been planning the next move and it was one which he would certainly have carefully worked out. George and Mary Stagg had both lived in Aston, then after marriage in Bordesley Green and later Erdington. Be assured that this represented a steady move up the social scale, an eventual Perry Barr country address, should it become available, even more so. In 1921 George somehow did just that, buying the pair of semi-detached houses known as Somerville Cottages in rural Brick Kiln Lane.

I would take an obvious guess that a fresh-air environment had been part of the medical advice offered to George when he left the army. Erdington was certainly getting close to that, but the area was being built up and George was aiming even higher. In keeping with every one of us who has aspired to the purchasing of a house, it was then a question of waiting for the market to throw up a suitable property in a suitable location and at a suitable price. Compared with what both George and Mary had once been used to in the industrial terraces, a move into Perry Barr must have seemed like aiming for the stars.

Escaping to the Country

Given all of this, the picture the press painted in 1924 of George as a rather hapless individual unable to hold down regular waged employment fails, I believe, to accurately represent either him or the reality of the general employment situation of the time. In the immediate post-war period, it was not only wounded men who found employment hard to come by as thousands of able-bodied men were unable to get better than short-term unskilled manual work. This was a situation that lasted, by and large, throughout the two decades before the next world war.

George was not exactly on easy street as both he and his wife were clinically unwell and there were always mouths to feed; nevertheless, compared with many of his social class, and particularly those who were war-wounded, he was doing relatively well. He had survived the war, had regular pensions coming in and, with the purchase of Somerville Cottages, had cannily acquired two country properties, one of which might well yield a financial return. With luck, this could generate a business income into the foreseeable future.

It would have been a huge challenge for Stagg to purchase a country property. As a very rough estimate, based on general house prices at the time, I believe it would ordinarily have cost around £400 to £600 for the pair of cottages, or in the region of £20,000 to £30,000 at 2022 prices. A snip nowadays, of course, but for Stagg, even if he had been 'scraping and saving', it was a tall order. I can see no way that he would have been able to pay cash down and, as he may have been a poor risk for a loan of any sort, he would have needed to find a vendor so keen to sell that he would be happy to come to an arrangement to receive long-term payment in generously small instalments. If I am correct, that is precisely the sort of property he found.

When I was tracking down contemporary properties in Brick Kiln Lane, I noticed that in the 1911 census several of the adult males living in the lane's cottages, namely Messrs Laurence, Asbury and Sutton, worked as farm waggoners. My conclusion was that each was likely to have been employed by the Perry Hall estate, which then owned large tracts of land in the area. It is a reasonable assumption that if each of the men in question worked for the estate, they lived in a property tied to it.

Apart from Mrs Stagg herself, the Laurences, who were to play an unwitting part in the events of 11 November, were the only family still recorded on election rolls after 1923. What became of the other families is open to speculation and it is quite possible, though unproven, that Stagg had bought adjoining cottages previously occupied by the Asburys and Suttons. The absence of clear property identification on the relevant 1911 census return does not enable this supposition to be confirmed.

If many, or all, of the properties on Brick Kiln Lane had been tied to the Perry Hall estate, then everything begins to fall into place. When such landed estates were put on the market the buildings, whether the grand house or labourers' cottages, invariably required significant modernisation and upkeep and were often sold off relatively cheaply or demolished.

Following this up, I subsequently discovered that the eighth Baron Gough-Calthorpe of Perry Hall, who had succeeded to the family's title and lands in 1910, had quickly lost interest in his Staffordshire estate, preferring to live on his other holdings on the Isle of Wight. By the end of the war, the Perry Hall estate was facing crippling tax bills, including unpaid death duties from the demise of the previous Baron in 1910, and was consequently broken up in 1920 and sold off.

This would be in common with many landed estates in the period after the Great War when dozens of 'aristocrats' were in deep financial trouble having operated beyond their means for years, so running up huge amounts of debt. The fear of having to settle such debts was a theme successfully mined by Julian Fellowes when he devised *Downton Abbey*. A further problem, which emerged during the war, was that a great many estate workers had joined the armed forces leading to a general labour shortage, so forcing owners into paying increased wages which inevitably added to their problems.

To help meet national war debts, the post-war Liberal–Tory coalition government increased income tax and death duties, and big pickings were expected from places like Perry Hall. These were pickings that a great many owners could not afford, and it was quite probable that Baron Somerset Gough-Calthorpe was hit hard. Unfortunately for him and others, Prime Minister Lloyd George, a man from an extremely humble rural background in Caernarfonshire, had no problem with squeezing the toffs. The result was that many large estates underwent what we would today term 'fire sales' by getting rid of employees, and their wages, along with any depreciating assets such as the accommodation tied staff lived in.

George Stagg, who must have been keeping his eye on the Perry Hall situation, appears to have been a beneficiary of such. If I am correct in this assumption, the need of the estate to sell might have reduced the purchase price to around, or even below, half of the market value I have previously estimated for similar properties elsewhere. It would be no surprise if the vendor's agent had been happy to come to an instalment payment arrangement. It is all speculation, but I feel it makes perfect sense.

It was also something of a golden opportunity for a man like George Stagg who had difficulty in finding regular work but who had a keen eye for the main chance. We might nowadays call it the 'escape to the country solution', whereby moving to that dream home is even better if it comes complete with a building or rooms that can be let out.

In this case it was not an annexe or a 'BnB' possibility but letting out the mirror-image house next door. Finding a tenant for this property might well have been the key to Stagg's planning as the rental income quite possibly gave him the wherewithal to meet repayments on the cottages with perhaps a little left over. Rental income has always been notoriously unreliable, so to acquire a tenant as regularly well paid as Tommy Ball would have been something of a godsend and no doubt the amount George charged would reflect that good luck.

Not that he might have lost sleep about a bit of overcharging; before the war, as we have seen, he was earning barely a fifth of what Tommy Ball was now bringing in. It is possible that the arrival next door of a physically fit, famous, upwardly mobile and cash-wealthy young man may have given rise to some feelings of envy. The considerable upside was that it gave George something of a money tree.

Given Tommy's regular and seemingly guaranteed level of income, it would have been a big decision in summer 1923 for George to have given the Balls notice to quit. With Tommy gone, George would have been forced to go back into the market to find another tenant.

This failure to apply the eviction became a key point at Stagg's trial, but I see it as a logical reaction to the anticipated loss of anything he may have been getting from his eldest boy who was planning to emigrate. The application procedure the lad had to go through to be admitted into Australia was lengthily bureaucratic and Stagg, as legal signatory to any arrangement, would have known of his son's intentions for some time. The anticipated loss of this 'housekeeping' and the likely difficulty in finding another tenant as able to meet his bills as regularly as Tommy could not be ignored.

Although Beatrice Ball confirmed in court that they had stayed on because they had not been able to find alternative accommodation, I am not in the least surprised that the eviction notice was never enforced.

'Down Under'

George John Alan Junior left England at the end of October, aged 16, aboard the *Largs Bay* out of London bound for Brisbane and was eventually to settle in Townsville on the north Victoria coast. I had initially assumed that the emigration was a knee-jerk reaction to the events surrounding Ball's death, but it had nothing to do with it as when the shooting took place the young man was somewhere in the middle of the Atlantic.

Emotionally difficult for the family to accept as young George's decision may have been, it was not an unusual situation as 'Pommies' were buying cheap tickets to Australia until into the second half of the century. In any case, it was not unusual in those days for many families to experience the disappearance of 'one of the boys' to find fame and fortune who knew where, and many families grew up with a mysterious missing uncle. It happened in mine when one of my father's eight brothers disappeared for long periods from the early 1920s. He made intermittent, brief, spare-room reappearances at our house over 30 years or so, drifting out alone of an evening to spend what little money he had in the Villa Tavern on Aston Church Road. Once the money had run out, he vanished again with no one ever any the wiser about where he went, what he did or what eventually happened to him.

The cold comfort to George and Mary was to know where George Junior ended up and, in Mary's case, to remain in written contact with him and, in time, his new family 'down under'. Less happy was the fact that after October 1923 Mary never saw him again, never met his wife and never gave her Australian grandchildren a hug.

Mary Ellen Cannon

It is now therefore opportune to look more closely at the woman George Stagg married.

Mary Cannon had experienced ill health since childhood, having to contend with lifelong diabetes for which, until at least the later 1920s and probably much later, she was unlikely to have had access to regular medication. As the treatment of the disease with clinically manufactured insulin was not introduced until 1923, when she was 37, it is doubtful whether she would have had any effective means of stabilising the condition before then. It is worth pointing out at this stage the key fact that untreated diabetes typically results in a deterioration of the eyesight.

When insulin was made available in 1923, it was under licence from the patent holder, the University of Toronto, at an initial nominal cost of one Canadian dollar per dosage to wholesalers, to which we can add the supply chain's costs and all commercial profits. We are not to know when, or if, it became regularly affordable to Mary, but following the advent of the NHS in 1948 when she was in her 60s might be a reasonable guess.

Mary was born in December 1884 in Aylesbury, Buckinghamshire, and shared an Irish heritage with her future footballing neighbour. Her father, John Joseph Cannon, was an itinerant blacksmith from Roscommon County who had married an Ellen Whiting in Portsmouth in May 1875, when she was pregnant with their first child John Joseph Junior. In addition to Mary, the couple went on to have three more children: William in 1882, Lillian in 1888 and Elizabeth ('Lizzy') in 1892.

Cannon, like George Stagg Senior, was often on the move, including spending time in India where second son William was born, and online family memory also has Mary in India for a time. If correct, his time overseas along with the Portsmouth marriage causes me to conclude that he may have been a naval man, either directly under the flag or, more likely, employed as a dockyard civilian.

At the time of the 1891 census, the family was domiciled in the Nechells area of Birmingham at 10 Northumberland Street, not far from where my maternal family lived. Northumberland Street was a typical Brummagem mid- to late-Victorian factory workers' terraced street with front rooms being one step up from the pavement and having a cobbled rear yard with coalhouse and almost certainly an outside toilet shared with other properties.

Overcrowding, including three generations of families, would have been endemic and the roadway, in the absence of motorised vehicles, would have doubled as the children's playground. Surprisingly for such a previously mobile group, the family was still there at the turn of the century, which probably suggests a consistent shortage of money.

By 1901, Mary was employed in one of the 200 or so small Birmingham backstreet factories involved in the 'press pin trade', making fixings for badges, though the word 'factory' often dignifies what was, in reality, a collection of backyard sheds. It was common practice in factory work in those days for retiring employees to provide, if available, a ready-made replacement from their family and, as the 1911 census records her younger sister Lizzy being in the same trade, it is possible that Mary gave up her job to her sibling when marriage and children arrived. Part of the family 'bargain' in those days decreed that the eldest female daughter should, in good time, take on responsibility for accommodating any single parent; this is perhaps why Ellen Cannon ended her days lodging with Mary and George.

A Silent Wife

Mary's part, or lack of it, in her husband's eventual trials is one of the key issues of the story.

We are given to understand that she was, apart from George, the only witness to the shooting and, quite possibly, to the argument that preceded it. According to her husband, and implicitly corroborated by Beatrice Ball, Mary appeared to have witnessed at least part of the scene from an open bedroom window and had entered into a brief, spirited dialogue with Tommy.

Though the level of visual clarity she enjoyed is, as we shall see, uncertain, she may have heard much of what passed perfectly well. She also had a confirmed brief exchange of words with Beatrice when she went into the Ball house while her husband went for a doctor and would have seen Tommy's dead body on the settee.

From the tone of the evidence given in court by Beatrice, it is apparent that, regardless of how the two men got on, the relationship between the two women was anything but cordial. I suspect this could have been the real reason behind the supposed antipathy of the two families towards each other and which became a central feature of the 1924 trial: the ebb and flow of backyard politics between the womenfolk in our part of Saltley certainly determined how the menfolk were supposed to behave towards one another. My pals from other parts of the street said much the same and I have no doubt it had been similar in most of the densely packed terraced streets.

Mary was perfectly within her legal rights of 'spousal privilege' not to give evidence at her husband's trial, but given the stakes at play we may find it difficult to understand why she did not. Although I think we can safely assume she would have spent time privately giving her version of events to her husband's counsel, she was not formally questioned by the police, nor required to submit a signed deposition.

George was to say at the petty session hearing on 28 November 1923, he did not want anyone else alongside him. We know, therefore, he meant Mary to stay out of things, and 'spousal privilege' gave him the right to forbid her to speak. Maybe that was also her wish. Once the case reached the Winter Assize, however, in front of a judge able to pass a death sentence, the stakes had risen considerably and the option of putting Mary on the witness stand must have been seriously considered.

She may, of course, have been frightened to appear in the threatening formality of open court, and perhaps lacked the confidence to face questioning. As counsel will generally prefer not to call witnesses who may be vulnerable to aggressive cross-examination, the defence team, having weighed up what she could add to their case, or potentially detract from it, may have advised her to stay clear.

For conspiracy theorists, maybe her version of events did not match the defence's case. Here we turn to something that was forensically investigated in 1978 by United States psychological researchers Brian Clifford and Jane Scott. They were able to show that a distance from a crime scene of greater than 15 metres, especially when aggravated by poor lighting, which is technically defined as less than 15 lux, invariably results in the possibility of a witness offering a significant misrepresentation of events.

The shooting, as shown by the subsequent police crime scene investigation measurements, would have taken place on the fringes of the Clifford–Scott distance 'rule' and certainly at, or beyond, the far extremities of cast light from, presumably, a low-level bedroom gaslight.

It is highly unlikely that the Somerville Cottages would have come equipped with the new-fangled electric lighting and there was no street lighting or any equivalent of modern external security lighting. We should also bear in mind my previous note regarding the possibility of Mary, through her diabetes, having suffered from deteriorating eyesight.

It was quite possible, therefore, for Mary to have heard what was being said but not to have had a clear enough view of things to present any value to the defence case. If there was even a slight variance in her account to the testimony given by her husband, then to place her in front of a clever prosecution lawyer would present problems.

On the darker side, maybe she was made aware of the rumours that had quickly spread about her alleged affair with Tommy and she either wished to avoid the inevitable press interest or was being shielded from it. Had the rumours arisen in open court cross-examination, even as a passing reference, they would have been 'fair game' for the press to broadcast and with God knows what reputational consequences for years into the future.

Unless a member of the family offers an informed 'angle' on her silence we will never know.

Part 3

Why?

Possibilities

Although a prosecuting counsel in court did not have to prove a level of planning to secure a guilty verdict, it is certainly worth discussing the handed-down assumption made by many people that Stagg had meant to kill Ball and had planned to do so. Within this apparently straightforward view, however, there are several scenario possibilities.

The first possibility and, I believe, the one most favoured by contemporary public opinion, is that Stagg had long before taken a dislike to Ball and had fully intended to murder him, planning to do so when a suitable opportunity arose, and had engineered a confrontation to do just that. Stagg's story of a tussle with Ball across his garden gate was a complete fabrication and Ball had been an unsuspecting and passive victim who was 'just passing by' and was shot before he could be aware of any danger. After all, Stagg was a trained 'shot' and had been armed with a loaded gun, so could presumably have 'picked off' his neighbour quite easily.

A second option is that Stagg planned a confrontation during which he intended to commit murder, but the action was stage-managed in a manner which gave him a solid case to plead self-defence. To validate this story, it would have been important for Stagg to convince a jury that Ball had been inebriated and was habitually aggressive in nature following a couple of drinks.

The third possibility is that Stagg, with the intention of frightening Tommy, planned and engineered a verbal confrontation only. He had no intention of shooting Ball but carried, for effect, the controlling 'prop' of a loaded gun. The idea was to make Ball cower a bit and agree to step back from whatever it was that Stagg objected to about his behaviour. The outcome may also have been designed to have the side effect of persuading Ball to look harder for accommodation elsewhere. The whole thing went catastrophically wrong with a fatally accidental discharge from the gun.

Fourthly, take the gist of the paragraph above but alter the final sentence to show that when things began to go wrong Stagg deliberately shot his neighbour.

Fifthly, let us assume Stagg's story of a chance meeting at his garden gate was absolutely the truth, but when things got out of hand, one, or both, lost their temper and during an ensuing scuffle Stagg deliberately shot Ball.

Sixthly, we can also consider that Stagg's story of a chance meeting, as per the previous paragraph, was true but when things got out of hand, he was genuinely forced to defend himself against Ball's physical attack, shooting him only in self-defence and as a last resort.

Finally, Stagg's story of the chance meeting and tussle was the absolute truth as he described it in his deposition, including his claim that the gun discharged accidentally. In court, he maintained, unlikely as people might find it, 'It is my story, and I am sticking to it.'

Balances of Probability

Many readers will no doubt have some experience in professional life, of having to determine the levels of truth in conflicting accounts of an incident. My own instinct, for the record, was always to eliminate the extremes of opposing claims, then proceed on the basis that the truth lay somewhere in between. Based on available evidence, anyone adjudicating on a dispute, say within a workplace setting, would be required to take as their guiding principle the establishment of a 'balance of probabilities' that such and such happened.

What one does not have to demonstrate in civil life is that such conclusions were proven 'beyond reasonable doubt'. By contrast, a prosecution case in a court of law must persuade a jury that the case is proven 'beyond reasonable doubt'. It is a huge difference.

As you progress through the book, you may wish to consider which, if any, of the seven scenarios outlined above, or a combination thereof, you consider might satisfy either a balance of probabilities or be beyond reasonable doubt.

You may, of course, come to a view that is not suggested here.

Means, Motives and Opportunities

'Means, motives and opportunities' represent the cornerstones of criminal law in the United States and in many other countries and they have, to an extent, embedded themselves in modern popular culture as essential ingredients in establishing criminal guilt.

In British law, however, a motive for committing a crime does not have to be demonstrated in order to prove guilt even though there invariably exists a public expectation of a 's/he did it because …' reason behind most crimes. This expectation has been enhanced over the years by a drip feed of popular plays, books, cinema films and TV shows.

Most, if not all, of these establish 'why did s/he do it?' plot lines to keep the viewer/reader enthralled before a suitably dramatic denouement. The ongoing narrative is invariably peppered with clues and red herrings to help the viewer/reader fathom out, or fail to, why, and by whom, the deed was carried out. In certain TV 'cop' series, it is an accepted dramatic strategy for the writer to introduce in the first five minutes several potential murder suspects who might all have the means, opportunities and motives to carry out the deed. As a 'spoiler', I would suggest going for the 'guest star' with the best-known name.

At this stage, it is worth pointing out that the judge at the Stafford Assize in 1924, though seemingly adversarial to Stagg during the hearing and reluctant to grant the jury's plea of 'mercy', accepted in his summary that the prosecution had not established a motive. Unfortunately for Stagg, this apparently even-handed statement did not prevent the judge from suggesting one.

So let us 'play the game'.

Means

This is the easiest of the 'tests' as there is no shade of doubt that Stagg owned a hunting gun and had admitted killing Tommy with it. In due course, we shall return to the gun.

Opportunities

This is, on the face of it, also an easy one to answer, but the imagined ease of opportunity only serves to confuse the actuality.

Stagg and Ball lived in an unlit, isolated country spot where there was probably no shortage of opportunities to commit, literally, dark deeds. As mine host confirmed, a trip to the Church Tavern was a regular evening out for Tommy and Beatrice, so Stagg would probably have had a reasonable awareness of the Balls' timings when returning from the public house and, had he wanted to shoot Tommy, he could have easily planned to lie in wait and do so. The problem was that Tommy was with his wife and witnesses to murder are generally inconvenient to the killer.

Nevertheless, lying in wait is certainly the view that has been, by and large, accepted by posterity and one story that has survived is that Stagg accosted Tommy by the latter's garden gate as he was coming towards his cottage. The inconvenient fact, however, is that the shooting did not take place at Tommy's gate, but around 30 feet away at the field entrance gate to George Stagg's garden.

We also know from Beatrice Ball's deposition that George Stagg certainly did not lie in wait as they returned home, still less did he accost them. Beatrice confirmed that the couple had gone into their cottage, Tommy had then opted to take his dog for a walk, lost sight of it, returned to the house to see if it had returned and had then gone out a second time. The action took place at George's garden gate as Tommy was walking past it while looking for the dog.

Stagg could hardly have anticipated that sequence of events, still less have engineered it.

Motives

Although not of critical legal value, the establishment of motive, had there been one, is the meaty part of the story and I will refer the reader to the main lines of speculation that existed at the time or have emerged since then.

Some Chickens and a Pigsty

Many people have willingly taken the bait dangled by Beatrice's testimony that the reason for Stagg's antipathy towards Ball was the latter's errant domestic chickens, which apparently strayed across the unfenced boundary between the two gardens. The dispute was advanced by her as the reason for Stagg issuing the Balls with a notice to quit their cottage.

To 'up the stakes' on this issue, Beatrice initially alleged at coroner's court, and quite probably in her initial talk to the arresting police officer, that Stagg had said, 'You all ought to be poisoned', 'you' presumably meaning the chickens, the dog and their owners. This was modified at the later petty assize hearing to 'they', rather than 'you', that is, only the chickens, not the dog or the owners. That is a critical difference that many chroniclers have chosen to ignore.

According to Beatrice the dispute then rumbled on via a dispute over whether the Balls were then entitled to house the chickens in their garden pigsty. The real issue was probably that the sty was constructed without landlord Stagg's permission, and Stagg's concerns that any pigs to be eventually sent along by Beatrice's butcher father might stray, messily, into his garden.

The Scotsman's rather grounded court reporter tellingly dismissed these domestic issues as 'small matters of dispute', but the stories took hold and 'it was all about chickens' is still used today as indisputable fact and the prima facie reason for the shooting.

The issue, anyway, could have been solved by the simple good-will erection of a small fence between the gardens. It is a moot point whether that responsibility lay with Ball or with Stagg. Under normal circumstances, it would certainly be the chicken owner's responsibility to keep his fowl out of his neighbour's garden and fairness might indicate that Ball should probably have taken measures to do so. As Stagg, however, owned both properties it could be argued that he should have borne landlord's responsibility, and thus the costs, for such an action. Well, that one could run and run, and Stagg was probably not the sort of man to take kindly to having to sort out a nuisance he considered none of his making. Still less would he have been keen to pay to do it.

As Simon Burnton sagely summarised in his online article, 'The problems seemed that as a landlord Stagg was a difficult man to please and Ball, as a tenant, seemed a little thoughtless.' This is, I believe, the most intelligent conclusion possible to that area of dispute.

Ball's Dog

Into the bargain, Stagg had also allegedly described the Balls' dog as a nuisance, but what often appears to have been overlooked, and is clear from his deposition, is that Stagg himself also kept a dog and from a contemporary photograph, unpublished at the present family's request, it looks to me like a Scottish Terrier. This is, of course, a breed that may often be relied upon to make plenty of persistent noise. The breed of Ball's dog is unknown, but a smudgy photograph in Paul Lester's book purporting to be Ball's dog, unpublished here as the original is untraceable, appears to show another Scottish Terrier. As neighbouring dogs do have a habit of setting off each other, it might be difficult to attach any sort of nuisance blame to either dog, let alone owner.

Ball's Lack of Sobriety and Domestic Violence

Rather than admit to having issues with Ball's chickens, Stagg maintained his August 1923 notice to the Balls to leave their cottage was because of Tommy's habitual drunken violence towards Mrs Ball. In claiming this in court, Stagg and his counsel were certainly aiming at the moral high ground.

Unfortunately for research, the written notice to quit appears to have disappeared from history; it was recorded on the evidence sheet at Stafford and I have been round in unsuccessful circles to try and locate it. This is a great pity as it would, presumably, have specified exactly what it was about Tommy's alleged behaviour that Stagg objected to. The original would have been handwritten and been in the care of recipients Tommy and Beatrice, thence the Stafford court authorities. I doubt very much whether Stagg would have taken the trouble to write out a duplicate, so for the moment that trail is cold.

We will never know whether Beatrice was a victim of domestic violence, and we perhaps should not be overly sidetracked by an issue that was never proven. As Beatrice denied she was a victim, and no evidence to the contrary was presented in court, we must accept that it did not occur.

If it were untrue, it remains, of course, possible that Stagg believed it was happening. As readers will well know, a great many happily cohabiting couples have been known to argue, and sometimes loudly, perhaps with a little slamming and banging for effect. Maybe Stagg had heard something through the walls and jumped to the wrong conclusions, but even if his errors of judgement offered him a reason for evicting the couple, it is not the same as making a case that he would be sufficiently outraged to want to kill his neighbour.

Date

An angle which we might reasonably want to consider, though there is no evidence it was raised in court, is whether any level of antipathy between the two men was aggravated by Stagg's mood on Armistice Day, and I have previously outlined the number of family deaths that George Stagg would have had to come to terms with over the previous seven years.

As a matter of historical interest, at a time when the event was still universally commemorated on the 11th day of the month rather than on the nearest Sunday, this was the first time since the end of the Great War that the 11th had fallen on a Sunday when few people were at work. Attendances at ceremonies were high as survivors and bereaved gathered to share their memories and emotions. The largest in the area was held in Birmingham's Victoria Square where, amongst others, the City Police marched past the crowd.

There would have been ample opportunity, for those who wished, to attend smaller gatherings outside and inside local churches. This was especially so as the stone cenotaph memorials, complete with the names of the local dead, with which we are now so familiar, had begun to appear across the country. There was no escaping what day it was and it offers the possibility that here and there a wounded ex-combatant's mind may have been emotionally disturbed.

Even had it been raised in court, however, the 'Armistice angle' would not necessarily have worked in the prosecution's favour. With so many homes living with the return of a loved one physically or psychologically damaged by the effects of war, it was quite possible that a wounded ex-combatant like Stagg might have benefited from a sympathetic jury pointing to mitigating circumstances. Having researched the members of the jury, I do think this may have played a part in discussions.

Insanity

Taking the notion of an ill mood a little further, it could be said, and probably was, that Stagg's commitment to Broadmoor some five years after the event solved the puzzle by offering 'madness' as a reason for the crime. It is a neat way of wrapping things up, and all things are possible, but a declaration of some form of mental illness in 1928 is in no way evidence of a state of mind in 1923.

In any case, 'madness' or 'insanity' are rather broad convenience terms which require more precise definition. Without the guiding benefit of the exact clinical diagnosis made of him in 1928, and which is still withheld by the West London NHS Trust despite my best efforts to secure it, we cannot fairly speculate on any link.

Envy

I must confess that when I began this study, I was drawn to the possibility that envy may have lain behind things as I took Stagg's reported ill health and lack of prospects to be in sharp contrast with Ball's youth, health and wealth. There may, of course, be something relevant in that line of thought, but they were only suspicions based on my highly unscientific generalisation of human behaviour.

Such suspicions, I decided, did me no credit. Envy is an emotion, which, I suggest, many of us have felt but it does not necessarily equate to, or prove, dislike, and if envy explained murder some of us would be doing a lot more of it.

The Elephant in the Room

We must inevitably turn to the talk which swept through Aston and which, if correct, might serve as the most obvious explanation for any underlying animosity Stagg felt towards Ball.

Immediately following the shooting, strong local rumours emerged that Ball had previously formed an adulterous relationship with Mrs Stagg, 18 years his senior. *The Villa News and Record*, in its obituary tribute to Ball, rather coyly states 'it is not within the province of a club journal … to make any remarks on an occurrence that is being so widely discussed in the daily papers and of which so many rumours are being bruited abroad'. It is reasonably obvious to which 'rumours' the publication referred.

The rumour mill was indeed quickly in full operation. My father's view based on what he had heard as an impressionable 11-year-old, and on building sites and in working men's clubs for years beyond, was succinct, if a little crude, and I apologise: 'He was having it off with the bloke's missus.' I can hear him saying it. You should understand that once Dad had expressed an opinion, even a second-hand one, it officially became fact and that he stuck to this view for ever afterwards may say rather more about him than about Tommy Ball. Urban myths are cheap, especially where the imagined nocturnal escapades of young, invariably overpaid, footballers are concerned.

From where might such a rumour have come? Anyone who has spent time in sports' changing rooms or in the company of sportsmen travelling to and from matches will have no doubt from where any 'banter' regarding players' imagined private lives emanates. I suspect there was an amount of 'locker-room' ribaldry aimed at Ball concerning 'the woman next door'. The problem is when such ribaldry escapes from its 'in-joke' club confines and sprouts legs in the streets and pubs.

A good source once told me of an acquaintance, a former Aston Villa employee, who believed the gossip to be correct. The gentleman in question had worked at the club during the 1930s and would have known club employees who had been there in the early 1920s and maybe one or two of the older players who were still around. He would, therefore, quite likely have been in receipt of what was still relatively recent club gossip, and his views would have made interesting listening.

This is a bit frustrating, as in 2007 when my father was 95, the club gave him, me and my lad an afternoon out as guests of honour at a home match. During the time we were there, we had cause to meet the gentleman mentioned above.

At the time I had not begun this research so unknowingly missed a wonderful opportunity for a few discrete words to ascertain who or what his sources were. On the other hand, I did get a wonderful shot of him and Dad posing in front of a wall photograph of the mutually adored Billy Walker, and I enjoyed prematch chats over a cup of tea with two personal heroes Peter McParland and the late Alan Deakin. Despite Villa predictably losing to Portsmouth, Dad enjoyed himself immensely and returned home proudly clutching a small gift from the club.

Intriguingly, I later came across a 2011 internet entry which offered a first-hand view of one of Stagg's great-nephews who wrote that, apparently, the family itself had believed the Stagg–Ball argument had been about an affair between Ball and Mary Stagg. He went on to write, 'However, that has never been proven', and that is, I think, where we should leave it.

Part 4

The Killing

In Brief

The action that led to Tommy Ball's death began in the late evening of Armistice Day, Sunday, 11 November 1923, when Tommy and Beatrice Ball went out for a drink at the still extant Church Tavern Beer House, then a country public house in Church Lane, Perry Barr. They left at what was then the national closing time of 9.30pm and sometime afterwards, which could have been anytime between 10.30 and 11.00, Tommy found himself embroiled in an outdoor argument with George Stagg. The disagreement somehow led to Stagg, who had with him a loaded hunting gun, shooting Tommy dead.

The police case was that Stagg had deliberately fired the gun in Tommy's direction knowing the action was likely to cause injury or death and was thus 'wilful malice aforethought'. Stagg claimed that the firing of the gun was accidental and maintained he had felt physically threatened by what he believed was Tommy's drunken language and behaviour. The reasons for the argument and the precise action that led to the fatal shot have never been satisfactorily established.

In attempting to answer these questions, we need to piece together known fact and probability while eliminating improbability, some of which has become established folklore.

A Quiet Night Out

For Harry Wood and Percy Redman, the evening of Armistice Day was something busy to get through before being able to retire for a well-deserved night's sleep. Instead, they became unwitting deponents in a murder investigation. Harry, licensee of the Church Tavern, probably looked forward to Tommy and Beatrice's visits to his establishment and would have surely taken regular opportunity to exchange a few words with them at closing time. In this instance, it may have been to hear a bit of 'between you and me' from Tommy on Villa's win at Notts County on the previous day. Being a purveyor of titbits of privileged inside information from Villa Park would certainly not have been to Harry's disadvantage in attracting custom.

To reach the public house, the Balls would have walked about a quarter of a mile west along the unlit and unmade Brick Kiln Lane on to the Walsall Road before taking a 'Midland Red' bus south towards Aston, alighting after no more than a couple of stops. They then strolled into Church Road, which is situated on the southern edge of what is now Perry Park, and walked past the Aston Unity cricket grounds on their left and the church of St John the Baptist on their right. The church was situated obliquely across the road, and only a couple of minutes, from the Church Tavern; eight days later, Mrs Ball would be back at the church following her husband's coffin into it.

Harry Wood duly signed a deposition confirming that the Balls arrived at his public house at about 7.45pm and were both 'perfectly sober' and 'peaceable' all the time. He said that Tommy had half a pint of stone ginger beer for his first drink, though, as he did not serve the couple after the first order, he did not know what else. He further added that they called in once or twice a week and, to the best of his knowledge, Tommy would only have three or four half pints of beer and they sometimes left before closing time. He confirmed that after 'last orders' on the 11th he spoke to the couple outside 'for about ten minutes'.

Percy Harold Redman, from Smethwick, a conductor with the 'Midland Red' bus company, was seeing out another late shift, hopefully without any ex-army drunks to have to deal with on Armistice night. He knew regular passenger Tommy 'by his reputation' and confirmed that the footballer and his wife were both 'as normal' when they boarded bus number OE 3151 from Perry Barr at about 9.50 or 9.52pm. They got off at Brick Kiln Lane about five or six minutes later, 'a minute or two before ten'. 'They were both perfectly sober,' said Redman.

The impact of these testimonies was, of course, to contradict Stagg's post-incident assertion that Ball was inebriated when he came home that evening and was often in such a state. At the Stafford Assize in March 1924, Villa trainer 'Freddie' Miles, a man whose word carried a high level of credibility, was to offer evidence of Ball's general sobriety and good living. This was important to the club as well as to Stagg's prosecutors as the Aston Villa board was then well known for its disapproval of any player exhibiting keen drinking habits. It also added to the popular view that Stagg had invented Ball's apparent inebriation.

Beatrice Ball's Story

Though she did not claim to have seen any of the incident between the two men, and her testimonies were based on what happened afterwards, there is no doubt that the key evidence in court was given by Tommy Ball's widow. Beatrice offered a brief statement to the coroner on 13 November, then gave a fuller statement on day two of the inquest a week later on 20 November, the day after she had seen her husband buried.

For anyone anticipating clarity, Beatrice's depositions are not an easy read and clearly reflect the stress she was under. As the one she gave first was within two days of helping to carry her dead and bleeding husband into their cottage and the second was made on the day following his funeral, it is not unreasonable to suggest that Beatrice was in a state of shock on both occasions. With the greatest of respect to her, her memory in places may have been understandably at fault and she may also have been a bit flustered by the formalities of the occasions and especially the presence of a jury.

The sequencing given by her of her actions is, particularly within the 20 November statement, a little confusing. Set against what we know from other depositions, her time estimates beyond 10.15pm are questionable and there are some circumstantial differences between what she said at each sitting of the coroner's court. When you reach the latter part of her 20 November statement, you may be excused for thinking that Beatrice had witnessed more of the confrontation than she was to admit to.

To the delight of the press, she also sensationally claimed that Stagg had aimed a shot in her direction, though the further I went into things, the more bizarre this claim appeared to become. It was never used in court as evidence against Stagg, nor was he ever formally accused of attempting to murder Beatrice, which raises all sorts of questions, which I will attempt to answer as we progress.

To avoid too much undue confusion, you should also be aware that when Stagg referred to a 'first' and 'second' shot, he was meaning a shot he alleged to have fired into the air as a warning to Tommy and then the fatal shot. When Beatrice referred to 'first' and 'second' shots, she meant the fatal shot as 'first' and then the one she alleged was aimed in her direction.

In case you were wondering, given the evidence they found, the police were satisfied that no more than two shots in total were fired and even though she was in her house only yards from the action, Beatrice claimed not to have heard Stagg's warning shot. Should you choose to believe her, it might suggest Stagg invented the story of a warning shot. Either that or she invented the one aimed towards her!

I have presented below a *verbatim* copy of her depositions:

13 November: 'I was in the kitchen preparing supper. I heard Mr Stagg shouting. I did not hear my husband. I then heard the report of a gun. I was then frying vegetables. I ran out and saw my husband. He was staggering towards my gate. He was coming from the direction of Stagg's gate. He fell just by my gate as he got there. He said "Oh Belle he's shot me." I stooped down and felt blood on his chest. I ran in the direction of Stagg's gate screaming. I have a friend up that way [author's note: this would have been Ellen Laurence]. **As I ran there was another shot** [author's emphasis]. I felt the wind pass me. It came from the direction of Mr Stagg's hedge. I ran back to my husband and then I saw Mr Stagg standing by the hedge at the side of his gate. I then ran towards Laurences and tried to get assistance there but could not. I then went back to my husband but before I got to him I saw someone coming down the lane with a light. It was Mr Stagg. He said "don't be frightened Mrs Ball. I haven't hurt you have

I?" He then said "let me help you lift him into the house. He's bleeding." He then got him in. He then went off for a doctor. He did not say anything then as to how it had happened. We have lived next door since January. There has been trouble between us over the fowl. He gave us notice to go in August. We did not go because we could not find another house. Mr Stagg did not come in in the earlier part of the day. There had been no other disagreement except about the fowls.

She also alleged Stagg had once said 'you all ought to be poisoned' [you will recall me pointing out that at the Stafford trial she was to amend this to 'they', i.e. the fowl only, all ought to be poisoned]. And to a question from the coroner's jury, 'Stagg has never threatened to shoot me or my husband or the dog.'

20 November: On day two of the coroner's hearing Beatrice made a fuller statement: 'I had one Guinness and my husband had three half pints of ale … We left … at half past nine, closing time. We stood talking to the Boss of the Tavern – Mr Wood. We left at about a quarter to ten and walked towards the bus in the Walsall Road. We got on the bus by Lord Calthorpe's lodge. We got off at Brick Kiln Lane. This would be between 10 and five past. There is no pavement whatsoever. We go through a gate at the side and the back. There is a single gate at the side of the prisoner's cottage.'

She continued: 'My husband and I got home shortly after 10.00. We both went in. We shut the door. My husband went out about five minutes later to take the dog for a run. I was preparing the supper things. He came back to see if the dog had been in but I said not and he went out to look for it and I went on preparing the supper.

'I heard Mr Stagg shouting about two or three seconds. I did not hear my husband's voice. I saw my husband staggering towards our gate from the direction of the prisoner's gate. I then saw my husband fall by the big slab in front of the gate. I went towards him. I felt warm blood on my hand. The blood went on my arm, jumper, skirt, stockings and shoes. I then ran to get assistance from the top of the Lane. I have friends there. When I got opposite Stagg's gate another shot was fired, it came in my direction. I felt the wind of the shot go past my shoulder. I then ran in the opposite direction screaming all the way. After the second shot was fired I went back to my husband. I shook my husband and asked him [Stagg] to help me. I was facing up the Lane and saw prisoner by the side of his hedge. He was standing inside his garden … I ran down the Lane away from Walsall Road. I was screaming. I went to the Laurences cottage – that is the first cottage – to see if I could get help. I told them what had happened and ran up the Lane again.

'I then saw Mr Stagg. He was coming down the Lane with a lantern lighted. He was about five yards past my gateway when I met him. I thought it was Mr Laurence, I asked him to help me. Prisoner said "it's only me Mrs Ball – don't be afraid, I haven't hurt you have I? Let me help you get Tom in the house, he's bleeding." We both carried my husband into our house. Prisoner said he'd fetch a doctor and went. He subsequently came back with the Doctor and Police … Prisoner has never expressed any regret to me for what has happened … My husband was sober. I was sober. I have lived very happily with my husband since marriage. We have never come to blows. He has never struck me or kicked me. Nor have we had high words. I have never known him drunk.'

In relation to their failure to move out following notice to leave she said, 'Prisoner didn't seem very happy about it.' On the question of their relationship with Stagg she added, 'We have had trouble over the fowls and prisoner said my dog was a nuisance. The prisoner kept a dog … there is no division between our garden and Staggs. We kept fowls that strayed sometimes and prisoner complained. We then kept them up [i.e. locked up] – this was in June. Mr Stagg objected to me putting the fowls in the pigsty. The pigsty belonged to me … prisoner said I had no right to put them there.'

In response to several questions by defence lawyer Mr Sharpe, Beatrice said, 'Mrs Stagg spoke to me from the bedroom window after the first shot was fired … I did have a conversation with her through the bedroom window after the first shot was fired, she said we were a lot of night howlers … I was not aware my husband was talking to Mrs Stagg when I went out … I did not hear my husband say to Mrs Stagg or prisoner "I'll have some trouble with you in the morning" … I did not say "go and fetch David". I know a man named David Timmins who was a friend of my husband … I said "you had better get in, can't you see that Tommy has been shot?" It was immediately after that conversation that I ran up the road and was fired at.'

Beatrice also admitted under questioning that Mrs Stagg came into the house when Stagg had left to find the doctor. 'She kept going in and out till he came back … Mrs Stagg did not say "it's a nice time to come home and kick up a row" … I did not say "It's nothing to do with you, we can come home what time we like" … She did not reply "It's not only one night but every night" … She did not say "I have to be up at 6 in the morning" and I did not say "you've nothing to do when you do get up" … My husband did not threaten to come up and bash Mrs Stagg's brains out … I did not hear the children cry … My husband and I often come home after 10 at night … and went to the Church Tavern about once a week.'

In order for her to make the latter responses, the questioner (Stagg's defence lawyer) must have been primed in advance by a conversation with Mary Stagg. Despite the almost comedic overtone of 'I said … she said', the reported dialogue does support my view that if there were strained relationships between the two households it is quite possible that it was the women who had taken the greater dislike to one another. It also supports a supposition that Beatrice was party to at least some of the action.

She was to add that since the shooting she had been staying at accommodation above her father's shop in Aston.

George Stagg's Story

When he was charged after the shooting, Stagg made a statement to the police which was treated as his deposition and on which he was subsequently to base his court defence. This survives within the National Archives and I quote it *verbatim* in full:

'There was no malice wilful or aforethought. It was just an accident. My dog was barking as he [Ball] was going past my garden gate to his cottage and he was shouting at the dog to stop it and I jumped out of the armchair where I had been dozing. I shouted at the dog to go in and lie down. He was chained up and Mr Ball was under the influence of drink. He shouted to me to "go in and go to bed or I'll bash your brains out". I said "now Tom go in and go to bed, there's a good chap" and Mrs Stagg was up at the window, she had gone to bed and she shouted at the window to go in and not make a noise and not wake the children up. The children had gone to sleep and he said to my wife "I'll come up and bash your bloody brains out" and came to climb over the gate to break in. The garden gate was locked. I locked and bolted it and always has been since we have been there. I'd got the gun in my hand when I went to the gate to see what was the matter. I thought it was funny a dog was barking and I told him to get off the gate and go to bed and I fired to frighten him. He went away and came back in a minute or two and tried to get over the gate again. I pushed him back with the muzzle of the gun and he caught hold of the gun and tried to wrench it off me and as I wrenched the gun away from him I stepped back and the gun went off. A sudden jerk and off it went. I immediately went out and done all I could for him. I helped to pull him up and put him on the sofa and immediately went for the doctor and informed the first police officer I met. When I was lifting him on to the sofa with Mrs Ball she exclaimed "Oh Mr Stagg I know you didn't mean it, I'm sure it was an accident. He would not have hurt Mrs Stagg although he kicks me about." Which he has done several times to my knowledge.'

Making a 'confession' yet introducing an element of personal nobility in how he dealt with the crisis by assisting Tommy into the garden, helping to carry him into the house and then seeking a doctor was a good minimisation tactic on Stagg's part. As a former police officer, and used to dealing with malefactors, he had doubtless learned that it was a good idea to get on the right side of the police by making their job a bit easier with a ready admittance of any level of responsibility.

Nowadays, there is often a discount in sentence available for admissions of guilt; in those days the advantages was simply to appear honest and co-operative from the beginning, hopefully giving the impression that you were not quite as guilty as had at first appeared. It is worth noting that in so doing Stagg had effectively admitted – at the least – to manslaughter and had certainly, and knowingly, condemned himself to a substantial prison sentence.

As you will now be aware, there were certain contradictions between the accounts given by Stagg and Mrs Ball.

The Depositions

I have made passing reference to depositions, which are written records of what certain persons have said when questioned during a post-crime police investigation. Such persons have not necessarily seen the crime take place but may be able to offer contextual information which can be used to prosecute or to support the person in the dock.

Depositions are initially recorded as neutral; the act of making one does not automatically mean that the deponent might be required to give evidence in court, nor is it in the gift of a deponent to opt to 'take sides' in a forthcoming trial.

Some depositions in this case were dictated to court officials following the coroner's initial hearing on 20 November and were witnessed and signed off by the coroner, Mr Lewis, but most were not made until the morning of 28 November, the day allocated for a hearing at a local petty assize (I will explain the differences between the various court hearings in due course). These later depositions were dictated, sworn to under oath and signed in front of the day's sitting magistrate, a Mr Rabene. Counsel for the prosecution and counsel for the defence were also present on the latter occasion, each of whom were able to request clarifications of things the deponents may have said.

After 28 November, the depositions were forwarded to the Director of Public Prosecutions (DPP), a position created in 1880 and forerunner of the Crown Prosecution Service, whose job it was to decide whether the charge made against Stagg was appropriate and whether the available evidence might enable 'the crown', i.e. the prosecution, to secure a verdict. It might otherwise be a waste of public money.

The then DPP was a Sir Archibald Bodkin, a former judge who was apparently noted as being a painstaking reader of legal papers. He was to agree that it was appropriate for Stagg to appear at an assize court before a judge who had the authority to pronounce the death sentence, and that the case against him would stand a realistic chance of being proven.

Once the DPP had decided to proceed, the depositions were sent to the regional 'circuit' courthouse at Stafford and made available to the defence and prosecuting counsels to enable them to plan their cases and strategies and to decide which deponents might be best suited to credibly support their case by standing as witnesses in the pressures of open court.

I was delighted to be able to obtain from the National Archives copies of all witness-signed deposition records and other relevant documents, such as the record of Tommy's post-mortem, the report from the psychiatrist who supervised George Stagg while in prison and, as shown in appendix 2, the list of court exhibits. These were substantial documents and ran to 49 handwritten pages. Their principal value was that they cut through much folklore and guesswork in clarifying what witnesses had, or had not, signed to under oath. They also gave the lie to one or two 'false news' instances where supposed events have lingered as a misrepresentation of fact.

The depositions were not without their challenges. They were transcribed longhand by court clerks and there are errors of grammar and spelling; there are also handwriting issues and occasional words have defied my interpretation. The initial transcription of Dr Garman's deposition, for example, is virtually unreadable. Dr Garman was the man who conducted the post-mortem on Tommy Ball's body and part of the problem, I suspect, was that the terminology the doctor used was beyond the duty clerk's experience. As Dr Garman subsequently made a second, legibly transcribed and fuller, statement, I have evidently not been the first person to struggle with the original document.

When considering the depositions there are caveats to consider. As it was up to legal counsel to decide what they most wanted the court to hear, there may have been aspects of the written statements that did not surface under open examination. Similarly, in the absence of court records, what also remains unknown is the cut and thrust of council examination and cross-examination as well as the verbal surety with which each witness dealt with the situation. It is possible that, here and there, answers made under close questioning in court may not always have matched the level of conviction suggested in a deponent's previous oral account.

Fake News

A story picked up in several press accounts was the apparent 'friendly conversation', as it was described in *The Illustrated Police*

Review, which was said to have taken place on the morning of 11 November when George 'obliged' Tommy by taking round a copy of one of the Sunday newspapers.

This presumably carried a report of the previous day's Villa match at Notts County, so might naturally have promoted a discussion between the two men. Tommy might have enjoyed the conversation for he was said to have played a very good game, *The Villa News and Record* subsequently reporting that the County forwards had been 'baffled and bent' by the Villa defenders, with Ball and Blackburn as the 'chief stoppers'.

Taking the above meeting at face value, I initially found it curious that neither Beatrice nor Stagg mentioned it in their depositions. In fact, Beatrice made a point of saying that Stagg had not been to their house that day.

Technically, this would have been quite correct as the meeting was said in the press to have taken place in the yard outside, though I take Beatrice's statement as suggesting Stagg had not called round at all.

As neither George nor Beatrice mentioned it, how the press found the information, and how they knew the meeting was 'friendly' is beyond my capacity to explain and I am inclined to conclude that the meeting may not have taken place. Had it happened, Stagg's counsel would surely have made good use of the information in court to claim the two men enjoyed an amicable neighbourly relationship.

Perhaps this simply circulated around the case as rumour and in its aftermath has been used to set up Stagg's craftiness in lulling Tommy into a false sense of security.

In similar vein, a story also circulated that Stagg had, that morning, somehow sought out an Arthur Pitchford, a 39-year-old 'horses keeper' who also lived in Brick Kiln Lane, and asked him where the nearest doctor might live. If correct, the story has some dramatic currency in suggesting Stagg was already working out what he was going to do once he had shot Tommy.

Unfortunately for conspiracy theorists, the tale was totally apocryphal as the meeting with Pitchford took place after the shooting when he and his wife were returning home 'about 10.40pm'. Stagg asked which was the nearest doctor but did not say what he wanted the doctor for. Pitchford told him to go to Dr Garman and noted that Stagg 'seemed in a hurry and spoke in a very low voice'. Pitchford added, 'I have never had any conversation before with him'.

In truth, nothing is known for certain about what Stagg or Ball did during Armistice Day until the Balls' fateful visit to the public house. Perhaps the two men attended a ceremony?

In the Vicinity

Ellen Laurence, the neighbour whom Beatrice had tried to rouse, and who lived down the lane at 'the cottage' with her husband Joseph and daughter Dora, said that she heard a shot at about 10.30pm 'coming from the direction of the Staggs and Balls'. This was followed by screaming and the arrival at her gate of Beatrice Ball. Ellen Laurence went on to say, 'She was screaming in the lane. She told me her husband had been shot and my husband telephoned the police.' Given the distance of around a quarter of a mile, Mrs Ball would have had to travel to get to the Laurence house, the telephone call to the police must have been made at around 10.45–10.50, that is, at least 15 or 20 minutes after Mrs Laurence had heard the shot and ten minutes or so later than Beatrice was to testify. You will have noted that Mrs Laurence mentioned her having heard only one shot.

Mabel Rose of Moor Cottage, Hamstead, had been walking across nearby fields with her sister Louise. Her deposition states, 'At about 10.15 we were going over the fields joining Brick Kiln Lane. We were about 500 yards away when I heard a shot. We could tell it came from Brick Kiln Lane direction. We went on. We then heard a second shot. It was a short time between the two shots. I should say about two minutes. We heard a dog bark and a woman scream. We heard the woman scream after the second shot. I walked about 20 paces between the two shots. I am no judge of distance.' The sisters' timing of the first shot was 15 minutes before the one heard by Mrs Laurence. It gets very confusing.

What the Rose testimonies do suggest is that the shooting part of the altercation between Stagg and Ball was over very quickly. Very importantly, Stagg would not have had time to have gone back into his house to collect a replacement cartridge, as he was to claim, and then load and fire the weapon. Aided by a degree of 'witness contamination' when discussing their statements, the pair's depositions were unsurprisingly virtually identical.

The most notable aspect of the Rose depositions, perhaps, is that both women said the screaming began after the second shot, so I think it likely that the two shots they heard was the sequence admitted to by Stagg, the second being the fatal one. Beatrice, of course, had claimed to have only heard one shot before she left her kitchen and said that the second shot was aimed at her as she began to run up the lane. It is highly probable, of course, that Beatrice screamed at various points in the narrative and quite possible that Mary Stagg, standing at her bedroom window, did so also. To confuse matters, we have noted that Mrs Laurence heard only one shot, which fails to tie in with either Stagg's or Beatrice's story.

123

'A Gun of Belgian Make'

Neither the make nor model of the gun were ever formally recorded; there is no clue in either the witness depositions or, surprisingly, in the list of court exhibits.

From the deposition description given by the expert witness who carried out subsequent ballistic testing, a John William Fearn of Ellesmere Road, Alum Rock, we do know that Stagg's weapon was a 12-bore, plain-cylinder, bolt-action hunting shotgun. Most hunting shotguns were equipped with long barrels and a substantial 28in barrel length or longer was common. This might broadly make sense of Stagg's description of both men at one point having hold of the gun during their tussle.

Given that 53-year-old Fearn was an employee of Webley and Scott, a prominent Birmingham small-arms manufacturer, I initially made the reasonable assumption that the gun in question was one of their weapons. Nor have I been the only chronicler to jump to this conclusion as Mark Cowan travelled the same road in his 2010 *Birmingham Mail* online essay. I think most people would have done so. To my surprise, however, I found that *The Birmingham Gazette*'s court reporter at the petty session of 28 November stated that the prosecuting counsel had referred to the gun as being 'of Belgian make'.

If I had been correct about the gun's Birmingham origin, and it is worth retaining that possibility, the weapon may have emerged from the city's famed gun quarter under, to give it the full trading name, the Webley and Scott Revolver and Arms Company Limited brand. The company was based in Weaman Street, which was on 'D' Division's 'beat' and, as they produced side arms for the city's police service up to 1979, it is likely that Stagg would have been quite familiar with the company and its products. With his police knowledge and contacts, he might well have known how to get hold of a gun either above or below the counter.

Circumstantially at least, this points to the gun being of local make and, remembering that Stagg had been gone from police service nine years before the shooting, it begs the key question of when it was acquired. If bought before 1914 it was in no way purchased for the purpose of shooting Tommy Ball, though if bought in the late summer of 1923 that was an entirely different matter. It is quite plausible that Stagg might somehow have got his hands on the gun when he moved into the Perry Barr countryside. Perhaps the Perry Hall estate had spares they were selling off. Maybe one came gratis, stored away and forgotten in a corner of one of the cottages he bought.

If the gun was 'of Belgian make', my first thought was that perhaps it was a war souvenir. Soldiers serving abroad have always coveted foreign-made guns as mementos, but these have generally been pistols, more easily hidden in kitbags than shoulder arms. In any case, the weapon Stagg had was a hunting gun and not a military rifle, though it could have begun its life as that.

In the immediate post-war period, the Belgian arms industry seized a market niche by specialising in mass-producing single-action shotguns. Many of these were 'converts' from acquired, and mainly German, military weapons, of which there would have been no shortage in Belgium. They were sold worldwide well into the 1920s, including into the British market. Belgian guns were generally easy to identify as they bore distinct proof marks, which not only indicated the maker but also the period during which the model was manufactured. That evidence would have been quite visible, but we have no record of it.

After doing some research, my best guess, and it is only a guess, is that, if Belgian, the gun may have been a Mauser originally built in Germany in the 1880s for military use. This was the time when bolt-action guns were becoming standard infantry issue, as per the British Lee-Enfield. One of the early Mauser models, an '1871', was, in the correct jargon, widely bastardised by Belgian manufacturers, for example the Liege United Arms Company Ltd, into a single-shot, bolt-action model.

It is interesting to note that some current collectors are at pains online to advise that anyone owning a rebuilt Mauser of the period should load it or attempt to fire it with extreme caution and preferably under supervision as they are notoriously unreliable and dangerous. Given Stagg's assertion of an accidental discharge, this information gives food for thought.

If a Mauser, the original gun would have had a 33in-long rifled barrel for shooting bullets, but these were often shortened during the conversion process. The 'rifling' was an internal barrel grooving enabling expelled bullets to fly reasonably truly and which, on conversion, was removed to render the gun capable of firing so-called 'hunting cartridges'. That the adaptation was sold extensively into the British and Commonwealth rural markets during the early 1920s increases the possibility that Stagg might have obtained one after he moved to Perry Barr.

As we have noted, it is not clear whether Stagg was licensed to own the gun. Unsurprisingly, there was a glut of military weapons, souvenirs and otherwise, which had illicitly found their way from mainland Europe during and following the Great War. The 1920 Firearms Act was framed to restrict the numbers of civilians able to casually bear arms as there were too many men around who knew full well how to use them. This was not least in the tougher parts of cities like Birmingham and, in case anyone still believes them to be TV fiction, the Peaky Blinders and other gangs really did exist and were around and active in parts of the city at the time our drama in Perry Barr was taking place.

To understand how the action on 23 November may have unfolded, it is of use to have a rudimentary understanding of how a 'single-action' gun is operated. The main thing to bear in mind is that it requires the manual reload of a new cartridge before each shot can be fired. This is done through what is known as 'bolt action', whereby a cartridge is introduced and then pushed securely into the firing chamber of the gun via a metal bolt mounted to, usually, the right-hand side of the gun. This action also expels most, or all, of any remaining piece of spent cartridge from the previous firing.

Although the gun is then activated for firing, the trigger has a built-in safety resistance that slows the finger pull and ordinarily protects against activation by accident. The delay might also give the shooter a short reflective time to consider whether he/she really wants to fire it. Resistance is measured in pounds; thus, any given gun is said to have a resistance of 'x' pounds. It was quite usual to have a poundage variation between seemingly identical batch weapons, especially those made in the 19th century.

Ammunition

I have referred to this type of gun firing cartridges, not bullets. Cartridges are rounded fabric cases filled with a fibre wad and gun powder and shot in the form of dozens of small metal pellets, and they vary in size according to the model of gun being used. These were initially held initially held together in a fibre wadding; in flight some pellets shoot off in all directions, but most go towards or into the target as an almost solid mass; the nearer the target, the more pellets simultaneously hit it. Mr Fearn testified that the cartridges used by Stagg held 234 pellets. Close-range impact on the target would have the effect of a single piece of metal causing one main entry hole, accompanied, as Ball's post-mortem was to suggest, by pieces of wadding and fragments of the cartridge casing.

Beyond a given range the pellet mass disintegrates, providing more of a spray impact on the target. Any cartridge fragments remaining in the gun after firing would be expelled on to the ground on reloading. Some wadding and pellets might therefore be found on the ground between shooter and target, as the police in scouring the gardens at Somerville Cottages were subsequently to discover.

In the hands of a proficient shot who could reload quickly, which we would expect Stagg to have been, a hunting shotgun would be a formidable deterrent to any poacher who suspected his potential victim might be carrying one. Anyone likely to be a target, were he close enough, might sensibly attempt to grab the barrel and force the gun sideways. At night, a likely target, who could not clearly see what was happening in front of him, but could hear only the distinctive click of the bolt reload, was in serious trouble.

If the shot hit a human or animal at close range, there would be considerable internal damage to bone and organs, rather like that, as we shall see, described within Tommy's body during post-mortem examination. On impact, the shot would cause a forward spurt of blood and the travel of the mass of shot would also result in an exit wound causing a significant backwards spray of blood.

Tommy Ball posing for one of Albert Wilkes's classic Aston Villa player portraits

A map of Aston showing :
1. Brick Kiln Lane [now Beeches Road]
2. The Church Tavern, site of Tommy Ball's final night out
3. The Church of St John the Evangelist, Perry Barr where Tommy Ball and Beatrice Richards were married
4. The Boar's Head, where Tommy Ball's post-mortem was conducted
5. Aston Lane, home of the Richards family in 1923
6. Woodall Road, where Tommy was placed into lodgings in 1920
7. Canterbury Road Police Station where George Stagg was charged and later tried before a police court
8. Villa Park
9. Highcroft Hospital where George Stagg died

George Stagg in Seaforth Highlanders No 1s prior to embarkation to France in November 1914

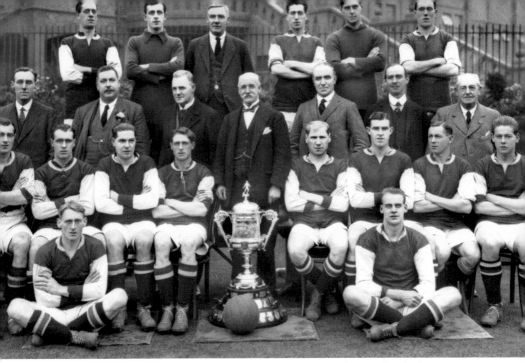

Aston Villa Football Club team group. 1923/24. With the Lord Mayor of Birmingham's Charity Cup. Back row l-r: Percy Jones, Tommy Jackson, H Gooch (assistant trainer), John Johnston, Cyril Spiers, Tommy Smart. Middle row: Alfred Miles (trainer), Captain P W M Bate, J E Jones, Frederick Rinder (chairman), Frederick, H Spencer (directors) E W Strange (assistant secretary), G B Ramsay (secretary). Front: Dicky York, Billy Kirton, Ian Dickson, Len Capewell, Frank Moss, Tommy Ball, Arthur Dorrell, George Blackburn. On ground: Tommy Mort, Billy Walker.

Andy Ducat and Sam Hardy, legends of the changing room

Tommy Weston, the long-serving left-back whose position in the team Tommy Ball was unable to take

Canterbury Road Police Station in which George Stagg was charged and later stood before a police court

Tommy Ball's coffin is carried into St John's Church. Villa captain Frank Moss is centre with, behind his right shoulder bearing the coffin, Arthur Dorrell, Tommy Mort, possibly Len Capewell, then Tommy Jackson. The gentleman at second right of the picture is Dr Milne while the mourner holding the bowler hats appears to be Andy Ducat

Tommy Ball's well -tended grave as it stood pre-Covid in the summer of 2019 following restorative work by Dot Ryan

The Duke of York takes to the pitch before the match vs Bolton Wanderers on 25 January 1924; he is accompanied by the Aston Villa chairman, Frederick Rinder. The magnificent new Trinity Stand can be seen behind the pair

Villa Park as it was when the author first attended in the 1950s. The iconic pre-1914 Witton Lane grandstand can be seen on the left and Archibald Leitch's 1924 Trinity Stand is on the right. Between the two is Frederick Rinder's 1939 Aston End terrace, subsequently known as 'The Holte'

The Trinity Road external staircase

*The Prisoners'
Dock at the
Stafford Winter
Assize*

*The Highcroft Hospital main
building still dominating
its neighbourhood in the
summer of 2021*

Part 5

After the Event

The Doctor

The doctor who Mr Pritchard advised Stagg to find was 53-year-old John Bernard Garman, who lived at Barr Hill House, a large property in Great Barr on or near to the Walsall Road north of Tower Hill.

If we are to take both Pitchford's and Garman's timings as accurate, it would have taken Stagg around 20 minutes to walk to the doctor following his meeting with Pitchford. For a man in an agitated state of mind and with a bad leg and respiratory problems and carrying a hurricane lantern, that would represent quite an effort and my feeling is that it may well have taken five or ten minutes longer.

Dr Garman confirmed that Stagg arrived at his house at about 11pm and wanted him to go with him to Brick Kiln Lane where there had been an accident. Garman asked what had happened and Stagg said there was a man shot while trying to get over a gate. Garman asked what a man was doing with a gun at that time of night and was told by Stagg that he himself had hold of the gun and that in attempting to push the man off the gate the gun was discharged in the struggle. Stagg had said that he had fired a shot in the air to frighten the deceased away and he then loaded again and tried to push Tommy off the gate with the gun. Garman confirmed that Stagg was very upset and feared the man was dead.

On turning into Brick Kiln Lane in Garman's car, they fortuitously saw PC Thomas Bickley, a 'beat bobby' on duty, and at Stagg's suggestion called to him and asked him to follow the car. PC Bickley's deposition confirmed that Stagg had said, 'Ball has been shot by the gate.' When they arrived at Somerville Cottages, Ball was lying dead on the couch with his clothes covered in blood.

Interestingly, although eventually appearing for the prosecution, Garman in his deposition was to refer to 'the scene of the accident', not the scene of the killing, murder, etc.

The Police Take Over

Bickley, who followed the car by foot, had 11 years' experience as a policeman but even so was probably a little out of his depth on this one. Having seen Ball's dead body, he telephoned through to the Canterbury Road station, presumably from the Laurence house, involving another walk of 15 minutes or so to get there and a similar time to get back. He spoke to his immediate superior, a Sgt Joseph Davenport, who at some point drove, or was driven, to the scene.

It is not clear whether Davenport had been in receipt of Mr Laurence's earlier call, but if the timing of his arrival at Somerville Cottages, as given in his deposition (see below), was anywhere near correct, he must have been reacting to the Laurence call and not to that made well after 11pm by Bickley. Nevertheless, he must still have been at the station after 11 o'clock or Bickley could not have spoken to him. Bear that in mind when reading the following.

Davenport takes up the story. 'At 10.40 I went to Brick Kiln Lane. I went to deceased's house and saw Dr Garman and prisoner – also Mrs Ball. Deceased was lying on a couch dead.'

Davenport's timing here was extremely dubious. He did not make clear whether he had responded to Mr Laurence's call made at around 10.50pm or to that made by Bickley considerably later. Had he spoken to Bickley, whose eventual call was made well after 11pm, he was obviously still in the police station at that point and could not possibly have set off at 10.40 as claimed. As he arrived at Somerville Cottages after Garman and Stagg. The probability is that '10.40' was incorrect by anything up to an hour. That the only other person to have mentioned '10.40' in a deposition was Mrs Ball raises considerable doubt concerning the veracity of Davenport's statement.

Davenport claimed that in his presence Mrs Ball said, 'Oh Mr Stagg, you ought not to have shot him.' He asked Stagg where it happened and received the reply, 'By my gate. I did it.' Davenport then arrested Stagg, leaving him with PC Bickley while he himself took Mrs Ball to a friend's house, which must have necessitated a walk back to the Laurences and another 15- to 20-minute walk each way.

On return, Davenport went into Stagg's house where he found a gun standing muzzle upwards by the side of a chest of drawers in the front room. It was handed to him by Mrs Stagg and a total of 19 cartridges in a stone jar was handed to him by one of her daughters.

Most contemporary accounts say that Davenport then took Stagg to 'West Bromwich' police station, so suggesting somewhere further afield from Perry Barr, but the venue was Davenport's 'home' station in Canterbury Road. This was situated within the wider West Bromwich local authority district and lies about an equidistant ten-minute walk from Woodall Road where Ball had lodged and the Aston Lane property where the Richards family lived. The substantial and rather forbidding building is still there today, though it was decommissioned several years ago and, at time of writing, awaits a buyer.

According to Davenport, before leaving the cottages, Stagg used the light of his hurricane lamp to draw the sergeant's attention to blood spots on his garden gate. These, he noted, were on the side nearest the road, on the top of the crossbar, between the poles and on the brick step beneath the gate. The clear inference was that Tommy had been shot in close proximity to the gate or even while attempting to climb it. At points between the gate and Ball's garden gate about 30 feet away, Davenport also saw several spots of blood, doubtless representing the journey made by Ball, with or without assistance, following his wounding. There were also blood spots on the ground outside Tommy's house, presumably made when Stagg and Beatrice carried the dead man indoors.

Charging

As he drove back to the austere Canterbury Road police station from Brick Kiln Lane at some time after midnight on the morning of 12 November, Sgt Davenport must have been a very relieved man.

Someone of national repute had been killed late at night on his 'patch' in violent circumstances, and within a few hours not only did he have the perpetrator safely within his vehicle but had received what appeared, on the face of it, to be a verbal confession. It was a 'result' obtained with little effort on his part. He could go back to his superiors at the police station with the metaphorical feather in his cap.

The only downside was that his prisoner had confessed only to firing a gun, not to any charge of murder. That had yet to be made. Davenport's deposition reveals that during the car journey to Canterbury Road Stagg attempted to make a statement but was advised by him to say nothing until he was cautioned and charged.

Until modern times, arrest and charging protocols had often differed widely between the many British police forces, of which there had been around 250 at the turn of the 19th century. To standardise matters, the then Home Secretary requested in 1912 that senior judges draw up national procedural guidance for police officers making an arrest, including when to caution and when to charge. These procedures, known as 'Judges' Rules', did not have the force of law, but in the interests of fair and equitable administration of justice, all forces were encouraged to adopt them. Judges at assize courts were given powers to reject any evidence that fell outside the spirit of the new rules.

Davenport was permitted by Judges' Rules to have charged Stagg twice, the first opportunity being when Stagg was initially apprehended in Brick Kiln Lane. Had Davenport arrested Stagg he would have had to caution him. This is a means of allowing a suspect the right to silence to protect him/herself from self-incrimination, but it also offers an opportunity for the arrested person to make an initial statement of his or her case, and, under caution, Stagg would have been within his rights to offer his side of the story.

As Stagg was not cautioned at this point, Davenport had no obligation to hear what he had to say, but we must remember that he was only the arresting officer not the investigating officer, so there had been no requirement for him to question Stagg at the scene. Given that Stagg had admitted firing the gun, Davenport may well have thought it not worth his while to hear anything more as there were more senior men at the station whose job it would be to do that.

Stagg, as a former police officer, would have been fully familiar with any advantages to be gained by a suspect vigorously putting forward his/her case before formal charging and he may have been hopeful of persuading the sergeant to advise his superiors to consider a lesser charge than murder.

By contrast, Davenport had spoken to Mrs Laurence and to Beatrice. From her, he would doubtless have been in receipt of plenty of spirited information on feuds, fallouts and threats of poisoning 'you all'. He also noted Beatrice's estimated timings, a track which the timings in his own deposition closely followed.

Whether Stagg had been charged on arrest or not, there was a requirement to read a formal charge in due course at a police station. Nowadays, a custody officer, having spoken to the arresting officer, ensures a prisoner is made aware of precisely why he has been brought in, but in those days, in order to validate the charge, it had to be formally made in front of a witness, normally a senior officer. The senior man may well have routinely told arresting officers how to verbally frame the charge.

As it would have been immediately obvious to the policemen that this was going to be a high-profile and well-publicised case, they had to get things right. Guided by Chief Superintendent Francis Tucker and witnessed by him, the full charge levelled against Stagg by Davenport was that 'feloniously and wilfully and of his malice aforethought he did kill and murder Thomas Edger Ball against the peace of Our Lord the King, his Crown and Dignity'. This was paraphrased in his notebook by Sgt Davenport to 'with the wilful malice aforethought of murdering Ball'. Davenport confirmed that Stagg had four children, two girls aged 15 and 13, a boy of four and 'I am sure there is a son on the way to Australia'.

The impact of the charge's wording meant that guilt could be established if it were shown that a wounding or a fatality was a foreseeable consequence of Stagg firing his gun in the direction of Tommy Ball. This, and (perhaps surprisingly) not motive or planning, would satisfy the phrase 'malice aforethought'. Even his carrying of the loaded weapon could be argued as proof that Stagg was prepared for the eventuality of shooting someone, whether that be Ball or simply a common thief who was prowling around outside. This would fulfil the 'wilfully' element of the charge.

It was only when the formal charge had been read out at Canterbury Road that Stagg was allowed to make a statement.

In the event, neither Davenport nor his superior at the station would have had any idea up to the point that Stagg made his formal statement that the prisoner was going to make cases for both self-defence and the unintentional discharge of the gun. Either claim, if effectively pursued in court, could make a charge of murder difficult to secure, and this was doubtless at the forefront of the DPP's deliberations in deciding how to pursue the matter.

Davenport's initial refusal to hear Stagg out is puzzling. Taken at one level, the arresting officer was being fair in protecting the rights of the arrested person to silence, but at another level it may indicate that, having heard Beatrice's side of things, Davenport had closed his mind to anything Stagg may have wished to say.

Without court records we cannot know whether any deviance from procedure was mentioned either in court or by the DPP. Nor is there evidence that the issue was raised at appeal. It is all very curious.

What if the Charge Had Been Manslaughter?

Given how the defence team presented its subsequent appeal case, I consider it almost certain that Stagg would have been prepared to plead guilty to the lesser charge of manslaughter.

A ready admittance of guilt would have rendered the case nicely cut and dried, and a county assize trial would have been deemed unnecessary. It would not mean Stagg had 'got away with it' as, if found guilty, he would have sat before a sentencing hearing which would have left him, at 1923 tariffs, facing a hefty prison sentence of anything up to 25 years. It was not a wonderful prospect, but it was not the gallows.

Although a 'manslaughter' charge might not have satisfied press or public opinion, it always remained a 'fallback' option for the Stafford Assize jury should they, after hearing evidence, not accept the 'wilful malice aforethought' charge as proven.

As Stagg's claim of self-defence could not be challenged by an eyewitness, I suspect his defence team confidently expected that an assize jury would be likely to advise a manslaughter verdict. In a highly revealing moment even the hawkish prosecuting counsel said during the trial that 'at any rate there was no escape from a verdict of manslaughter'.

Why then did the police, when not in possession of Stagg's side of the story, choose the more extreme charge? It is possible that by charging Stagg as he did, Davenport was under the direction of Tucker, his senior officer, who was hedging his bets with the not unknown practice of 'overcharging'. If it subsequently became clear that a lack of accrued evidence might conceivably make a jury reluctant to convict at the initial charge level, then the lesser one could be substituted. It was not realistic to do things the other way round.

Should 'manslaughter' have been the charge or outcome there were many then, and doubtless are now, who would have felt Stagg kindly dealt with. Even had Stagg been found guilty of manslaughter and gone to prison for a considerable length of time the correct press headline would, sensationally, have been 'footballer's killer not guilty of murder'. Cue uproar in the land.

I have little doubt that public opinion might naturally have expected Stagg to be given a form of retribution more extreme than long-term imprisonment. We have all been there; it is what modern criminal psychoanalysis terms 'law enforcement zeal' and we see it most notably today following terrorist incidents, child murders, the killing of a police officer in line of duty or, thankfully rarely, the murder of a citizen by a serving police officer. To suggest that this emotion was not at play in 1924 would be to defy belief.

Coping

We can only speculate over everyone's states of mind in the aftermath of events in the early hours of 12 November. As Tommy's post-mortem took place in a nearby inn on the following day, it is likely that his body remained in his house overnight. Beatrice, who did not travel to the police station, almost certainly stayed the night, bloody clothes notwithstanding, with the Laurences.

It does not take much to sympathise with her position as her husband was dead in dreadful circumstances and their hopefully bright future together had suddenly disappeared. There was also the unknown element of what the next few days would bring and how she might deal with the challenges. She must have felt terribly alone; her family needed to be contacted, as did the Ball family. As can be told from her deposition, she was certainly 'in a state' and in desperate need of support and guidance. There was also a lot of cleaning up to be done in the cottage.

To add to her stress, she had probably been told that she would be required to attend a coroner's court early in the week and would have to make a statement. As far as I am aware, she would have had no professional support that night or thereafter.

You may, or may not, also wish to cast a sympathetic thought for Mrs Stagg who had heard, if not clearly seen, a man being killed and, inside her neighbour's house, had a close view of the injuries on his dead body. She was left in her house with a toddler and two early-teenage girls whose dad was in jail and, for all she knew, might never be released. He might even have been facing a murder charge. Her eldest son, at the age of only 16, was uncontactable somewhere on the high seas en route to his new life in Australia.

There would have been a lot of tears in Brick Kiln Lane that night.

Part 6

Following Up

Crime Scene Investigation, 12 November

PC Bickley and Sgt Davenport, the two policemen who had attended on the previous evening, returned to the scene of the shooting with a superior officer, an Inspector Mollart. There, they conducted a search of Stagg's house and Bickley found the ends of two cartridges amongst the ashes underneath the parlour hearth in Stagg's cottage, saying, 'I had not been told by Stagg to look there.'

At this point we should recall Stagg's story that he fired two shots, one being a warning while Ball was attempting to mount the gate, the other the fatal shot. This was not challenged in court and the remains of the two cartridges found by the police in Stagg's parlour ash pan appear to have been accepted by all parties as being from the two shots Stagg claimed. As Stagg had admitted to this, it remains a mystery why they should have seemingly been clumsily hidden.

The officers were able to pass on the used cartridge remains to Chief Superintendent Tucker later that day, along with the gun and spare cartridges that had been retrieved the previous evening. Two days later, on Wednesday, 14 November, Tucker passed these items back to Inspector Mollart to enable ballistic testing to take place.

Post-Mortem, 12 November

Meanwhile, Dr Garman was authorised by the coroner to undertake a post-mortem on Ball's body. This took place at the Boars Head public house on the Aldridge Road, around a ten-minute drive from Somerville Cottage and a short walk from the Church Tavern.

In its day, the Boar's Head was a rather stately country inn, since rebuilt and now a large restaurant dominating the junction of Aldridge Road with College Road and virtually within the shadow of the modern M6. Garman timed the investigation at 9pm, so perhaps mine host closed the bar to paying customers earlier than usual, though possibly much earlier in the day to allow suitable room preparation to take place. He could not have been too pleased to have to welcome an extremely bloody corpse on to the premises, but doubtless the public purse compensated him accordingly.

This seems not to be the only connection between the Boar's Head and Aston Villa. My *Heroes and Villains* writing colleague John Russell once noted that in 1885 Villa's third team had played a match 'at' the Boar's Head. It may be that this arrangement, perhaps in a field adjoining the pub, was long-running, but I do not know.

There was soon to be a third connection as, for the convenience of everyone involved, if not the landlord, the two subsequent sessions of the coroner's court hearing were also to be held there. A further possible connection has also emerged on the pages of *Birmingham History Forum* with the speculation that the pub was later managed by 1950s Villa stalwart Jimmy Dugdale.

Garman gave evidence of the post-mortem at the second sitting of the coroner's court on 20 November. As previously noted, much of his original deposition is virtually unreadable, having been drafted by someone with poor handwriting and who was evidently unfamiliar with the spelling of the anatomical phraseology used by the doctor. It was seen as necessary for the deposition to be redrafted in advance of the petty session hearing on 29 November.

Nevertheless, one small section of the original deposition is entirely legible and it is probably the most important: 'I formed the opinion that the muzzle of the gun must have been between two or three feet off the man's shirt. If the muzzle had been against his clothing, I should have expected some sign of staining.' In this sense 'staining' meant singeing.

It is worth quoting the remainder of the second deposition in detail:

'On 12 November at 9.00pm I made a post-mortem examination of the body at the Boars Head. I found the clothing over the chest perforated – the two ends of the tie were perforated by a hole about the size of a two-shilling piece approximately conciliar. There was a hole corresponding to this on his shirt, undervest and flannel chest protector. When I removed the clothing there was a hole in the skin slightly larger measuring one and a half inches across – approximately circular in shape. There was a hole through the left side of the chest bone which involved the cartilage of the fourth left rib. This hole was four feet four and a half inches from the sole of the foot and I think five inches from the top of the chest bone. The lobe of the left lung projected into the wound. The back of the wound was through the pericardium and the left side of the heart was completely shattered. The back of the wound was horizontal in the erect posture. I found in the heart a wad of a 12-bore cartridge. I found two other wads loose in the chest behind the lung. There were a few shots in the cavity of the chest. The main charge had hit the fifth rib behind the mid-auxiliary line which it had fractured and been deflected downwards into the muscles of the axilla. The main part of the charge was enveloped in the fabric of the tie.'

I would draw particular attention to the next section of the statement:

'I also found in the thorax the metal part of a shirt button. I formed the opinion from the back of the wound that the right shoulder was advanced towards the muzzle of the gun which must have been held in a horizontal position.'

Finally, he said, 'All the organs of the deceased were healthy. The cause of death was shock and haemorrhage caused by a gunshot wound.'

A common error made in the retelling of the story is that Tommy was killed instantaneously. For the record, and despite the injuries suffered, Dr Garman never said that death was instantaneous. In fact, it could not have been as Beatrice confirmed Tommy had spoken some last words to her which, according to police measurements, was at a point around 23 feet away from where he was shot.

Inexplicably, the coroner recorded an opinion of an instantaneous death. This is perplexing as he had witnessed and signed off Beatrice's initial statement containing the information about the circumstances under which Tommy had spoken his last words and had possession of Dr Garman's post-mortem report.

In terms of establishing what happened on the evening of the shooting, the most important evidence to take forward was the doctor's views that Tommy was hit with a 'clean' shot from a metre or less away with the muzzle of the gun facing him at almost 90 degrees, though not touching him, and he appeared to have braced himself, right side forward, for the expected impact. Despite the poor night-time visibility, Tommy must have known that he was about to be shot.

Ballistic Testing, 15 November

Police Superintendent William Henry Mollart and John Fearn, the Webley and Scott works manager, were tasked with carrying out ballistic tests on Stagg's shotgun. These appear to have been conducted in the vicinity of the two cottages, either in the garden area or in one of the neighbouring fields. Fearn was probably selected for the role because of his company's supply contracts with Birmingham City Police and with due formality he had to be handed the gun in situ by Mollart before he could carry out the tests.

Fearn later stood in court at Stafford as what we would today term an 'expert witness'. As recently as 1911 he had recorded on the census his employment as a 'filing clerk' at the gun company. This occupation sounds rather more clerical than technical, but by 1923 he had evidently enjoyed a significant promotion to the position of works manager and was able to speak on the workings of firearms with some confidence.

Indeed, Fearn's deposition opened by saying, 'I have an expert knowledge of the making and firing of guns' and he went on to offer some important contextual information. 'Five-sixteenths of an inch is the travel of the trigger required to fire the gun which is known as a long drag pull – the weight of the pull is eleven pounds. The average weight of a pull of an ordinary shotgun is about five pounds.'

He continued, 'I found about two-thirds of an exploded cartridge case in the chamber of the gun.' In court Fearn was handed the cartridge remnants retrieved from Stagg's fireplace and noted that it was possible that the exploded cartridge parts still in the gun matched some of those remnants found in Stagg's ash pan.

Fearn then described the nature of the tests he had conducted. For a target, he had used pieces of cardboard backed with coats and he fired a shot at each. The first shot was fired with the muzzle touching the target, the gun was then held three feet from the target and fired, then four feet six inches away, then nine feet away and finally 18 feet away.

The card targets were presented in evidence at both the petty assize and at Stafford. The shot fired at three-feet distance produced a hole measurement of one to one and a half inches, which was close in size to the entry wound on Tommy's body as measured by Garman who had also estimated a two- to three-feet distance apart.

The shot fired by Fearn while touching his target slightly burned the card, but as Garman did not note any burning to Tommy's clothing, this appears to rule out a shot made any closer than two feet. From this one might infer that had they been tussling across the gate, one or other, or both, would have taken a significant step backwards, thus more or less as Stagg described events.

It leaves open, however, the intriguing possibility that when the shot was fired there may have been no tussle across the gate at all, so allowing Stagg a 'clean shot' at his adversary. At this point, we should remember that the post-mortem had suggested the fatal shot was made with the gun pointing directly at Tommy's chest. Had that been the case, and remembering also that all the blood staining was on the field side of the gate, or on top of it, it presents us with two alternatives. Either Stagg had opened the gate and walked on to Tommy's side of the hedge, then shot him, or Tommy may have been in the act of climbing the gate with his upper body raised above the gate's crossbar when the shot hit him.

The Heavy Trigger Pull

Mr Fearn did have the experience of firing the gun several times during the ballistic testing on 13 November, so, in giving courtroom evidence, would have known what he was talking about, and this leads us to an issue which was to prove critical to the way the case was argued.

He testified that Stagg's weapon had an extreme resistance requiring an unusually heavy trigger pull of 11 pounds, which represented a 'trigger travel' of five 16ths of an inch. This resistance was just over double the five pounds which was his own company's factory norm for a similar weapon. I still harbour my suspicion that Stagg would have 'gone Brummy' with his choice of weapon and it is this referencing of his own company that prompts me to wonder whether the gun may, after all, have been a weapon from Fearn's factory, but one which did not correspond to the intended trigger pull for the batch in which it was produced. As far as I can ascertain, such production anomalies were common within the industry.

Whatever the make, the principle of heavy pull meant, firstly, that it might need an experienced shooter to discharge it efficiently, and, secondly, that the slowness of the process would ordinarily have given the shooter sufficient time to consider whether he or she really wanted to fire the gun, especially if the target was human. The prosecution case would be made considerably easier if they could convince a jury that the fatal shot fired by Stagg had been quite deliberate; he would have known full well who his adversary was and where he was positioned. Knowing that, he still pulled the trigger. Malice aforethought, me lud.

In his defence Stagg was to claim that only the first, warning, shot 'into the air' was deliberate, while the second shot resulted from an accidental knock to a sensitive barrel unexpectedly activating the trigger during the struggle with Ball. That a weapon might be subject to a heavy pull and be at the same time 'knock-sensitive' appeared, on the face of it, to be a significant contradiction in terms. We should, however, take note of the fact that George Stagg was later to demonstrate at his Stafford trial, by striking the barrel on a gate crossbar, how easy it was to accidentally activate the trigger.

Measurements

While he was in Brick Kiln Lane, Mollart did some measuring of distances to Somerville Cottages from the Walsall Road and from the Laurences' cottage. He also followed up the previous Monday's investigations by taking measurements around the cottages.

The distance up to the Staggs' bedroom window where Mary was alleged to have witnessed events was 10ft 10in, which, had it been daylight, would presumably have given her a good view, but in darkness less so.

The distance from the Balls' back door to the spot where Tommy fell was 28ft and that spot was 23ft from the gate at or near where the action happened, so seemingly confirming that, unless Stagg had carried Ball's dead body between the two points, death could not have been instantaneous. That Stagg was standing near to his hedge when Beatrice emerged from her kitchen appears to offer a further indication that her neighbour, a man in apparent poor physical condition, had not carried a dead body across 23ft and then skipped smartly back to where he had started from.

The position that Beatrice claimed to have seen Stagg standing at when she emerged from the house was 17ft 6in from his kitchen door and 23ft from the point at which Tommy collapsed. If she was correct, and it was a big 'if', Stagg had moved himself around five feet away from the point where he claimed to have shot Ball.

Although we can make some effort to understand what this data may have told us about the action, we have absolutely no evidence to show whether or how any forensic assessment of the information was used in court. Nor do we know for certain whether any attempt was made to correlate Fearn's evidence with that contained within the post-mortem, but the connection is so obvious that it must have been made.

Part 7

Three Weeks in November

The Law Moves Speedily

Readers familiar with the pace at which the legal system operates today will be amazed at the speed with which proceedings were expedited in 1923 and 1924. The three preliminary stages of the process were completed within 18 days from the time of the shooting, while the entire case history, including appeal hearing, was completed in around 14 weeks. As we shall see, speed of process was further emphasised at the Winter Assize when the entire trial, including verdict and sentencing, took only one working day to complete.

There were three obvious reasons for such a speedy timetable. Firstly, assize dates were calendar-fixed and there was always a need to expedite cases in time to be fitted into court schedules and to avoid backlogs of business. Secondly, such expedition ensured that prisoners were not sitting around filling essential cell space at public expense for weeks or months at a time. Thirdly, it was important for the wider public to be shown that the authorities were getting on with things and that justice was being done.

Lacking modern communications technology, the potential downside was the pressure on police, the DPP and the prosecuting and defence counsels to prepare and execute cases to the high standards that justice demanded. You may therefore speculate that the perceived need for speed may have been at the expense of a little care in police investigation, report production and case preparation. You may agree with me that procedures were not designed in the interests of parties likely to be severely emotionally affected by events; in particular, readers cannot fail to have the greatest sympathy with the stresses this timetable placed upon Beatrice Ball.

Press Reporting

Before we come to a rational explanation of the legal process following Tommy Ball's death, it is worth stressing how tangled the contemporary press reports left the entire process. Most of the dozens of provincial newspapers in existence would not have been represented at any of the courts and instead relied on syndicated accounts of the various legal hearings from the London, Birmingham or Stafford presses. These were then subedited with varying degrees of skill into available space and not necessarily by the following day. The international '24/7 information ricochet' we live with today was the best part of a century away.

Often there was no re-editing of the timescales used by the on-site reporters, so that, for example, a 'parent' newspaper's mention of 'yesterday in court' might be left untouched by a provincial newspaper's editorial team even if their paper, many of which were 'weeklies' generally coming out on a Saturday, was printing the piece several days later. The phrase 'yesterday in court' was you will understand a recurring research nightmare.

Equally confusing was the practice employed by many newspapers, and presumably for reasons of space, of conflating two or more of the November hearings into one. It was pot luck which of the separate court titles was then chosen by the subeditors, who often slipped into the common convenience of calling any hearing a 'magistrate's court'. This was particularly confusing when the *Illustrated Police News* for 22 November mangled together the news from the separate coroner's and police courts into, seemingly, a single 'magistrate's court'. The same publication also confidently misinformed the reader that the 'petty session' (which, ironically, was a court presided over by a magistrate) would take place 'tomorrow', i.e. 23 November, when in fact it was scheduled for five days afterwards.

Another research challenge has been in identifying the location of each court. Apart from identifying Stafford as the venue for the assize hearing in 1924, no attempt was made to identify a particular venue for each of the subsidiary hearings, which took place in November 1923. Each was habitually credited with being held 'in West Bromwich', but given the local authority boundary changes that have taken place over the past century this has proved distinctly unhelpful.

To confuse things further, the phrase 'petty session', which was the correct terminology for the hearing on 28 November, is often completely absent from the more recent online accounts, presumably because the terminology has no modern currency. For a similar reason, the Winter Assize held at Stafford in February 1924 is nowadays often referred to as a 'crown court' hearing. Whilst the approximate equivalence of a circuit assize to a modern crown court is broadly correct, those latter bodies were introduced only in the 1950s. In 1924, no one would have been familiar with the terminology 'crown court' and any online researcher seeking a 'crown court hearing' for that year is doomed to disappointment.

Staffordshire Coroner's Court Day One, 13 November

After a short night in the cells in Canterbury Road, Stagg was transferred to Birmingham Prison at Winson Green, not too far away from West Bromwich township. In accordance with established procedure, he was placed in the hospital wing to come under the surveillance of a medical officer appointed by the DPP. This was to determine whether he was mentally fit to understand what was happening to him and thence to stand trial, and I will include the report made on him later in the narrative.

The death was immediately referred to the Staffordshire coroner, whose inquest was heard on 13 November. The coroner's job was to preside over an inquest to establish the cause of death and the circumstances surrounding it and, as required for cases of suspected murder, the hearing was conducted in front of a citizens' jury. Although Stagg had already been charged by the police with murder, the coroner's jury had the authority to endorse this by confirming that there was sufficient evidence forthcoming for him to he be indicted and the jury could also require the coroner to name him as the suspect.

At that time, a coroner's jury could comprise anything from 12 to 24 men of good standing within the community, though no women were eligible. Given the speed at which the proceedings were arranged, the certainty was that each juror was resident either within the locality or close to it. Doubtless they were all familiar with the Aston Villa club and several were quite possibly attendees at matches and had seen Ball play. What is uncertain is that they would be approaching their task dispassionately.

The coroner in this instance was a Mr Gerald Champion Lewis and a Mr G. Sharpe, a local lawyer 'from West Bromwich', had been appointed to represent Stagg. The court met twice, initially on 13 November and then on 20 November. The initial brief hearing established identification of the body, heard any available witness depositions and took any relevant statements. The hearing was adjourned pending post-mortem, ballistic and crime scene reports and the preparation of further depositions.

The inquest was held at 2.30pm, but the venue, as ever unhelpfully described by contemporary press reports as being 'in West Bromwich', remained unclear to me for some time. It was apparent from posts on The *Birmingham History Forum* that coroners' records for West Bromwich pre-1939 can be extremely elusive but given the post-mortem took place only on the evening prior to the inquest, it made sense that the inquest would be staged in, or near to, Perry Barr.

Initially, I thought it might have been held within the Canterbury Road police station. As a great many stations were purpose-built with a dedicated courtroom, they could be used for such a purpose, but Canterbury Road, although then only about 20 years old, did not have this facility, so I had to look elsewhere. When coming across a press report of another coroner's hearing around the same date and I saw this was held in a public house, I had my clue.

What, then, could have been more convenient to all parties, excepting, perhaps, the landlord, than to hold the court at the Boar's Head where the post-mortem had taken place? This was confirmed by Rory Powell of Sandwell Archives Service who very kindly did some digging on my behalf and found a report in the locally distributed *Free Press* for 16 November 1923, which confirmed the location.

The only witness to be called was Beatrice Ball who confirmed her identity and gave evidence of identification of the body. It is no surprise that the *Illustrated Police News*, for once, perhaps, reporting with some accuracy, recorded her as being 'in deep distress'. Having no time to obtain a mourning outfit, Beatrice was reported as wearing fawn with a black hat. That she was able to attend at all was a testament to her strong will. Stagg was not present, nor did the law require him to be, and in any case his statement was not yet ready for the court to hear.

Amongst the attendees was the Aston Villa chairman, Frederick Rinder, club secretary George Ramsay and director Thomas Bate. Rinder was allowed to make a statement on the club's behalf and expressed deep regret at what had passed, praising a 'nice, quiet, unassuming young fellow ... very popular ... and very efficient as a player'.

With the inquest effectively stalled for want of further information, the coroner decided to adjourn the hearing until the following Tuesday. At that stage he may not have known that Tommy's funeral would take place the day before that sitting.

It would appear, to modern eyes, to be insensitive in the extreme to require witnesses, particularly Beatrice Ball, to submit themselves to the stresses of giving evidence in a public court within 24 hours of attending what was inevitably going to be an emotionally charged funeral. Nowadays, there are strict protocols governing such timings, but this was a different age.

Aston Villa FC vs Liverpool FC, Football League First Division, 16 November

To say playing a match on the Saturday following the shooting would have been difficult for the Aston Villa players is an understatement. It would not have been too easy for the visiting Liverpool team either. Nowadays, Villa would certainly have requested a postponement and, other commitments permitting, Liverpool would have doubtless gone along with it. Things were different then and we are dealing with a society where death, often measured into thousands, had recently been an everyday reported occurrence. So, life went on.

27,000 spectators turned up to watch a match, which would have begun in a sombre atmosphere. The *Derby Daily Telegraph* was one of many newspapers to record the fact that a flag above the ground, presumably the Union one atop the central barrel roofing of the then main stand on Witton Lane, was lowered to half mast and that players of both sides wore black crepe 'armlets'. It is not reported, but one imagines that a short prematch period of silence was observed rather than the applause often favoured today to mark the death of persons associated with the home club.

Things evidently warmed up as there was considerable crowd unrest. *The Birmingham Gazette* of 19 November noted that the referee had been 'in bad odour', which is a novel way of putting it, and for his pains was 'accorded a special demonstration betokening anything but pleasure', a tradition still keenly observed at the ground. Several 'sharp' decisions by the referee had put the crowd in a mood of 'open hostility'.

If your team had three penalty appeals turned down in the space of five minutes, each for alleged hand ball, I doubt if you would have been happy. Indeed, many of the spectators behind the goal had been 'frantic' in their appeals, especially when the referee refused to consult his linesman at any point. A pity they had not yet got round to using those newfangled moving picture things to get on-field decisions right.

The *Sunday Mercury*'s account the following day toned down things by headlining it a 'thrilling game' and reporting that the fans simply booed the opposition for their unfair tactics. *The Birmingham Gazette* reported that the club handled the terrace unrest sensibly, however that was achieved, and later ensured that the referee was smuggled out of the ground without mishap; the *Sunday Mercury*'s reporter did not mention the escape.

The match was dominated not only by the referee but by a strong wind with which neither team was fully able to come to terms, this giving the first-half advantage to Liverpool and the second to Villa. Our *Birmingham Gazette* reporter, doubtless mindful of recent events, judged that Dr Milne, who had replaced Tommy in the team, let the side down a little as he was not fully familiar with Villa's 'offside trap'. The 0-0 result, Villa's sixth draw in 17 games, meant they disappointingly slipped to fourth place in the table.

The heart-warming postscript was that a public collection held in the ground to benefit Tommy's widow raised £127. The modern equivalent would be around £7,400, more than enough to buy her a new house in the suburbs. I doubt, however, whether Mrs Ball or any members of the wider Ball and Richards families were invited to the match.

The Villa team that day was a 'classic' early- to mid-1920s line-up playing in the traditional 'W' formation: Jackson; Smart, Mort; Moss, Milne, Blackburn; York, Kirton, Walker, Capewell and Dorrell, each of whom might have had their minds on their forthcoming duties 48 hours later as Tommy's pall-bearers.

The prematch dressing-room atmosphere can only be guessed at and captain Frank Moss's words to the team must have been particularly difficult to put together. Mind you, we are talking about a captain who was once allegedly admonished by a referee for going verbally 'over the top' in cursing his own players, so I expect he came up with a suitably brief and inspirational message. I doubt whether a point for the draw created much joy in either camp.

When the return match was played at Anfield on the following Saturday, Villa, fielding an identical side, had the satisfaction of a

1-0 victory courtesy of a Len Capewell goal which, for the record, was not a penalty.

I was curious to know whether Dicky Johnson, Tommy's old mate from his Felling days, was playing in the Villa Park game. He was not, but readers who keenly follow football history may be interested to learn that the Liverpool side was Scott; Lucas, McKinley; Bamber, McDevitt, Pratt; Wadsworth, Forshaw, Walsh, Chambers, Hopkins. As an author's note for footballing geeks, although *The Villa News and Record* had Shone at inside-right the *Sunday Mercury*'s report had Forshaw replacing him.

Tommy Ball's Funeral, 19 November

The funeral, held at St John the Evangelist, Perry Barr on 19 November, stirred tremendous public interest. As *The Villa News and Record* noted, 'the road [to Perry Barr from Mr Richards's butchers' shop from whence the cortege left] was lined with sorrowing spectators'. The number was put at 'thousands'; it must have been quite a sight.

It is recorded that William Richards, Beatrice Ball, Tommy's mother Effie and two of her other sons, David and James, then aged 35 and 28 years respectively, attended the church as 'chief mourners'. I cannot find any reference to Mr Ball Senior, or brothers John, Hubert and Norman, being present. As with Tommy's wedding, travel and accommodation costs would have been high. Nor are Beatrice's three sisters mentioned, but they must have been there.

One imagines that Mr Richards bore part of the funeral costs and it would be surprising if the club had not contributed generously; the cost of the masonic work alone would have been steep. As I have noted, the mason who prepared the grave's monumental work was better informed than many Villa-supporting historians, as well as the 1923 editor of *The Villa News and Record*, in correctly spelling the deceased's name as 'Thomas Edger'.

What the club certainly provided were floral tributes and they doubtless footed the bill for a centrepiece, recorded as a 'fraternal offering' from the players, in the form of 'a large square of moss to represent a football ground, with white and yellow chrysanthemums worked into the shape of a football, and claret and blue ribbons at the corners'. Other floral tributes were sent by the West Bromwich Albion, Walsall, Middlesbrough and Birmingham clubs and by the Aston Manor Cricket Club, whose ground remains today situated just over the road from the church.

Aston Villa was principally represented by its chairman, Frederick Rinder, and also present were George Ramsay and assistant secretaries William Strange and 'Billy' Smith. The club's directors were also in attendance, including legendary former captain John Devey, under whose leadership Villa had won the Football League and FA Cup 'double' in 1897.

There were representatives of the Birmingham County FA, of the Birmingham and District Works Association and from the Sunderland and Coventry City clubs. Besides Devey, many former players doubtless attended, though only the names of the Sunderland-born 1913 cup-winning hero Charlie Wallace and of the formidable 242-goal Harry Hampton are handed down by chroniclers. It has been suggested to me that the gentleman standing between Frank Moss and Dr Milne in the photograph featured in this book may be 1920 FA Cup-winning captain Andy Ducat. Indeed, as he knew Tommy personally, I would be surprised if he had not attended.

The service and graveside prayers were conducted by the Rev. Cecil Watts-Read and the organist was a former football referee,

Mr T. Statham, who played 'In Memoriam', though whether the version written by Caradog Roberts or that by Frederick Maker is not known, and Handel's 'Dead March'.

The names of pall-bearers drawn from the current playing squad reads as a list of all-time Aston Villa 'greats'. Len Capewell, George Blackburn, Dicky York, Tommy Mort, Arthur Dorrell and Billy Kirton carried the coffin into church. Frank Moss, Tommy Smart, Dr Victor Milne, Tommy Jackson and Billy Walker with assistant trainer and former goalkeeper Harold Cooch carried it from the church to the graveside.

It was probable that Villa's entire playing staff had been present as one of Albert Wilkes's photographs, available on the Colorsport website, features a group of them following the main cortege into the church. Included in the group are Cyril Spiers, Ian Dickson, George Clark, Joseph Corbett, 'Jock' Johnston and our old friend Percy Jones. Strangely, though reserve team coach Cooch was a pall-bearer, I have found no mention of Freddie Miles being there.

Over the years the grave has suffered periods of severe neglect and occasional vandalism but has been periodically restored by the efforts of Villa supporters. Particularly prominent has been Jeff Hillier, who 'kept watch' for many years and is credited with a restoration of the site, and it has more recently been looked after by my correspondent Dot Ryan who has spent a considerable amount of time keeping things in good order.

The churchyard, which also contains a handful of Commonwealth War Graves Commission interments, sadly suffered considerable neglect for several months during the Covid crisis when the gates were locked to visitors. When visiting in the late summer of 2021 I needed to move a canopy of weeds to see Tommy's grave, though Dot has subsequently been able to return and make things presentable once again and council operatives have been active in general clearance work around the site.

It is not difficult to imagine that with such a crowd turning out for the funeral there was good opportunity for someone to make money. Sure enough, sellers were indeed busy 'working the crowd' with a distinctive memento of the occasion, which came from a seemingly unlikely source. The author of the memoriam poem being pedalled was a 55-year-old world-renowned Birmingham chess master named Frederick Richard Gittins.

Gittins has no proven connection to football, but there has been online speculation that he may have been related to the old-time Small Heath FC defender Walter Gittins. For what it is worth, F.R. Gittins lived for much of his adult life in Eversley Road, Small Heath, close to the Muntz Street ground used by Small Heath FC/Birmingham until 1906. After a successful chess-playing career, Gittins had become an internationally proclaimed author on chess problems and their solutions. In 1897, he published a bestselling text *The Chess Bouquet*, first editions of which are expensively offered for online auction from time to time.

In view of the modern collectability of his book, it is ironic to note that in the years before the Great War, Gittins had fallen on hard times and to make ends meet serialised a second volume of *The Chess Bouquet*. Things had been so bad in 1909 that he had published a rather forlorn autobiography entitled *Life on Nothing per Week*. By way of response, some fellow chess enthusiasts organised a testimonial fund to help him out. By 1911 he was back in work but as a travelling salesman.

With a keen, some might say desperate, eye for a commercial opportunity, Gittins penned the somewhat melodramatic, and in its way quite curious, 'A Memorial Poem to Thomas Ball'. This was published on card by the Commercial Printing Company of Newhall Street. You may find it informative to read this in full (grammar shown as printed):

'Twas on a Sabbath Evening
In drear November days
Two friends were heard 'Creating'
In Perry Barr's bye-ways.
High words just fed the anger
The young man's life is fled
A shot and then another
And Thomas Ball was dead!!!

Tis sad to think of her now left
Alone to fight in 'life'
Without Protector's kindest care
Of husband unto Wife.
Though fame was His
And cash not short
They proved alas in vain.
And Aston Villa lose a man
Who always played the game.

Of poor Stagg's fate nought can we say
The Law impels to silence.
The motive too is quite obscure
Until they break the Se the wide world o'er
And lonely hearts the wide world o'er
Will pity all concerned.
In this sad tragedy near Brum
Of which we have just learned.
Requiescat in Pace

Perhaps not the best poetry to have been written but sturdily within the heroic fashion of the times. Scrutiny reveals several interesting lines, not least in the author's drawing of several conclusions about the events. Despite saying that the case is sub judice, 'the law impels to silence', Gittins then proceeds to reveal that two shots were fired. This information was already being commonly passed around, but by broadcasting as fact that the second shot was the fatal one Gittins could, technically, be seen to be prejudicing the following day's inquest and any forthcoming criminal trial.

He also refers to Ball and Stagg as 'two friends', which rather contradicts the later perception, as promoted by the judge at Stafford, that the men did not like one another. His mention of 'obscure motives' correctly hints at the absence of a good reason for murder. As any future jury member might certainly have read the poem, both phrases were probably also in breach of sub judice.

Although entitled 'A Memorial Poem to Thomas Ball', the real curiosity value in the work lies in the unexpected hint of sympathy for the killer ('poor Stagg'). This view is at odds with what is historically presented as the prevalent public mood and Gittins certainly offers a degree of sympathy never, to my knowledge, picked up on by later Villa chroniclers. His lines are so carefully chosen that I am tempted to think that Gittins and Stagg were known to one another and that Gittins was hinting he had a bit of inside information on the Stagg–Ball relationship.

That Gittins may have lived on one of Stagg's 'beats' and remained in touch with him is possible, but it is a thin thread and cannot be proven. It must be said, though, that rather than a paean to Tommy Ball the poem reads more as a defence of George Stagg.

Staffordshire Coroner's Court, Day Two, 20 November

With almost callous disregard for witness emotions, the second coroner's hearing took place on the day following Tommy Ball's funeral. The proceedings were to allow the coroner to take police investigation, ballistic reports and the post-mortem into account and to hear further witnesses. The almost predictable prospect of the jury returning the view that Stagg should be indicted meant that the presence of a magistrate was required at the hearing.

One must have considerable sympathy for Beatrice Ball having to appear the day following the overwhelming emotional experience of attending her husband's very public funeral. It is salutary to consider that nowadays, courtesy of the 2003 Criminal Justice Act, the Crown Prosecution Service is obliged to observe clear guidelines over their dealings with bereaved families in homicide cases. No such consideration existed in 1923 and how, the day after witnessing the burial of her husband, Beatrice Ball could have been reasonably expected to offer lucid and safe testimony is beyond me. It was patently not fair either to Beatrice or to the man who might be indicted on the strength of her evidence.

Perhaps Stagg's legal representative, Mr Sharpe, had an awareness of Beatrice's emotionally fragile state and chose not to question her too aggressively. By contrast, *The Birmingham Gazette* of 21 November states that she was closely questioned by the coroner, and it is interesting that other chroniclers have picked up that he was reportedly sympathetic towards Stagg's version of events, though overruled by the jury's verdict.

The press, predictably, became excited by her evidence, especially the alleged shot aimed at her. Other witnesses were also heard and, in his absence, according to *The Aberdeen Press and Journal*, Stagg's statement to the police, as shown earlier, was read out by Mr Sharpe. This included the section making clear that he wished no one to speak for him, which closed the door to anyone hoping to see Mrs Stagg enter the witness box.

The Londonderry Sentinel of 22 November, doubtless publishing an abridged syndicated account of Stagg's written deposition, said simply, 'Accused had his gun in his hand and Ball, who was under the influence of drink, tried to wrench it away. In the struggle the gun went off.' Were it so simple!

Even if there were reservations on the coroner's part, the jury decided, as was their prerogative, that 'wilful murder' had been committed. The DPP had taken due interest in things and had expressed the view that dependent upon the jury's verdict the case could be referred to higher authority.

The next step was for the Staffordshire police, working with the magistrate in attendance, to establish a 'police court' to facilitate Stagg's passage through the criminal justice system. As this was arranged to take place the following day, and a room had already been made available within the Canterbury Road station, the coroner's jury's verdict had clearly been anticipated.

Staffordshire Police Court, 21 November

A police court was essentially a legal formality designed to take the coroner's findings and allow the police, in front of a presiding magistrate, to formally charge a defendant with whatever the coroner's jury had decided was appropriate. The indictment would then be speedily forwarded into, and through, the assize system firstly to the more junior local 'petty session' and, dependant on how things went, on to the higher authority of a county assize.

I have already remarked that in researching the case I have been surprised by the speed at which the law operated. The eight-day time frame within which the coroner's court, police court and petty assize hearing followed each other is a case in point, although the police and assize court hearings were little more than formalities. To labour a key point, the speed of action poses the question as to whether evidence had been fully evaluated either by the police or by the two legal counsels. I do not think either George Stagg, Beatrice Ball or the wider Ball family were well served by the process.

The police court was presided over by a local magistrate, a Colonel Arthur Rabene, and Superintendent Tucker was called on behalf of the DPP to apply for Stagg to be remanded in Winson Green for a further week to enable arrangements for the assize trials to be expedited. This was granted, so enabling the DPP some brief time to examine the existing depositions, the post-mortem report and an evidence sheet (Appendix 2) that included the gun, the used cartridge ends, a discharged cartridge case, the bloodstained garden gate and four pieces of card from the 'distance testing' ballistic trials of the previous Wednesday.

George Stagg made his first appearance in a dock to confirm his name and address. The considerable interest created by the case demonstrated that the Canterbury Road station was unprepared and unsuitable for both the numbers wishing to attend and the celebrity into which it had been forced.

Facilities were a bit too small to comfortably cater for press and public demand and the room chosen for the hearing was described by the *Derby Daily Telegraph* as 'resembling an improvised office', which it probably was. Anyone approaching Villa Park on a matchday from the Handsworth/Birchfield direction might want to take a short detour to spend a few minutes outside the now deserted police station and imagine the crush of journalists and sightseers on that day in 1923.

Stagg was described in *The Birmingham Gazette* as a tall, rather lean figure, grey-haired and almost bald with haggard features and looking 'considerably more than his forty-five years'. He was theatrically seated in a dock hastily knocked together earlier in the week by one of the officers who could do a bit of carpentry. The same source said that Stagg, perched on the rostrum, looked like a man ready to make an open-air speech. He evidently wanted to do nothing of the kind as he was reported to have sat throughout the proceedings saying nothing, staring upwards, never making eye contact with anyone but tightly gripping the rail of the dock. He appeared to present a very dejected figure and made no objection to a furtherance of his period of remand.

Stagg was duly sent back to prison and the case referred to the petty session for a formal criminal hearing. Given that petty session magistrates had no power to sentence in cases of murder, it meant that such a hearing had the authority to refer on the case to the next stage in the process before a county assize court. Here, the judge, if he so chose, would be able to pass sentence of death.

Death Certification, 22 November

Once the coroner's inquest was over, the West Bromwich registrar, a W.N. Price, could be informed and a death certificate produced.

Taken from Tommy's death certificate, the cause of death as per the findings of Coroner Lewis and his jury were:

> 'Haemorrhage & shock due to a wound in the chest caused by a shot fired from a gun by George John Alan Stagg at the same place on the same day. Murder.'

Whether the inclusion of the word 'murder' was to the coroner's satisfaction or whether its inclusion was insisted upon by registrar

Price is unclear, but if the latter, then Lewis would have needed to agree with its inclusion. I am most uneasy about this as its inclusion on a death certificate reads to the layperson as if murder was already an established legal fact. One needs only to follow the route taken by the Hillsborough hearings from 2017–19 and what many saw as a distinct and inexplicable contradiction between a coroner's court finding and that of a criminal court.

There would be little doubt that, given the coroner's verdict, the public and Ball's family would have taken Stagg's guilt as literal three months before he stood trial in the criminal court. There would have been an expectation for the Stafford jury, being offered identical evidence, to record an identical verdict.

It is worth considering, however, that in the present day an arrest for a crime is often eagerly taken by interested parties as evidence of guilt. This is especially so in high-profile cases when the public mood is keen for speedy retribution.

You may not be surprised to learn that the registrar joined the queue to misspell Edger as Edgar. You may, though, be surprised to learn that the coroner, who would have been given ample time to study the document as drawn up, did not pick up on this.

Staffordshire Petty Session, 28 November

This court, very broadly equivalent to the modern magistrate's court, acted as a catch-all for a magistrate to hear local crimes. The clue was in the name, 'petty' being an adaptation of the Norman French 'petit' or, in legal terms, 'small' crime. A great many serious crimes initially found their ways into the petty court, but this was an obligatory step in the process of determining whether such cases merited an upwards referral to a county assize court. In Stagg's case such a decision was inevitable.

The hearing took place on 28 November and, according to the deposition statements taken on the day, the location of the court was 'Perry Barr Courthouse', but I have little idea where this was situated. The contemporary press, as ever, was unhelpfully non-specific by offering the location as 'West Bromwich'. Sessional courts were often held for convenience in a police station, but as Canterbury Road had proved inadequate for the previous police court hearing it was unlikely to have been used for a busy petty session where several unrelated cases, involving the to and fro of a great many people, might be heard during the same day. A more adequately equipped courtroom would have been required and for that reason, I think we can also rule out the Boar's Head.

Rebecca Jackson, archivist at Staffordshire Record Office, told me that under usual circumstances the case would probably have been conducted in the magistrate's courtroom in Lombard Street West, which lay within the West Bromwich township. This possibility is compromised by the indisputable fact that the remaining witness depositions, heard on the morning of the trial, were signed off by the session magistrate at what is clearly shown in the original documents as 'Perry Barr Court Room', subtitled the 'committal court'.

To hear depositions at one venue then transfer papers, deponents, counsel and court officials to another within the same day makes it unlikely that the depositions were heard in Perry Barr in the morning and then the case heard later the same day in West Bromwich town, but maybe that is what they did. In the wider scheme of things, the venue is perhaps of little significance but for a researcher it presents an irritation, and any clarification would be welcome.

As today, the presiding justice of the peace was a member of the public considered prominent and sensible enough to conduct

THE ARMISTICE DAY KILLING

affairs. The presiding magistrate was again Arthur Rabene, who earlier in the day heard further depositions from the witnesses, each of whom appears to have been examined by both him and by the defence and prosecution counsels. The defending counsel was again Mr Sharpe 'of West Bromwich' who this time reportedly gave Mrs Ball a bit of a grilling about the alleged domestic violence of her husband. The prosecuting counsel was one G.R. Paling 'of London' who questioned why Stagg should have been sitting in his parlour at night with a loaded gun. Clearly, Mr Paling was not a countryman.

The formal charge against Stagg was confirmed and he made one statement: 'I most emphatically state that I am not guilty. I made a statement to the police which is true in substance and in fact. I don't wish to say anything further in this court or to call any witnesses.' The case was duly passed 'upstairs' to the Lord Chancellor Viscount Cave, who, on 23 December, decided that the case would be heard at the Stafford Winter Assize the following February. Witness depositions with notes of any questions asked of the witnesses were again collected by the DPP and made available to the higher court, including new legal counsel who used them to facilitate the development of their cases.

Part 8

'Feloniously, Wilfully and with Malice Aforethought'

Of Sound Mind

Before a murder trial could proceed, medical surveillance was maintained for several weeks to determine whether a prisoner was 'insane on arraignment', that is, whether he/she was mentally unfit to plead and was incapable of understanding what was likely to be going on around him/her at trial. In instances of 'unfitness' in those days the accused would usually, without trial, be incarcerated indefinitely in an asylum.

Should a jury find at trial that the accused was 'guilty but insane at the time of the act' then asylum incarceration and not prison would follow, as happened to the accused in another case tried at Stafford during the same week as Stagg. If there was no evidence of insanity, someone found guilty of murder would be facing either prison or the scaffold.

Stagg was potentially well served by the man to whom his case was allocated at Winson Green. Dr Maurice Hamblin Smith was no jobsworth prison doctor but a psychologist with an international reputation. With nearly 30 years' experience of assessing inmates at seven different prisons, Hamblin Smith had become the country's most eminent criminal psychologist and a pioneer in his field. In 1924, he was medical officer of Birmingham Prison, a lecturer in criminality at Birmingham University and a persuasive writer on the 'new science' of psychology. In 1922, he had written the internationally acclaimed *The Psychology of the Criminal*. I have been able to obtain an early copy; it makes a fascinating read.

Based on his experiences and with a slogan that 'men are not machines', Smith was to become an agitator for prison reform and was convinced that the route to eliminating criminality lay via the close study of the criminal mind.

His formal report on Stagg was dated 11 January 1924 and it confirmed that the prisoner had been 'under close observation since he came here first on 12 November last. I have seen him each day and have had a number of long interviews with him.' From the information provided, it seems as if Stagg spent his prison time in the hospital ward where 'he occupies himself with small jobs of work'. That, to Hamblin Smith, was an important point when deciding on fitness to stand trial.

The report says:

> 'He is somewhat depressed but not to any abnormal degree in the case of a man who is awaiting trial on a serious charge. He converses readily, rationally, with good intelligence, and with apparently good memory. He has no delusions or hallucinations. I have observed nothing which would indicate insanity. He is quite fit to plead to the indictment at his trial. His physical health is not good. He suffers from heart disease of an old standing. The action of his heart is rapid, and he suffers from "shortness of breat" on slight exertion. He states that he was wounded in the

left leg, during the war. On the calf of the left leg there are two healed scars which are such as would be caused by the entrance and exit wounds of a bullet. He also states that he suffered from pulmonary tuberculosis, and that he was in hospital with this disease in 1917, for about two months. I find no evidence of this disease being active at the present time.'

Based on his considerable experience of testing and of conducting structured conversations with prisoners pre-trial, and then correlating his findings with the outcome of their subsequent criminal trials, Hamblin Smith was certain that he could, pre-trial, place a prisoner into one of several categories that might indicate a predilection towards 'intentionally and consciously' committing criminal behaviour.

The factors he believed might move a person towards criminality were alcohol abuse, poverty, hereditary issues, 'redivision' (repeat offending), a lack of education and 'mental defectiveness'. It is worth idly considering into which of Hamblin Smith's categories Stagg might be placed. Apart from having no knowledge of the levels of schooling Stagg had undergone or whether his family had a history of mental problems, I do not see an 'easy fit' other than possibly some level of childhood poverty. Stagg might not have featured highly within Hamblin Smith's view of potentially criminality.

Amongst other things, Hamblin Smith used a form of assessment by which he encouraged the patient to indulge in 'free expression' conversation on topics of their choice. It would defy belief had Stagg not, at some point, attempted to create an opportunity to rehearse his version of the events of 11 November to his assessor; he may even have hoped that Hamblin Smith would 'put in a good word' for him. As Hamblin Smith's role was only to make a judgement on sanity and not to give prisoners rehearsal time for their day in court, he would doubtless have been skilled enough to avoid any conversation which might be designed to bring him onto the patient's side.

Even had Hamblin Smith come to a view of Stagg's predilection, or not, to commit murder there was no expectation that he should make such views known to the police or to the courts. His responsibility was only to indicate a patient's fitness to stand trial. That he spoke positively, as shown above, about Stagg, we can safely assume that in 1924 George avoided categorisation as mentally defective, 'sub-normal' or psychopathic. There appeared no question in Hamblin Smith's mind that Stagg was suffering from any form of diminished responsibility. He was therefore able to stand trial as charged, would be held entirely responsible for his actions and, if found guilty, sentenced accordingly.

Although Hamblin Smith never claimed that he was able to come to an opinion on a person's likely guilt, you can be sure that he became very good at doing just that, though any views he might have had he kept to himself. In any case, psychoanalytical evidence was not then recognised by the courts and, even had they wished to do so, neither defending nor prosecuting counsel had the right to informally ask Hamblin Smith his opinion on likely guilt.

Still less would he ever be asked to take the stand as an 'expert witness'. To act in court for or against a patient by divulging information given in confidence would catastrophically damage his future ability to gain client confidence, thereby making untenable his position within the prison service and signalling the end of his professional career and reputation.

Despite what I have said about the importance of Hamblin Smith maintaining a position of scrupulous neutrality, some readers might be tempted to think that the 'good memory' and 'no delusions' references in his report were coded language for whoever might need to read it.

A Royal Visit

Aston Villa was hardly out of the headlines in early 1924 and it was not all bad news, at least at first glance. In the middle of the furore over Tommy Ball, the club's attention was temporarily diverted by the anticipated opening of Mr Rinder's latest project. This was the construction of the so-called New Pavilion, better known to contemporaries as the 'Trinity Stand' and to more recent supporters as the 'Trinity Road Stand'.

This magnificent building has been widely acknowledged as the masterpiece of the veteran 'go-to' stadium architect and builder Archibald Leitch, whose work was in evidence at grounds all over the country. In the post-1980s rush to construct larger, maybe safer, stadia, often on new sites, many of Leitch's other great designs are gone, most notably perhaps, though not exclusively, at the former Roker Park, Highbury and White Hart Lane grounds. Arguably, the most notable remaining example of his work in England can be seen at Goodison Park, the home of Everton FC, but there are many others.

The club had wanted the opening of the stand to be conducted by royalty and the highly popular Prince of Wales, the future Edward VIII, was their favoured choice. One has, of course, to make a formal request for a 'royal' to open a building and you are not necessarily given who you want, but who is available.

Thus, Villa did not get the Prince of Wales but unknowingly secured another future King, his younger brother 'Bertie',

Duke of York. In entirely unexpected circumstances in 1936, 'Bertie' was to become King George VI. This turned out to be highly appropriate as his eldest great-grandson and, one presumes, a future king is now reputedly a keen supporter of the club.

To what extent the killing of Tommy Ball had taken the gloss off the completion of the New Pavilion project is not known, but to Rinder and the board the royal visit must have been a welcome opportunity to divert public attention. I think we may permit ourselves to be a little wistful and, had Tommy Ball survived to meet royalty, imagine how the family at home in Usworth and the Richards family in Aston would have reacted to it.

The grand opening on 26 January, therefore, offered a wonderful opportunity for the club to focus public attention on its ambitions and the local Aston footballing public was drawn to the occasion. Over 56,000 turned out to see the Duke of York on the pitch meeting the Villa team before a match against the ever-strong Bolton Wanderers side. As Bolton were FA Cup holders, winning the famous 'white horse' match of 1923, and Villa had realistic ambitions of winning the trophy in 1924, it was an attractive choice of fixture. Villa won 1-0 courtesy, again, of a Len Capewell goal.

On the face of it the opening of the new facility was good news. Unfortunately for the club, the celebrations temporarily masked a less happy issue. As amply demonstrated by Villa-supporting architectural expert Simon Inglis, it later became apparent that in financing the new stand Rinder had dug a little too deeply into the club's coffers. It was a big blow to his reputation and in the shadow of this, in July 1925, his enemies on the board took the opportunity to secure the great man's temporary banishment.

Aston Villa was not to be the last club to be laid financially low by the architectural ambitions of a club chairman I might add, but happily the Trinity Stand proved its worth over time. It survived to become, whether viewed from the roadside or from pitchside, one of the most iconic edifices in world sport. Like many a young supporter I was entranced in the 1950s by my first sight of its gracefully curving balcony painted in claret and blue and the magnificent half triangular central roof gabling, which showed off the club crest. By comparison with modern stadia the stand now appears in the memory to be small, but in 1924 it was one of the largest in the country, if not the world, and still retained its aura when I watched the three World Cup matches played at the ground in 1966.

It also became the heartbeat of the club's support, though the modern Villa fan may smile in condescension at me recording the awe generated by the sound of the trilby-attired season-ticket holders in 'the Trinity' stamping their feet in quick, loud unison. This was always a signal for action and eagerly picked up on by the team; 60 or more years ago, it was that noise, rather than the singing from the Holte End choirs, that got things going.

Despite promises to the contrary, the stand was controversially demolished in 2000 as part of the ongoing modernisation of the ground, an act described by many supporters as being nothing short of corporate vandalism.

As a small side issue, diminished cash reserves made it no doubt necessary for Villa to explore new means of income. Given Rinder's views on sobriety and set against the background of George Stagg's allegations against Tommy Ball, it is ironic to note that on 31 March 1924, the very week that Stagg's conviction was commuted, the club received a licence to sell alcoholic drinks in the ground on matchdays.

Rex vs Stagg, The Winter Assize, Stafford, 19 February 1924

George Stagg's trial at the Stafford Winter, or 'Epiphany', Assize was held at the courtroom in Stafford in front of a judge with powers to pass the death sentence. The handed-down date of the trial has for some reason tended to be 16 February, ignoring the fact that this was a Saturday and the assize did not formally convene until the following Monday, Stagg's case being heard on day two.

Assize courts were formed in medieval times and dealt with the most serious types of crime such as treason, riot, murder, burglary, bigamy and violence. Such cases were often dealt with initially at a petty session, but as they were deemed punishable at levels exceeding a magistrate's authority, referral to the higher court ensued. Following the then usual model of local law enforcement, the assize courts were geographically based within an administrative county and generally, though not exclusively, in the 'county town'. As, in 1924, Perry Barr was within Staffordshire, Stagg's trial was held in Stafford and not in the more conveniently situated Victoria Assize Court in Corporation Street, Birmingham.

An assize met periodically, sometimes twice a year, for example 'winter assize' and 'summer assize', or, as at Stafford, as seasonal 'quarter sessions'. They sat for an unspecified period, often over weeks, until all referred cases had been dealt with. In the early 1920s, before a dozen assizes were each grouped into one of six geographical 'circuits', Stafford then being part of the 'Oxford Circuit'. Assize courts were abolished in 1972 and much of their work is now, broadly speaking, conducted by Crown Courts.

Assize courts generally shared the use of members of their circuit's approved list of legal practitioners, known as a 'bar', to prosecute or defend cases. Prosecutions were conducted at public expense while up to 1903 defendants had to pay the salaries of their counsel. Poorer defendants who were often expected to conduct their defence without legal support might find themselves facing professional prosecutors, and the resulting mismatch of skills in presenting arguments did not usually work to their advantage. The Poor Prisoners Defence Act gave eligibility for legal aid from the public purse to persons who were deemed to have a reasonable defence against charges made, but heaven help those who appeared to the DPP to be guilty as charged and not worth wasting the money on.

The perceived likelihood of 'the poorer you were, the more chance there was of you being hanged' was one of the reasons why movements for the abolition of capital punishment gained traction in the early 20th century. One expects that, as Stagg's case involved a mixed plea of self-defence and ill luck and the deposition evidence was not decisive, the provision of legal aid would have been forthcoming and enabled him to have a defence team drawn from the bar.

It was always possible that, for the opportunity to appear in such a high-profile and potentially widely reported trial, Stagg's defence team may even have enthusiastically offered their services pro bono, or free of charge to the public purse, but this has not been established.

Stafford Crown Court was situated within the town's architecturally grand Shire Hall, which had been constructed in imposing neoclassical style in 1798. The courtroom still exists, though in 'mothballs' , and is planned to form part of a new Staffordshire History Centre.

The usual story is that huge crowds had assembled outside the courtroom on the day of Stagg's trial and that 'hundreds' were locked out. *The Staffordshire Advertiser* tells us differently, saying that, contrary to expectation, there was not a large public assembly outside the court. As the number allowed into the public gallery was limited by the court's small size, there was perhaps some locking out, but probably not quite as much as traditional accounts suggested. Another myth broken.

In contrast to accounts of Stagg's appearance at the police court, *The Staffordshire Advertiser* describes him as 'a tall man of military appearance', which simple words give an entirely different impression of a man who is usually presented to history as 'broken'. It may well be that Stagg had been advised by his counsel to smarten up his appearance and present himself as a sympathetic old soldier of some dignity and bearing.

Mr Justice Rowlatt

The work of an assize was generally presided over by one or more judges, men only, who were assigned to a given circuit and who might share the load in hearing the cases. At the Stafford Winter Assize the duty load was allocated to two men, a Mr Justice Bailbache, information on whom I have been unable to trace, and the rather better-known Mr Justice Rowlatt, into whose lap the George Stagg case fell and about whom there is no lack of surviving opinion.

Sir Sidney Arthur Taylor Rowlatt, 1862–1945, was possibly the highest-profile judge in the country at the time. He was a member of the Oxford Circuit Bar and had previously worked at Stafford and other circuit courts as a barrister. The appointment was probably not good news for Stagg as Rowlatt was not a man who, reputedly, suffered contradiction to his opinion, though he was not without a sense of humour. According to one of his obituaries, he had once, reportedly, admonished a jury in a fraud case for coming to 'a very silly verdict' and when duly acquitting the defendant had advised him sternly, 'don't do it again'.

Rowlatt's main work came not from the circuits but from complex taxation cases and he was recognised as the leading arbiter of his day of such cases. I was interested to learn from another obituary that he had a reputation for making up his mind about cases very quickly in proceedings, though not always recording on paper the rationale for his judgement before he gave it.

This may, up to a point, be understandable as speed in getting things out of the way was a prime consideration at assizes, and trials that could be sorted out within a day or less were most welcome. This put pressure on judges to have their summarising words to the jury ready in mind and, in anticipation of a jury's decision, to know what sentence they might pronounce. It would no doubt be helpful if a judge's closing summary contained direction to the jury regarding how they should find.

It was not unusual for judges to keep a given trial going until into the evening rather than have it mess up the following days' schedule. Rowlatt was credited in an obituary with having presided over 416 complex tax cases of which only 128 entered a second day.

It is perhaps useful to know that Rowlatt had recently made a big name for himself leading an investigation into wartime links between alleged native terrorists in British India and the German government. Based on his consequent 1919 report and recommendations, the government passed the Rowlatt Act which gave those living anywhere in the Empire very few opportunities to prove their innocence should they be accused of sedition, that is, discussing, plotting or encouraging rebellion.

The strategies Rowlatt had recommended be adopted included arrests without warrant, secret trials without jury, the accused remaining in ignorance of the identity of their accusers and being denied access, pre-trial, to the precise evidence for their arrest. There were also to be restrictions on press coverage of their trials.

Perhaps Rowlatt was unlikely to be patient if a case he thought he had 'cracked' from the outset was dragging on a bit. Those barristers at Stafford who had presented to him previously would have known full well how to go about their business and jurors who were familiar with him would know a speedy verdict was required and maybe be able to pick up any hints from the bench as to which way they might be expected to find.

The judge was clearly delighted by the light workload presented at Stafford this time and began overall proceedings on Monday, 18 February, as was customary, with an open session attended by all participating lawyers, jurors and the press. *The Staffordshire Advertiser* informs us that he told the assembly of his delight that, following 40 years of working at Stafford, there were only 17 cases 'on the books' this time. 'It really was wonderful how little crime there was today in this part of England,' he said, and he applauded the fact that there were no cases of bigamy, 'an extraordinary thing in these days'.

He went on to suggest that most of the cases to be heard were of minor significance, by which he may have meant 'I've got them all sorted out'. The 'minor' cases included financial misappropriation, demanding money by menaces and breaking and entering, but the few more juicy offerings included a couple of attempted wife murders, an alleged infanticide and the Stagg case or, as he put it, 'a charge of murder of a dreadful kind. No doubt they had all heard about it.'

You may be open-mouthed to learn that he then proceeded, with press and jurors present, remember, to run through an open summary of each case and, in so doing, probably suggested that he had the answers already worked out. For example, he announced to the assembly that one of the attempted-wife-murder defendants he was about to try was mad, whatever that meant, and another had acted under considerable stress. Though it was all most helpful in informing jurors how business could be dealt with quickly, it seems to modern eyes to have been of dubious legal probity.

Remembering that Stagg's case was not to be heard until the morrow he informed his courtroom audience that 'the man who was accused undoubtedly did it … but under what circumstances they would have to investigate'. For certain, everyone would have known Stagg had admitted to killing Tommy, but I doubt whether Rowlatt's pre-trial public assertion of culpability would pass muster in a modern British courtroom.

Note also that Rowlatt was not recorded as issuing, and probably was not required to, the modern warning in a high-profile case that jurors should ignore all that they had previously read or heard on the matter.

It would have been most unlikely that any of the jurors had not read quite a lot about the incident, including the subsequent coroner's and minor court hearings, and would be well acquainted with the press attribution of Mrs Ball's testimony and of Mr Stagg's defence.

British courts have always been adversarial by nature with both sides working for a 'result', but we have a reasonable expectation for the judge to stay above that conflict. Indeed, part of the reasoning for setting up a Court of Appeal in 1907 was to provide a check on the behaviour of many 'old-school' 19th century judges who apparently took it as normal to actively influence the processes of prosecution, defence and jury decision.

I invite the reader to judge whether Rowlatt's interventions in the Stagg case compromised that neutrality and had any significant bearing on the trial's outcome.

Just for the record, it may be of interest to know that Rowlatt's third son, who himself would become a noted tax lawyer, partially mirrored Stagg's wartime experience by being shot in the leg. In his case, the severity of the wound led to amputation. He was also awarded the Military Cross.

Vachell vs Coventry

To add to the trial's crowd appeal, the reputedly 'flamboyant' C.F. Vachell, the 'celebrity lawyer' of his day, led the prosecution with the Hon. Geoffrey Lawrence. No one has quite explained how Vachell was 'flamboyant', or why he was a celebrity, but there is no doubt that he was a very clever and highly experienced advocate and he probably put on a good show for the gallery and reporters.

He also had an interesting local 'backstory'. Born in Cardiff in 1854 to a prominent local family, by the age of 27 he was living and practising as a young solicitor in, of all places, Aston. By 1891 he was evidently on the way up as a barrister-at-law. As his census record shows he had moved to lodgings in well-to-do Sutton Coldfield and had by then 'taken silk' in becoming a Queen's Counsel member of the Oxford Circuit Bar. Ten years later, as a King's Counsel, he had conclusively moved into the big time, living as a self-employed barrister-at-law at a prestigious 104b Great Charles Street address in Birmingham's city centre. Over the following decade, he was prominent as a recorder at several of the Oxford Circuit assize courts, including Gloucester, Shrewsbury and Stafford itself.

Though by the time of Stagg's trial Vachell had been living in central London for a few years, there is no doubt that he knew the Midlands, its police forces and its assize courts very well indeed. Approaching 70 years of age, he was also quite probably familiar with Judge Rowlatt's court style and knew how to play to His Justice. As a former resident of Aston, he would certainly be keenly aware of the almost devotional affection in which the Aston Villa club was held by its supporters and the likely strength of local feeling to have Ball's killer 'nailed'. Long since an honorary Midlander, Vachell died in Evesham in 1935.

Stagg's defence team was led by Sir Reginald Coventry, 1869–1940, of Croome Court in Worcestershire, now a National Trust attraction and in recent years rescued from dereliction by that organisation. He was formerly a deputy lieutenant of Worcestershire and a well-connected descendant of the earls of Coventry, doubtless being on nodding terms with several of the landowners on the jury. He was assisted by a Mr J. Wylie, himself a busy barrister who had been appointed to act in other cases at the assize.

Coventry was to prove no match for Vachell as, despite having been recorder at the Stoke-on-Trent petty quarter sessions, his experience was generally with less complex cases than the one in hand. Although aged 54 at the time of the trial, he had only obtained his 'silk' as King's Counsel two years beforehand and was, in terms of experience at this level, significantly junior to Vachell.

Whereas Vachell had already made a name for himself, the Stagg trial could reasonably have presented a career-defining opportunity for Coventry, hence my view that he may have been acting in a pro bono capacity. What he would not have expected was that the trial was going to broaden his professional experience a little further by leading him to an appearance before the Court of Appeal.

The Witnesses

A frustrating research challenge has been in establishing which deponents appeared in court at Stafford to give oral evidence, and what they said. Although newspaper accounts have been helpful up to a point, and give enough clues to enable one to work out certain things, they invariably do not go beyond a cursory description of what a witness had said in court and offer nothing close to a complete record of proceedings. I have attempted several avenues of research, but information regarding the whereabouts of court reports, should they survive, and which might contain the information I was seeking, has led me round in circles, with each possible repository suggesting I contact the others.

By convention, the first choice of witness went to the prosecuting counsel, and it is apparent from newspaper reports that Tommy's widow Beatrice Ball, John Fearn, the Birmingham firearms expert, and Dr Garman appeared for the prosecution, and it is reasonable to suppose that Sgt Davenport and Inspector Mollett, the two police officers principally involved, did so also. Aston Villa trainer Alfred Miles famously appeared as a 'character witness' defending Tommy Ball's reputation.

There is no known reference to suggest anyone stood for Stagg, and, as he had made it clear from the outset that he did not require such assistance, it is safe to say that everyone who was required in court appeared at the prosecution's behest. For reasons we will come to, Stagg's defence team, unlike the prosecution, was unable to call character witnesses, which was to leave him very isolated.

You may, however, consider that Dr Garman could have usefully stood for him, and possibly local residents the Rose sisters and Arthur Pitchford.

The Defence Case

Eyewitnesses. This was Coventry's strong point as only the defendant was available to the court as an eyewitness. Beatrice Ball had not seen what happened and Mary Stagg, as we know, had claimed spousal privilege not to take the stand. As there was no one who could directly contradict his evidence except by speculation, insinuation or hearsay, it was important for Stagg to avoid any pitfalls during cross-questioning and keep to a well-rehearsed script of being the honest victim of circumstances: 'That is my story and I am sticking to it'.

The Loaded Gun. Nor could the prosecution categorically disprove Stagg's explanation that he had loaded his gun as a genuine and regular safeguard against poachers, or that the meeting with Ball was anything other than accidental.

Self-Defence. As immediately before the shooting Ball had allegedly made several verbal threats against both Mr and Mrs Stagg and had attempted to illegally enter his neighbour's garden, then Stagg could be represented as acting in legitimate self-defence throughout the incident.

Ball's Inebriation. To support the notion of self-defence, Coventry considered it important to emphasise Stagg's view that his neighbour was acting under the influence of alcohol. *The Staffordshire Advertiser* represented this line of defence by quoting Stagg's words under court examination: 'Ball was more or less an habitual drunkard [who was in] a violent, aggressive, intoxicated condition … trying to force his way in [to my premises] … in order to commit some act of violence.'

An Accident. If the possibility that the gun discharge had been accidental could be shown in front of the jury, this might indicate there had been no intention of causing death or injury and so

185

cast considerable doubt on the prosecution case. As it happened, Coventry and Stagg had planned to visually re-enact the supposed tussle over the gate and, as will be shown, Stagg evidently carried this out with some aplomb, complete with trigger activation exactly on cue.

Relationship with Ball. Stagg emphasised that he had no intention of killing Ball because 'I had received nothing but kindness from him'. He also said that the notice to quit the cottage had been served not because of disputes over chickens, but because of Ball's apparent violence towards his wife.

As we know, this latter claim was vigorously denied by Mrs Ball, but importantly she had already backtracked on her initial damning testimony that Stagg had said, 'You all ought to be poisoned', so perhaps Coventry was hoping for a bit more of the same.

Mrs Ball's Testimony. As Coventry would have been aware that Beatrice's appearance in the witness box might be emotionally persuasive to the defence case, his tactic was to counter the impact of any testimony she might give by dismissing it as fanciful and inaccurate. As it was possible that Beatrice's memory for fact was unsound, Coventry would probably have felt very confident of being able to challenge her testimony and noted to the jury, 'It was reasonable to assume that Mrs Ball was hysterical at this time and that her memory was at fault'.

Contrition. Coventry's other major advantage was that he was able to emphasise the fact that Stagg's ready admittance to having shot Ball was not the response of a man trying to get away with something. In addition, Stagg's claim that he had given assistance to the wounded man, his subsequent quest for medical help, as endorsed by Dr Garman and Harold Pitchford, and his ready willingness to direct a policeman to the scene of the shooting were, similarly, not the actions of a guilty man.

Medical Evidence. A significant weakness in Coventry's case was the absence of defence witnesses to take the stand, though Simon Burnton makes the curious and intriguing point that 'the defence produced a doctor who having studied Ball's injuries said most emphatically that the gun could not have been at Stagg's shoulder.' The implication was that it was not a 'lined-up' and deliberately aimed shot. There is no doubt that, if correct, this was a more than useful piece of witness evidence and, again if correct, the witness Simon refers to could only have been the man who carried out the post-mortem, Dr Garman.

Unfortunately, Garman's written deposition lacks this precise information, and he was, of course, called as a witness for the prosecution, so if he had said that which Simon claimed, it must have been under cross-questioning from Coventry. Simon does not acknowledge his source but given the tone of Garman's deposition, especially in supporting the timings claimed by Stagg, it was entirely credible, as I have previously suggested, that the doctor could, perhaps should, have appeared for the defence.

The Prosecution Case

Although posterity tends to assume that the outcome of Stagg's trial was a foregone conclusion, you will have taken my earlier hints that it was anything but.

Intention. The nub of the prosecution case was to establish that Stagg fired the gun on purpose and, in so doing, knew that it might kill or injure someone. With the gun having a challenging 11lb pull, Vachell used the testimony of his expert witness, John Fearn, to suggest that Stagg had ample time to desist. Thus, in firing the gun, he would have made the decision to do so in the clear knowledge that he might cause injury or death.

Vachell would also have wanted the jury to believe that Stagg's decision to reload following the first, harmless, shot might further indicate that he then had every intention of aiming a second shot directly at Ball.

The Accidental Shot. He then had to challenge Stagg's testimony that the fatal shot had been accidental, and he worked hard to sow considerable seeds of doubt regarding this possibility. To establish the point, Vachell again made use of John Fearn, whose testimony implied that such a discharge was unlikely. As we shall see, in an intervention that appeared to take the watching press by surprise, the judge, Mr Rowlatt, was to take it upon himself to unsuccessfully try to prove Fearn's point for him, so no prizes for guessing where the judge's money lay.

Ball's Sobriety. Vachell needed to offset the defence case that the firing of the gun was proportionate to the physical threat Stagg found himself to be under. As he lacked an eyewitness to directly contradict Stagg's account of how the incident unfolded, it was not necessarily easy for him to argue 'beyond reasonable doubt' that Tommy did not pose a physical threat. The key to doing this lay in challenging Stagg's assertion that Ball was a habitual drinker who was inebriated at the time of the incident.

Character Evidence. The defence assertion that Ball was not only drunk on the night of the shooting but was also a habitual drinker represented, in legal terms, a 'smear' on his character. By so doing, the defence unwittingly, and clumsily, played into Vachell's hands as it enabled him the opportunity to preserve the dead man's reputation.

Vachell, as he was entitled, unsurprisingly took full advantage of this by using the evidence submitted by persons who had spoken to Ball on the night in question. The Midland Red conductor, Percy Redman, and pub landlord, Harry Wood, had already offered depositions which appeared to counteract the drunkenness allegation. Whether the two solid citizens took the stand, or their depositions were represented in court by Vachell, is not clear.

Vachell was also entitled to call anyone else who might offer credible character testimony to support the view that Ball was not a drinker. His trump card was the 39-year-old Aston Villa trainer, Alfred Miles, who knew Tommy both personally and professionally. Being nationally famous, he was, in public perception, in a different league to Redman and Wood and gave a glowing reference of a 'sober chap … always in the best of condition'.

Vachell certainly 'milked' Miles's evidence, emphasising to the jury, 'professional footballers were looked after very sharply by their trainers whose duty it was to see that they were kept in the best of condition and lived a proper sort of life'. One imagines that the club officials, especially Mr Rinder, would have been quite pleased to hear Miles's control over his players lauded in court.

By challenging Stagg's integrity over the core issue of drunkenness, Vachell could subliminally suggest that other aspects of the defendant's version of events were equally fanciful. The confirmation of Ball's apparent sober living also weakened Stagg's 'moral high ground' claim that his neighbour often beat his wife while under the influence of alcohol and certainly threw doubt on his claims that Ball had, on the night of 11 November, threatened to harm both him and Mary Stagg.

Under questioning, Beatrice Ball was also able to confirm her husband's sobriety and good domestic behaviour, denying the allegations of inebriation and violence on his part and confirming they had enjoyed a happy marriage.

Avoiding a Trap. For his part, Vachell was extremely careful in not impugning Stagg's character as, had he done so, Coventry would himself have been entitled to call up character witnesses on behalf of his client. Perhaps Coventry already had these standing by, and the last thing Vachell wanted was a coterie of bemedalled war veterans and former policemen queuing up to say what a patriotic, level-headed, honest, even-tempered fellow the defendant was.

There must have been many of Stagg's former colleagues, superiors and friends, possibly even our international chess champion Mr Gittins, who could have offered heavyweight supportive character testimony. As it was, Stagg was only given the opportunity, through his counsel, to tell the jury that he held 'five medals and two clasps, sir', and Vachell would not want any more of that sort of talk.

Historical Bad Blood. Vachell was in possession of plenty of information from Beatrice Ball regarding the alleged rancour Stagg had apparently shown towards his tenant over chickens, a dog and a pigsty and culminating in an eviction notice. Ill will was not technically admissible as proof of guilt in a 'wilful murder' case, but Vachell must have raised the possibility as the judge, whose summary instructions to the jury were to be quite explicit, appeared convinced that past falling-outs were key to the case.

Beatrice Ball's Evidence. If Freddie Miles had been a face card, Vachell also held the ace in the person of the deceased's widow. He did, however, need to play the card expertly and was to stage-manage Mrs Ball's contribution perfectly. She was, as widely reported, appropriately presented, both audibly and visibly, and her day in court at Stafford was suitably dramatic. Dressed 'in deep black [she] made a pathetic figure,' said a reporter. Her appearance and testimony, 'punctuated by pathetic sobs', was eagerly devoured by the press pack and her descriptive language, in particular her accounts of Tommy's dying words and of the shot allegedly aimed at her, were widely and sympathetically reported.

Unsurprisingly, the unsubstantiated allegation of an attempt on her life, although not pursued in court, made good press copy. At the time, stories from the Victorian-style 'penny dreadful' crime magazines were still culturally fashionable, so reporters and their subeditors were able to offer their 1924 readership the ever-popular mix of villainous, dead-of-night, deeds and a young, vulnerable female narrowly escaping death.

Doubtless it would help to sell papers, though, to her eternal credit, when Beatrice retired to a private life she did not, as best we know, try to 'milk' her brief celebrity to make money out of maintaining press interest.

A Risky Strategy. This leads us on to a clear contradiction in the prosecution case. Apart from Mrs Ball, all parties, including Vachell, appeared to have accepted Stagg's assertion that only two shots were fired by him, the second being the fatal one. Mrs Ball's evidence that the first shot killed her husband with a second shot aimed in her direction was therefore counter to the version of events accepted by the police, DPP and prosecution. Her persistence with the claim, which was presumably with counsel's agreement, I find baffling. The only obvious advantage I can see was in the press picking up on Stagg being a 'bad lot'.

Unfortunately, apart from his general comments concerning the overall veracity of Beatrice's evidence, I have found no record of how Coventry dealt in court with the issue.

Judge Rowlatt, however, in his summary to the jury, did not draw attention to the police case being at odds with Beatrice's testimony but was simply to refer to there being 'conflicting evidence' regarding which shot killed Tommy. Thus, the door was kept open for the jury to favour Beatrice's evidence.

Stagg's Character. Without being able to explicitly say so, Vachell had suggested that the jury should consider Beatrice's landlord an unfeeling man whose behaviour was unmannered and verbally cruel. He drew attention to the fact that Stagg, virtually over Ball's dead body, had claimed Beatrice had admitted to being 'kicked around' by her husband. He told the jury, 'It is impossible to suggest that at such an awful time as that the wife should [be asked to] put the reproach of violence and cruelty on her husband.'

By implying that Stagg was unfeeling and cold-hearted by nature, Vachell appeared to be gambling, apparently successfully, that rather than believing the rather dour and seemingly embittered middle-aged man who had killed a local hero, the jury would be more inclined to allow the visual and emotional impact of the attractive young grieving woman in black to influence their deliberations. If any members of the jury went into their private room post-trial with a level of sympathy towards Beatrice's account, then everything Stagg had alleged about events leading up to and surrounding the shooting itself was laid open to question.

The Ash Pan Cartridges. The curious case of the cartridges found by the police to be hidden in the ash pan has never been explained. Although they in themselves proved nothing that had not already been established, the damage was that it probably increased the suspicion that there was something fishy about Stagg's account of things.

Mr Rowlatt Intervenes

The truth surrounding Stagg's assertion of the trigger's sensitivity was always going to be critical to the case outcome. I find it improbable that Coventry could not have found someone from the gun trade, of which Birmingham was the national centre, or from the military, to offer a counter view to that of John Fearn regarding the crucial issues of the likelihood of an accidental discharge when the barrel was knocked on the gate.

In the event, it was Stagg himself who was given the opportunity to apparently prove his point, and in bizarre fashion. Vachell did not contradict Stagg's overall story of a tussle over the gate, but unaccountably, and in an act which appears to me to have stood outside both the letter and the spirit of the law, Judge Rowlatt decided to play a rather theatrical part in the prosecution case.

The unloaded gun was introduced into court as an exhibit, as was Stagg's garden gate. *The Scotsman*'s reporter wrote, 'The judge took the gun, cocked it and banged it a number of times on the bench [not the gate] without moving the mechanism'.

Far from destroying Stagg's story about the accidental discharge, the judge had, unwittingly, given him the perfect opportunity to prove it. Stagg was reported in *The Staffordshire Advertiser* of 23 February as having recreated the tussle with Ball in court, having a warder 'stand in' for Ball. Then, as described by *The London Hearts Supporters Club* magazine of 19 February, Stagg 'took the gun, cocked it, and going up to the gate … struck the barrel on the top of the gate with the result that it went off.'

The incident was widely reported and may well have come to the attention of the Home Secretary and those justices who were to sit on the appeal bench.

If Coventry's luck held, the jury, several of whose members had considerable experience of using firearms, may, on witnessing the courtroom theatricals, have been inclined to accept Stagg's account of things.

Opportunities Missed?

It appears to me that both the prosecution and the defence possibly missed three important opportunities to make their cases.

Firstly, there appears to have been a consensus in court that the two men did tussle physically, though Stagg's claim that Ball handled the rifle's barrel was not proven. You may be surprised to learn that the technology did then exist to enable the police to take fingerprints from the gun after they took possession of it, but there is no record of their having done so. If Ball's prints had not been found on the gun, it could have indicated that Stagg's story about the tussle, and by extension the accidental discharge, was false; if Ball's prints had been on the gun, the defence might reasonably have argued it was proof that Stagg's account was the truth. The evidence gained could have swung the case either way. Good police work it was not.

Quite the opposite, as the police could have taken the weapon away from the scene immediately but, to our knowledge, the weapon was left in Stagg's parlour overnight and subsequently handled after the incident by at least three persons, Davenport, Mollat and Fearn, plus, quite possibly, one or more members of the Stagg household, thus contaminating the key piece of evidence they had.

Secondly, both sides may have been well advised to look for any constructive indication from the crime-scene measurements and the post-mortem results to suggest where each man might have been standing at the point of the fatal shot. There existed precise relevant information within the post-mortem, the ballistics reports and the description of where blood stains lay on the gate. It was not 'rocket-science' forensics to match this information. It might have established where Ball was at point of impact and could have been critical in proving or disproving Stagg's account of things.

Thirdly, we have already noted that the police did not ascertain whether, and if so why, Stagg's nearest neighbours also owned firearms and routinely loaded them at night. This could have proved fertile ground for both legal teams to explore independently and there had been time available in which to do it. As it happened, Vachell was able to insinuate, without corroborative evidence, that Stagg was somehow unusual in keeping a loaded gun at his side at night, whereas Coventry was seemingly without empirical evidence to counteract the insinuation.

Influencing the Jury

Coventry's summing-up to the jury was predictable. He maintained that Stagg's testimony had been 'clear and consistent' and he said, 'The jury must be satisfied that there was no motive whatever for Stagg to commit the crime of murder, and the facts favoured the truth of the prisoner's statement that this tragedy was an accident.'

It was Vachell, possibly generally pleased with how things had gone, who was able to re-emphasise in his summary remarks that Stagg's account 'was the story of a man in a difficult position', which was, of course, an invitation to the jury to accept that Stagg's story was a fabrication.

Even though, or perhaps because, Stagg appeared to have proven the critical issue of the gun possibly discharging accidentally, the judge appears to have weighted his concluding remarks against the defendant. I doubt whether Mr Rowlatt took kindly to having looked a little comical, even if the situation was of his own making.

As widely reported, Rowlatt, in his case summary, instructed the jury not to show too much sympathy towards Stagg for his public service but 'to look at the facts dispassionately'. Taken at face value that statement might indicate an awareness that weight of opinion in the jury room regarding Stagg's intentions was likely to be divided.

Rowlatt also emphasised the key legal point. 'If it [the gun] went off by accident during a struggle it was manslaughter', but if the death was caused by 'the gun being pointed at the man and discharged on purpose' they must find Stagg guilty of murder. No obvious problem there but, were the jury to take the view that the shot was not accidental, there was no advice that has survived to cover the fine-line possibility of Stagg firing in self-defence while in fear for his own safety, and ultimately that of his wife. Nor, as far as we are aware, did he offer any instruction regarding whether Stagg's reaction to Ball's alleged threatening behaviour may have been 'proportionate'.

Rowlatt, somewhat surprisingly, advised that although there had been a conflict of evidence as to which shot killed Ball, 'and no motive shown', the jury could find a guilty verdict 'if a man might lose his temper against a person he did not like'. My interpretation of this is that the jury was being advised that in the absence of fact they might accept hearsay as evidence.

The last-minute introduction of this 'new' option by which Stagg could be found guilty could be interpreted as a legally contestable direction to the jury. That his approach may have been typical of the times is possible but not entirely relevant; what was relevant is whether he overstepped his entitlements.

Whether the jury was split on the decision based on the weight of evidence and/or had misgivings concerning how the trial had been conducted cannot possibly be known, but the subsequent recommendation of mercy, i.e. that Stagg should receive a custodial sentence only, suggests that at least some of the members were less than happy at the prospect of Rowlatt donning the black cap.

Many readers will conclude that Stagg got what he deserved. Others may feel the question of whether Stagg had been tried before an impartial and independent court, as was his right, is worth the debate.

Jury Service

The most interesting feature of jury service at an assize court a century or so ago was that each case did not bring with it an entirely new jury. Instead, a group of over 20 persons was nominated to cover the entire proceedings with the 'lucky 12' for each case drawn by lot. This hopefully ensured that everyone, more or less, took a fair turn. The nominated foreman would presumably sit on as many case juries as was considered reasonable.

Unsurprisingly, with assize work sometimes taking several weeks, only men with a readily available reservoir of free time could aspire to jury service, and there was some aspiration to be nominated as selection publicly demonstrated a certain level of social standing, as the list (to be shown) demonstrates.

Having achieved a place on the list was one thing but having to sit through and adjudicate on several, possibly complex or boring, cases was most certainly another. Drawing by lot made it theoretically possible that everyone might expect a little time off, but from my research it seems that it was not unusual for many jurors to pull social or experiential rank to avoid having to listen to more cases than they fancied.

The jury at Stafford would probably have been as relieved as Mr Justice Rowlatt to learn that there were only 17 cases to be heard but, to argue against my previous sentence, there may have been an element of enthusiasm to be associated with such a cause célèbre as the Tommy Ball case, especially as they would all have read about it in the papers and would come to it with some measure of prior knowledge and possibly an opinion or two.

As can be imagined, it would be usual within an assize framework for any given juror to sit before the same judge on several occasions, especially if returning to jury service over a period of several years.

This presented its own challenges as in the 19th century, to hurry things along, it had been common for judges to be proactive in influencing jurors in how they thought a case should be found. In any event, regular jurors in 1924 might have become familiar with a given judge's verbal hints, facial expressions and summarising pushes to recognise which way the wind ought to blow. This was doubtless of use in a case involving conflicting and complex evidence.

Coming to a Verdict

It was also quite likely that the more experienced, articulate or socially superior jurors would hold sway in influencing the verdict. As *The Birmingham Gazette* helpfully pointed out, 'the view of the foreman and the most experienced jurors tended to predominate. Decisions were usually arrived at quickly.' Bear that latter point in mind.

I think it reasonable, therefore, to assume that strong differences of opinion which could lengthen the proceedings may not always have been well received in the privacy of the juror's room. It is more than possible that forms of quid pro quo may, from time to time, have emerged to keep everyone happy and cause any dissident jurors to fall into line. For instance, an agreement to put forward a plea for mercy in a murder trial where jury opinion was split might, with its chink of light for the defendant, satisfy all shades of opinion.

It was not until the Juries Act of 1974 that majority verdicts were permitted. but it defies logic to suggest that all deliberations before that date had been unanimous, and there must have been ways and means of bringing all jurors 'onside' to enable the presentation of a verdict. A plea for mercy, therefore, was maybe a convenience to disguise a behind-closed-doors horse trade aimed to secure unanimity amongst the jurors. It also allowed an exit from court at a reasonable time, providing everyone with a clear conscience.

Requesting 'mercy' may also have offered a coded signal to the outside world that the verdict had not been unanimous. This might, for example, be in the case of defendants who evoked a level of sympathy, perhaps because of youth, previous good conduct, military service, standing in the community or when the use of force had been accidental or understandable. At least three of these possibilities may well have been in play during deliberations over the Stagg case.

It is worth noting that most accounts of Stagg's trial written in more recent years appear to consider that the time taken by the jury to come to a decision, around an hour and three quarters, was short enough to indicate a degree of unanimity concerning the verdict. This view is possibly based on how a modern jury might operate, but in 1924 the contrary appears to have been the rule and I have come across opinion that deliberations of one and a half hours or so were then considered to be an inordinately long time and indicative of some serious division of opinion.

Our doughty reporter for *The Scotsman* even suggested in print that there was some disagreement with the judge's seemingly clear direction to find a guilty verdict, though how he would have known that for certain is not clear.

Good Men and True

Having 'set the scene', we might now usefully examine the 22 men who comprised the Stafford court's list of jurors – no women, you will not be surprised to learn.

I have researched each as far as I have been able and present them in alphabetical order with, where known, age, habitation, social rank or occupation:

T.B. Adams Esq, an industrialist and philanthropist of Compton Hall, Wolverhampton.

J.F.W. Binns Esq of Smethwick.

Baron Sir Thomas Wilmot Peregrine Blomefield, of Lichfield, aged 75 years.

F.A. Bolton, a former amateur motor racing driver of Moor Court, Oakamoor.

C.J. Clay Esq of Stafford.

R.C. Clive Esq of Gravenhanger.

W.W. Dobson Esq of Seighford Hall, Great Bridgeford.

Lt Col Richard Fawley Butler, later Lord Lieutenant of Staffordshire, of Pendeford Hall, Wolverhampton.

Baron Sir W.H. Fielden of Dilhorne Hall, Stoke-on-Trent.

Baron Sir Francis Villiers Forster of Lysways Hall, Longden, aged 73 years.

J.C.G. McFerra Esq of Rickerscote House, Stafford.

Captain W.S.R. Levett of Milford Hall, Stafford.

Baron Charles Arthur Mander Esq, managing director of the family paint and varnish business and twice mayor of Wolverhampton, of Kilsall Hall, Donington, aged 39 years.

Sir A.F. Nicholson, owner of a cloth-weaving business, of Leek.

Lt Col William Swyfen Whitehall Parker-Jervis DSO, former professional soldier, of Meaford Hall, Stone, aged 44 years.

Col W.A. Weatherall of Rugeley.

C.H. Wright Esq of Tillington Hall, Stafford.

G.F. Fletcher-Twemlow Esq of Betley Court, Newcastle-under-Lyme.

J.F. Twemlow Royds, a landowner of Sandbach, aged 33 years. Although living in Cheshire, he was the nominated foreman.

Lt H. Twentyman Esq, an import company managing director, of Codsall.

Sir William V'Alters Gradwell-Goodwin, of Westwood Manor, Leek, a former mayor of Newcastle-under-Lyme, aged 61 years.

Baron Sir C.M. Walmsley, the 9th Baronet Walmsley, of Rugeley, aged 77 years.

Sympathy for the Defendant?

That list tells only part of the story; there are sub-texts. It is fair to say that the jury largely represented a mixture of landed privilege, business acumen and civic service; there appears to be no one who might be termed a 'peer' of the accused, so on the face of things it looked grim for Stagg. If we look a little more closely, however, it is evident that a core of jurors had backgrounds that could indicate propensity for a degree of sympathy towards Stagg's situation. For example, there were five men represented bearing military titles and at least nine, though possibly more, who lived on country estates at some remoteness to urban centres.

To labour the point, the latter group would be well attuned to the need to protect rural property and stock. They would almost certainly have been complicit in the usual security measure employed by their gamekeepers and tenant farmers to do so, in other words, the ownership and, whenever appropriate, visual display of a shotgun. Using rough methods to scare off intruders would hardly have been unknown to many of the jurors optimistically asked by Vachell to be dumbfounded by Stagg's possession of a loaded firearm at night.

Some of the others were likely to have a more direct emotional understanding of what Stagg had been through in his life and you will understand why his counsel wished to affirm his possession of military campaign medals. Nicholson, for example, had lost a son in the Great War and apparently never recovered from the blow. In 1925, he was to fund the building of a unique clock-faced war memorial in Leek known as 'Sir Arthur's pocket watch' and which he dedicated to his dead boy. Levitt had lost a brother in the war, Mander had himself been a major in the Staffordshire Yeomanry and had been wounded in Palestine and, for what it was worth, V'Alters's chauffeur had been drowned at sea. Doubtless many of the other landowners had lost relatives or men from their estates in the conflict.

Perhaps the juror who was most likely to have identified with Stagg was Parker-Jervis who, from 1899 to the end of the Great War, had enjoyed a career as a professional soldier in the King's Royal Rifle Corps, as the name suggests a rather specialist outfit. He was the same age as Stagg and like him had fought in an African imperial conflict, in his case the Second Boer War, and then on the Western Front. Also, like Stagg, he would have extensively used the Lee-Enfield bolt-action rifle and might have had a good idea of whether Stagg's story about the accidental discharge of shot in a bolt-action weapon was likely to have been true or false.

As, intriguingly, would have another of the jurors. By his title Colonel Weatherall had a military background; I can find no details of his service, but what I have discovered is that he was an active member of the still extant Staffordshire Smallbore Rifle Association. In 1906 he presented the Association with the Weatherall Shield to be awarded following an indoor shooting competition competed for by local affiliated rifle clubs. Out of interest, in 1924 the winners were Lichfield Rifle Club. The point here is that notwithstanding the levels of military know-how spread throughout the potential jurors we have a man who was probably very expert in the field, two if you include Parker-Jervis, and who, had he been sitting on the Stagg case, would have been more than able to offer authoritative opinion on whether the defendant's story of the accidental shot rang true or not.

The caveat to all of this is that we are not to know which of the long list of jurors served in the trial, but we can be certain that based simply on the law of averages a proportion of the jurors would have been countrymen or military men or both, and most jurors may have been affected by the Great War in some way. Several may well have been observing the trial with slightly different eyes than we might have expected.

Maybe, as I have suggested, some jurors were sympathetic towards Stagg's service record and his health problems. Perhaps some felt that his story was plausible; maybe some felt that Ball was the aggressor and that Stagg, in forcibly protecting his property, was acting at a reasonable level of entitlement. Perhaps some had doubts concerning Mrs Ball's testimony. The jurors knew that a 'guilty' decision would almost certainly result in Stagg being hanged, so anyone who did not see this as reasonable might well speak in favour of appealing to the judge's mercy.

Mercy

After around 90 minutes' deliberation the 12 chosen men duly returned their guilty verdict but 'strongly recommended the prisoner to mercy', a plea that does not sit easily with the conclusion that Stagg had committed 'wilful murder'. As I have previously pointed out, the time the jury spent deliberating was, in those days, indicative not of unanimity but that the verdict was far from cut and dried, and this was precisely the point made by Coventry when the case went to appeal.

Whatever had taken place in the jury room, I believe it possible that Stagg had come closer to escaping the verdict of murder than most people have since imagined.

Given this view, it is interesting to note that some contemporary journals, and many accounts written to date, claimed the jury had seen Stagg's self-defence story as 'fanciful'. Juries, we should remember, do not, and did not, publicly justify their decisions nor are/were they required/entitled to give media interviews afterwards. Press comment of any kind was therefore totally speculative, and the uncritical repetition of this claim has not helped our understanding of the story.

The Verdict

As we know, Rowlatt did not accept the plea. There is little doubt that had he done so it would have caused a level of outrage amongst sections of the public. Instead, he sentenced Stagg to death with the time-honoured words:

> 'The court doth order you to be taken from hence to the place from whence you came, and thence to the place of execution, and that you be hanged by the neck until you are dead, and that your body be afterward buried within

the precincts of the prison in which you shall be confined after your conviction. And may the Lord have mercy upon your soul.'

Even though he had passed a capital sentence, Rowlett, for unclear reasons, did not entirely ignore the jury's plea and agreed to forward the mercy request to 'the appropriate parties'. By so doing, he would know the case would reach the Court of Appeal and Review and thence, possibly, the Home Secretary. Nowadays, we might call it 'kicking the can down the road' and Coventry was probably already planning the appeal before Rowlatt had completed sentencing. Stagg, for his part, was widely reported as remaining unmoved as sentence was passed, though *The Birmingham Gazette* went a step further by describing him as looking 'dazed' by the verdict.

As a condemned man, it was Stagg's right to address the court, but, whether through pride, desolation or the acceptance that his bluff had been called, he declined the opportunity. If things continued to go badly, an unmarked grave in the grounds of Winson Green awaited him sometime in March. Maybe there was a guardian angel working for Stagg as Paul Lester's work reports that the taxi taking him back to Birmingham broke down en route.

Part 9

What Really Happened?

We have the facts of the case as known at the time of the Stafford trial and we know the outcome of the trial. We still do not know what really happened, though perhaps the reader has begun to form conclusions.

I thought long and hard about this and eventually decided to include a speculative though informed view based on setting known forensic evidence against the principle of 'balances of probability', as discussed earlier in the book. I emphasise the word 'speculative' and have little doubt that many readers will disagree with my conclusions. So be it.

To begin with, there are aspects of the case that have always concerned me:

Witness Testimony. The major challenges come with Beatrice Ball's recollections and with George Stagg's reconstruction of events. As noted, Beatrice, seeing her husband dying in front of her, handling his warm blood and helping carry him into the house, was almost certainly in shock throughout the incident and for some time afterwards. It would be no surprise, and certainly not a criticism, if the brutality of the situation had significantly distorted her memory. It would also be possible to present a case for George Stagg to have misrepresented the sequences of argument and action either through similar memory disorientation, or to support his case for self-defence.

We might usefully take account of the factor now known as 'weapon focus' which was first identified in 1947 by United States academics Gordon Allport and Leo Postman. This built on research that had been under way since British psychologist Sir Frederick Bartlett pioneered the theory of 'reconstructive memory' in 1932. Amongst other things, this suggests that the disturbing presence of a weapon at the scene of an alleged crime can lead a witness into a state of memory disorientation.

In research trials, this resulted in a tendency for witnesses to forget details other than the presence and/or use of the weapon, and this often resulted in the invention of situations that had never occurred. Although all the research in question took place after 1924, it is more than likely that police and lawyers had previously recognised aspects of the conclusions the academics were to come to.

The 1976 Devlin Report, which investigated the accuracy and importance of eyewitness accounts, advised that British juries should not convict anyone where the only such evidence was provided by a single person. As a result of this, eyewitness testimony as sole evidence of what may have occurred during a crime involving violence is now handled within the criminal justice system with great circumspection.

In 1978, another American academic team, Brian Clifford and Jane Scott, went a stage further with the formal identification of a 'violence distraction' syndrome. This suggested that witnessed acts of violence can significantly skew an onlooker's memory away from other occurrences in a way that might make their entire testimony questionable.

Timings. This is of the utmost importance. As I have hopefully already shown, the timelines given under oath were likely to be accurate only up to a certain point, that is, around 10.15pm. Beyond that, with Ellen Laurence's 10.30 timing of one of the shots probably the only correct factor, things become messy. The importance of this is that it challenges the veracity of the prosecution's construction of the narrative and suggests that aspects of certain witness statements were unreliable. A jury could make of that what they would.

I will spare the reader the close details of my examination of the depositions but have reached the following conclusions:

- To begin with we are on safe ground. The bus conductor knew his schedule well enough, and mine host Mr Wood knew what time to call last orders. Thus, the timings given from 9.30pm to around 10.10, when Tommy took out his dog for a walk, are certainly accurate.

- Beyond that point, Beatrice's timings are likely to be poorly remembered estimates. Regardless of the effect of the weapon on her memory, you might agree it would have been quite unlikely that, under the circumstances, she would have had the presence of mind to mentally note, and then remember, accurate timings.

- The Rose sisters were in an unlit field area and, should they have had timepieces, would have had difficulty in reading them. Set against Mrs Laurence's timing (below), their timing of the gunshots at around 10.17 may, I think, be as much as ten minutes before the actuality.

- If we so adjusted their timing, this would then dovetail with Mrs Laurence's deposition that she heard a shot at 10.30. Being indoors with, one assumes, a clock at hand, she would probably have got her timing right. That this was before Beatrice ran down the lane to see her suggests that Beatrice was well out with her estimates.

- You will recall that Beatrice gave a time of 10.25–10.30pm for when she and Stagg brought Tommy's body into the house, saying this was after she had returned from the Laurence cottage. Those timings cannot possibly be correct. After hearing a shot, Beatrice claimed to have gone outside, approached Tommy's prone body, been shot at herself, 'ran' in the dark to the Laurences' cottage, spoken to them and then returned along a steady but noticeable uphill stretch, pausing to talk to Stagg with his lantern and then helping carry Tommy's body indoors. This was a total distance covered by her of around 540 yards along an unlit, unmade road, and given the two conversations she had and the return gradient, this whole episode could not have taken less than 30 minutes, quite possibly longer. Mrs Laurence's deposition suggests that Beatrice did not arrive before 10.30 and from this we can safely assume the later successful laying of Tommy's body on the settee may have been achieved nearer 11pm.

- Arthur Pitchford, who spoke to Stagg in the lane after the body had been laid on the settee, would also be challenged by a lack of light to check the time and, given what had transpired, I believe his encounter with Stagg would not have taken place before 11.10.

- Given that Dr Garman was an experienced professional, you would have thought it highly unlikely that he would have got this timing wrong, and he said that Stagg arrived at his house at 11pm. He lived, however, somewhere along the Walsall

Road towards Great Barr, at least one mile, and quite probably more, from where Stagg met Pitchford. Even had Pitchford's timing been accurate, Stagg's arrival time at Garman's house would have certainly been well after 11pm, especially as he was finding an address he had never visited before. Given the time it might have taken Stagg, bad leg and all, to walk to Garman's house, and add the conversation with Pitchford, I believe it was possibly as much as 30 minutes later.

- Stagg then had to explain everything to Garman; the doctor would have needed to put on boots and coat and get his medical bag together and start his car after which they stopped en route to briefly explain the situation to PC Bickley. This puts the arrival of Garman and Stagg at Somerville Cottages at some point between 11.30 and midnight.

- PC Bickley, who had been stopped by Garman and Stagg on the Walsall Road, had to walk the quarter of a mile to Somerville Cottages and would have arrived several minutes after the others. He then, we assume, walked a similar journey to the Laurence house, the nearest point at which he could access a telephone, and made his phone call to Davenport.

- Davenport said that he left the police station at 10.40 on receiving a call (which was presumably the one made by Mr Laurence) and when he arrived at Somerville Cottages, which was around a 15-minute journey by car, Stagg, Garman and Bickley were already there. His arrival, therefore, was likely to have been shortly before, or even after, midnight, meaning he could not have left Canterbury Road until after 11.30.

Senior police officers, lawyers and the DPP needed only to cast a cursory, experienced eye over things to see that most of the timings within the evidence were open to question. It was not good investigative work, nor was it a good basis on which to launch a murder trial, especially as Beatrice Ball was the chief witness for the prosecution. Yet the prosecuting council was to draw attention at the appeal hearing in March 1924 to the veracity of her evidence.

Most concerning is Davenport's role. Given that he attested to having arrived at the cottages after Stagg, Garman and Bickley, he had, without question, incorrectly recorded the time he left Canterbury Road. His interview with Beatrice took place shortly after his arrival and this is the point at issue. His claim to have left the station at 10.40 tallies, for me, a little too closely with Beatrice's memory. Modern good practice recognises that witnesses conferring over an exchange of information can wittingly or unwittingly 'cross-contaminate' each other's testimonies, which can potentially lead to an 'owning' of each other's recollections, with one taking his/her lead from the other over matters of fact such as timing. Davenport, as arresting officer, and Beatrice were both key witnesses for the prosecution. Davenport would also have doubtless been keen for his report to demonstrate to his superior officers how promptly he had reacted to the situation.

With witness credibility in this case so important, I think you would expect a modern defence team to be 'all over' the evidence to find any chinks in the accuracy of depositions to then suggest there might be errors elsewhere in the prosecution case.

The Gun

There has always been an unsatisfactory feel about so little being known concerning the gun used by Stagg. As I have emphasised, the police did not visit other homes in the area to ascertain whether owning a shotgun, licensed or not, was common practice. In the modern world, I would suggest, the issues of obtaining and licensing a gun would have been fundamental not only to police investigation but to both defence and prosecution cases.

What we do know is that to the satisfaction of the police and the court, only two shots were fired, and those did not include the one Mrs Stagg alleged was aimed at her. That removes one important issue from our considerations.

Guarding his Property

Let me begin my reconstruction with a fundamental claim made by Stagg and which I believe, on the balance of probabilities, to have been correct.

First and foremost, I am convinced his argument that he habitually loaded his shotgun on a nightly basis for fear of intruders is entirely logical and convincing.

Livestock or not, guarding isolated properties against intrusion has always been a major rural issue, and it still is. Stagg had two such properties, a wife, three children and some paying tenants to protect and during much of his adult life, as soldier and policeman, he had been trained to anticipate and offset potential danger. Burglars and the like were not Sudanese warriors, but they may have been armed, possibly not alone and could present danger to life and property. As I have noted elsewhere, the Birmingham area housed plenty of men who lived parts of their lives beyond the law. Stagg was a trained soldier and, if danger threatened, he would have been confident in his right to keep a firearm, and in his ability to use it.

There is a big difference between Stagg planning dark deeds or being simply just another country dweller who got a bit nervous when darkness fell. Given where he was living, it would be more of a surprise if he had not obtained a gun to protect his family and property.

I believe it plausible, therefore, that Stagg did leave his cottage on the night in question fearing intruders. His account of having dozed off to be woken by a barking dog appears credible. Who hasn't been? After all, both he and Ball owned dogs, both possibly terriers, and as one of the reasons for keeping them would be to act as night-time sentries, why wouldn't Stagg have gone out to check when one of them began to make a fuss? You do not keep a guard dog and then ignore it when it barks.

Was it an Ambush?

As you will have gathered, I do not accept the view that Stagg had been awaiting the return of the Balls with the intention of having some sort of showdown. If that had been the plan, he would have known what time they would usually return from the pub and positioned himself in a place advantageous to it. It is evident that Stagg did not apprehend Ball as he arrived home, and neither did he lure Ball out of his house. Ball left the house voluntarily, not once but twice. His eventual meeting with Stagg appears, therefore, to have been, as Stagg claimed, entirely accidental. It was Tommy's ill luck that Stagg's dog barked at him and alerted its owner.

Moreover, if Stagg had planned to kill Ball from the outset, is it remotely feasible that he would engineer a situation whereby he would allow his victim to move within three feet of him? This was virtually touching distance and an old soldier like Stagg would have been more than aware of the military concept of making the 'killing distance' between a man and his adversary as wide as possible to obviate the risk of the other man being able to strike out.

It does not make any sense that, had things been planned, Ball was being given the opportunity to grip the weapon that was meant to kill him. Opportunities for clandestine killing were almost certainly present in the geography of the cottage area without any need for Stagg to put himself at such risk.

Coming from the Dark Side

Had Tommy walked across to Stagg's garden from his own property's garden he would perhaps have been fairly easily identifiable and things might not have gone as they did. That he did so virtually incognito on a dark night from the unlit fields outside a perimeter gate on the 'wrong side' of Stagg's property puts an entirely different complexion on things.

This is precisely the route into the cottage gardens that a burglar might have taken, not a direction from where he might have expected his neighbour to emerge.

Stagg would have taken a second or two before he realised who he was dealing with and would certainly have thrown out a verbal challenge to whoever it was. I can imagine that once he knew who it was a 'what the bloody hell are you doing out there' style of question may have been asked. If so, Ball's possible reply was likely to have been equally forthright, and things might have degenerated from there.

How Ball reacted to any challenge from Stagg across the gate is a matter of conjecture, but I think we can safely assume that neither his response to it, nor the ensuing 'conversation', would have been conducted in a patient or friendly manner. Each man would have a case for thinking the other was wasting his time and both, for differing reasons, were already 'on edge'.

A Man and his Lost Dog

There is a salient point here that to my knowledge has never been previously raised that Tommy may well have been extremely agitated because his dog had just run off. Not a big deal you might say, but that might suggest you had never owned a dog, still less experienced it running off on a dark night into seemingly limitless open countryside.

Anyone who has tramped through dark fields at night-time in winter vainly calling out a dog's name will relate to this, and I do speak from some experience in the matter.

Tommy had already gone back into his cottage to see if the dog had returned and there would have been more pressure on him from the knowledge that his wife would want him back in anytime now for the supper she was preparing. Tommy would have been in a heightened state of agitation, and I defy anyone to say otherwise. To be challenged by the bloke next door holding a gun would, quite understandably, not have gone down well and George was probably on the verbal receiving end of Tommy's anxieties.

A Voice of Calm and Reason?

Given that Stagg, just awoken and perhaps a bit disorientated, would also have felt his time was being wasted, it is not difficult to see how tempers might have easily risen and who knows what was then said? In the heat of the moment verbal threats of the alleged 'bashing your heads in' type might have been uttered by both men, as well as each 'suggesting' the other should calm down and go to bed. Include your own view of any colourful language used within these suggestions.

All in all, I find the overall scenario as painted by Stagg quite plausible, though the one aspect I would take issue with is George's portrayal of himself as the voice of calm and reason. I very much doubt this and would take the verbal build-up of tension as six of one, half a dozen of the other.

Certainly, voices must have been sufficiently raised to bring Mrs Stagg not only to her bedroom window but moved to open it, and maybe Ball did aim a 'nosy neighbour' suggestion or two her way.

Underlying Tensions

Thus, my view is that the incident came about through an accidental set of circumstances which were not well handled by the participants. What should have been a backyard verbal altercation degenerated into violence and it is certainly worth speculating whether some of the issues that lay in the background came to the fore.

Although making a list of someone's life problems does not offer proof of intent to commit violence, much less murder, I would be sympathetic to the 'Armistice view' that Tommy Ball had unwittingly come across George Stagg at a time when he was feeling particularly unhappy with his lot and more prone to react badly to any circumstance that irritated him.

It is certainly inescapable that in his life he would have experienced much that could have caused mental trauma. He had fought in three major battles and had doubtless seen a lot of men killed and maimed; he had himself been severely wounded in action and had lost a brother during the war, and a sister and his mother shortly afterwards. His mother-in-law who lodged with him had also recently died. Most concerning, I would imagine, was that he had only recently said his goodbyes to his son, knowing he might not ever see him again.

Setting this alongside Tommy's heightened levels of irritation over the missing dog and it may well be that the ill feeling of past backyard disagreements came to the fore within both men's behaviour. In a moment of reality, even the prosecuting counsel at

Stafford had been moved to say that both men probably annoyed each other. I think they probably had done so for some time.

Under the Influence?

As we know, Ball's apparent sobriety on that evening was confirmed by the pub landlord, by the bus conductor and by Mrs Ball, while his 'clean living' was to be later lauded by his trainer at the football club.

A lot can be skewed, of course, by the questions put to the witnesses. If, for instance, mine host at the Church Tavern was asked, 'Was Mr Ball drunk?', then a man who was no doubt well used to dealing with people who were inebriated and troublesome was, in the case of a chap leaving civilly and peacefully with his wife, almost certainly going to answer 'no'. Similarly, the man who might be well used to conducting inebriated drinkers boarding the evening bus after closing time would have seen nothing in Ball's demeanour to have suggested a problem.

'Under the influence' does not, however, always just imply a visible inability to walk in a straight line. If the question asked had been more searchingly oblique, for example 'Have you ever seen young men become aggressive in their behaviour following a modest amount of alcohol?', the answer from the publican might have been interesting. And if asked whether he had ever had to deal with passengers who had appeared quite well behaved on boarding his bus and then become confrontational, the conductor might have had some stories to tell.

Stagg's Field-Side Gate

At that time and into the present day, wooden paling gates have been a relatively easy method of offering a pedestrian access into a garden area.

'Palings', or slim vertical posts, are nailed or screwed on to the outside of a frame in the hope of presenting a neat, flat face to public gaze, while also denying easy footholds to anyone attempting to climb over from outside a property. Given that the design commonly used for garden gates did not alter throughout the last century, we might assume the rear frame was the ubiquitous three-plank 'Z' pattern. As the gates were generally built to allow one person at a time to pass through, a rough judgement would make most such gates little more than two feet wide.

If that were the case, George Stagg's garden gate would probably have consisted of up to eight evenly spaced upright palings, each being around one to two inches in width with narrow open gaps between each paling. The structure would be made more rigid with the fitting along the paling tops of an horizontal crossbar. The whole would sit between two slightly taller and thicker outer holding posts which were embedded into the ground.

The two outer posts of the gate were measured by Inspector Mollart at 4ft in height and the inner palings at 3ft 10in. The gate would be side-hinged into one of the posts and attached to the other by a latch-closing mechanism usually placed about 18 inches or so from the top of the post.

The gate in question stood above a stone step and could be padlocked, as Stagg alleged was always the case at night.

Was Tommy Shot while Standing on the Field Side of the Gate?

This is the first option to consider. We should note that the post-mortem concluded his body was maybe in a brace position when shot which, on the face of it, suggests he had both feet on solid ground.

Ball and Stagg, both of an approximately equal height of 5ft 10in to 5ft 10.5in, were considerably taller than the gate, but of crucial importance was the fact that the land on Ball's side of the gate (i.e. the field side) was measured at five inches below that on Stagg's side. Thus, when the men initially faced each other, Stagg would have been given a height advantage of five inches and would be looking slightly downwards towards his neighbour.

This becomes an important consideration when we recall that at the post-mortem Dr Garman said the fatal shot hit Tommy on a horizontal plane with an entry point measured to be at 'heart level', four feet four inches from the sole of his foot. To be able to get anything like a clear shot to hit his adversary at heart level, Stagg would probably have had to lean on to the gate with the gun mounted at his shoulder, thus positioned about a foot above Tommy's heart. Had this been the case, the shot would have been travelling at a downwards trajectory, say 45 degrees or so, and not at the horizontal plane concluded by Dr Garman.

If Stagg had stepped slightly backwards and discharged the shot on a horizontal plane, the differing ground level of five inches meant the shot, travelling over the crossbar, had around one and a half inches of clearance to enable it to have hit Tommy in the chest at heart level. That would have been a very lucky, or unlucky, shot. Had Tommy been standing behind one of the taller four-foot end posts, a horizontal shot aimed at 'heart height' would have first touched or smashed into the post end and possibly even deflected away from the horizontal. There is no mention anywhere of damage to the gate, nor of wooden splinters being found in the body.

Tommy's height would have been slightly elevated by the soles of his boots but if, as Garman suggested, he was bracing himself on his right side against the shot to his body it would have been slightly lowered, thus making a direct hit from a shot fired over the gate more improbable. Putting all of this together, I would suggest the probability that Ball was not shot while standing on the field side. There was, however, a blood spillage on the grass outside the gate, on the top of the gate and on the field side of the gate itself, so that has to be explained.

Was Tommy Shot while Standing on the Garden Side of the Gate?

Bearing in mind the possibility that Tommy was shot while having both feet on the ground, we should also consider whether he managed to get over the gate and was shot while in Stagg's garden. It is an intriguing possibility and some of the evidence might support it.

Assuming Tommy had managed to get over the gate, with both men of roughly equal height and standing on level ground, and with no gate obstacle between them, this would allow Stagg the opportunity to make an unobstructed shot directly at the heart, though with the gun raised at chest level rather than at the shoulder. In this event it would be likely that the shot would hit Tommy while travelling in a horizontal plane.

The possibility breaks down with the critical forensic fact that there was blood on the field side of the gate but none on the garden side.

Was Tommy Shot while Climbing the Gate?

If we reject the previous possibilities, we are left with the conclusion that Ball must have been shot while in the act of climbing the gate, thus broadly as Stagg had claimed.

Both Garman and Fearn had independently suggested the lack of burning on Tommy's clothing, and the size of the entry wound set against the results of the ballistic testing indicated that the fatal shot was fired with Ball around a distance of three feet away from the end of the gun barrel. This gives some currency to the possibility of the two men coming together to tussle across the gate before the shot was fired. Then, perhaps, both simultaneously took a step back from the gate as the gun discharged.

That possibility, however, challenges Stagg's claim that the gun barrel hit the top of the gate. If it had done so, it is almost certain that the shot would have fired at an upwards angle, which, however slight, was unlikely to have hit Ball on a horizontal plane.

Additionally, under those circumstances, it was questionable whether the two men would have been as far as three feet away from one another when the gun went off. It is more likely that a shot under those circumstances would have been detonated nearer to Ball, possibly even touching, thus singeing, his clothes, which was not the case.

On the balance of probabilities, therefore, I would rule out the 'tussling' scenario as claimed by Stagg.

But there is another possibility. The gate, with no obvious footholds on the smooth-fronted field side, may have been something of an obstacle for a 'normal' man to climb at night, especially as the five-inch land droppage on the field side would make it a little more difficult for a climber to get a foot purchase on the palings. Given, however, that Ball was a very fit and athletic professional sportsman, this may have presented an awkward but not formidable obstacle.

Had Ball attempted to climb the gate it is quite possible that at some point he was partially mounted with his left hand placed in a supporting position on the gate's crossbar and his upper body exposed. This could have allowed him to lean over the gate top while attempting to reach the latch, which would have been on Stagg's side, with his right hand. If so, one side of his body would have been tipping forwards at the shoulder and at post-mortem this may have suggested a brace position.

Alternatively, Tommy may have been in the climbing position described, heard Stagg reloading and instinctively braced his body forward.

Whatever caused Ball to position his body in that manner, there would have been a second or two when his upper body had been exposed to a horizontally aimed shot. Perhaps Tommy's upper-body moved forwards or a slight lowering of his right side coincided with Stagg's backwards step. When the gun was raised to Stagg's shoulder, it was coincidentally in line with the position of Tommy's heart.

The force of the shot would tip Tommy's body backwards with the blood spillage from the entry wound causing splashing on to the top of the gate, on to the field side of the palings and on to the stone step below. The spillage from a dynamic exit wound would land on the grass in the field.

The First Shot: Warning or Accident?

Stagg claimed that two shots were fired, and this tallied with the cartridge remains recovered by the police. The first shot, you will recall, was alleged by him to have been a deliberate warning to Ball to back off and was fired into the air; the second was claimed to be an accidental shot which proved fatal.

We know that at Stafford, with the help of a court official acting as Ball, Stagg had visually re-enacted his account of the accidental shot. This culminated with him striking the gate top with the gun barrel and activating the trigger, thus apparently proving the point.

Remembering that it was essential for Stagg to stick to his story, it would have been a risky strategy, especially under vigorous cross-examination and under the close gaze of the jury, for him to invent and act out a struggle that had never occurred. It was similarly risky to invent an accidental trigger activation that might not have worked in a court re-enactment.

I would therefore accept that an accidental shot, as capably demonstrated by Stagg in court, did occur at some point during the dispute. If so, and given the likely, even slight, upwards angle of the barrel on contact with the gate top, I consider it unlikely to have been the one which killed Tommy.

My contention is the confident court re-enactment was totally safe for Stagg to go through, complete with the claimed trigger movement exactly on cue, and it was not luck but expertly carried out because that is precisely what happened. Except that the discharge he was recalling was not the fatal shot but the one he had claimed to be a warning.

Once the initial 'pleasantries' had been exchanged, I can imagine the two men close to each other separated only by the gate and an enraged Ball vainly grabbing at Stagg's gun. I can visualise Stagg, in temper, fending him off and, maybe in temper, perhaps accidentally while pulling away, hitting his gun barrel on the gate top. Then, I believe, it went off, harmlessly and angled above Tommy, but to great dramatic effect.

The mistruth, I would suggest, was not that the gun discharged accidentally, but that this incident was placed out of sequence and where it better suited George's story.

The Reload

The effect on Ball of the first discharge would have been electric and I would accept Stagg's assertion that his neighbour initially made to walk off before his temper and righteous indignation forced him to return and again attempt to mount the gate. Within seconds, he would be over the gate and presenting a formidable threat to his neighbour.

Tommy may not have been drunk but the relatively small amount of alcohol he had imbibed might well have influenced his actions, especially given his existing agitation over losing the dog. For Stagg to appear to threaten him with a loaded firearm, and then for the gun to fire, was not a sequence of events likely to calm him down and Stagg was now the object of his righteous frustration.

Once the gun had detonated the first time, Stagg was, for a moment, without his means of protection. With his adversary mounting an attack, it was likely that his military training would have immediately set in and he would have attempted to reload as quickly as he could. I do not accept that, as he claimed, he went back indoors to reload. The strong likelihood was that Stagg would have been unable to walk, or limp even, about 30 paces back to the house, retrieve a cartridge from its stone jar, reload, return and continue the argument before Ball had got over the gate and caught up with him.

I would argue additionally that Stagg's military training would have ingrained the habit of having at least one additional cartridge about his person whenever he went out at night. As Philip Warner's book *Army Life in the Nineties* (that is, 1890s) stresses, this kind of spare cartridge 'insurance thinking' was drummed into infantrymen of the time, especially if they were likely to take a turn as camp sentries.

Is it conceivable that Stagg would go out into the dark to check on prowlers and not have at least one 'spare' about his person? I think not. Admitting to such was another matter as having an extra round in your pocket might have smacked of preparation for foul deeds. Stagg had been a policeman and would have known how to avoid incriminating testimony.

If he was able to reload in situ he would have gambled that Ball, still mounting the gate, might not have reached him in the two seconds or so a professionally trained man might need to reload plus the few extra seconds required of Stagg to activate the trigger. To the man with the gun, that time might seem like a lifetime; to the man without the gun, struggling over a gate, it was almost immediate. But for Tommy it was now 'fight or flight' and you may wish to ask yourself what, in his situation, you would have done.

It is more than likely that Ball would have seen and even handled Stagg's gun at some point after moving in next door; after all, the weapon protected him and Beatrice as much as it did the Stagg family, and he would have been aware that Stagg knew exactly how to use it. There might also have been some ex-army blokes around Usworth who had bolt-action guns 'on the quiet' and had perhaps done a bit of moonlight rabbiting. All things considered, I think it likely Tommy would know what a bolt reload sounded like and may well have reacted to it by bracing himself as best his position atop the gate would allow.

The clicking of the replacement cartridge into place was the signal that a second shot might be coming along and this one might not be into thin air.

The Second Shot

Faced with an extremely fit and angry younger man whose actions may have given a decent impression of inebriation, it was then Stagg who had to make the 'fight or flight' decision.

He might already have backed off slightly from the gate and could either try to outrun Tommy or stand and risk a physical 'tussle'. Whichever of these options he took there was only one winner, and it was not the older man who had a bad leg and respiratory problems. He may also have reasonably thought Ball might continue his rampage into the house where Mary was still at the window. To avoid a 'doing over', George's only other way out was to take the military option.

As Tommy was trained to get to the ball before his opponent, so Stagg was trained to hold his line in the face of the enemy. He was a twice-trained infantry soldier and, as Philip Warner, again, writes, 'There can be no half-measures in the Army; either you shoot straight and kill or you are probably killed yourself.' You may now wish to ask yourself what, in George Stagg's situation, and with his background, would you have done?

Stagg may not have deliberately aimed at the heart, and in the darkness probably could not have done so, but he completed his activation of the trigger pull. The range of around three feet from barrel to target was as near to point blank as made no difference, and with the inevitable consequences.

Balanced on the gate, there was no way Tommy could have avoided the shot or minimised its impact. When it came, the mass of wadded cartridge pellets hit his left chest in a horizontal plane, smashing the side of his heart and forcing his body to jerk backwards, so causing the blood spillages detailed earlier. Had George Stagg missed his target, lost his nerve or stopped to consider the legal implications, it might have been his blood spilt in his garden.

Making the decision to fire was a critical judgement and following the reload Stagg had a few seconds in which to make it. Had the scenario I describe been presented in court the prosecution would doubtless argue this equated to malice aforethought, while the defence might, with equal conviction, counter that it was proportional to the danger presented. You judge.

Aftershock

I had initially doubted that Stagg had gone through the gate to help his would-be assailant to his feet, but he must have done. That neither padlock nor keys were listed on the evidence sheet suggested that this element of Stagg's deposition was not thought open to challenge. The gate itself was certainly paraded as evidence, but presumably to illustrate the blood marks.

Once standing, Tommy did what so many do when close to death: he forced his body to move towards the place and the person that would give him comfort. He somehow staggered across the garden area into his own side. Unlikely though it may sound, I believe he did this journey by an almost superhuman lone effort.

I have it on well-informed advice that injuries to the heart do not necessarily bring instantaneous death and it is not unknown in criminal investigation for a person wounded there to continue to move 'until the blood runs out'. You may find this improbable, but I believe it highly doubtful that Stagg, with all his health issues, could have assisted Tommy nearly 30 feet across the gardens and then returned smartly to his own hedge before Beatrice came on the scene. Stagg's own deposition is silent on whether he helped Tommy across the garden, so I would infer he did not.

The shock that would have hit Stagg was the enormity of what he had done; there was no escape from the fact that he was in serious trouble, but his mind would have raced to find a way out. Few of us have committed murder but most of us are familiar with a need to find a way of minimising the look of something we should not have done. Before long, the police would be involved and the ex-policeman in him would quickly have realised that what was a reasonable response in a battle situation may not be seen as such by a civilian jury.

George would have to consider his subsequent account very carefully. After helping Ball to his feet, he would have needed a moment or two of thinking time to compose himself, and maybe also to control his breathing, so he stayed near to the hedge in the position Beatrice noticed.

Standing at his hedge and watching Ball stagger onwards, it might have dawned on Stagg that with his gun initially detonating unexpectedly he had, with a little tweaking, a ready-made explanation for the incident. It was a story he could recount to the police, to any doctor who came on to the scene and to an adversarial barrister without it necessarily appearing that he was making it up.

Beatrice's Reaction

Here, we have not been helped by Beatrice's deposition. On the one hand, she claimed to have emerged from the kitchen only in time to see Tommy fall to the ground, that is, having let enough time elapse before emerging for Stagg to have opened the field gate and helped Tommy up, and then for the mortally wounded Tommy to stagger 28 feet into their garden. On the other hand, she indicates that she heard part of the verbal exchange with Mary Stagg, which took place before the fatal shot was fired, possibly before either shot was fired. To confuse the issue further, she claimed to have heard only one shot.

I suspect, therefore, that she may have been in her yard before Tommy made his walk across the gardens but may not have clearly seen what was happening near Stagg's gate. And she may simply have forgotten anything she saw before Tommy collapsed.

Did Stagg Attempt to Shoot Beatrice Ball?

Like me, you may have wondered why the police did not seize upon Beatrice Ball's claim of Stagg having fired a shot in her direction and charged him with the additional count of attempted murder.

I had incorrectly assumed this might have made it a bit easier to convict Stagg, but it was the opposite. The key was that, with the remains of only two cartridges being found, the police had to accept that only two shots had been fired and that those, as evidenced by the Rose sisters, were in relatively quick succession. There was no ballistic or witness evidence of a third shot and any such claim in court would be vigorously challenged by a defence team.

I would expect the DPP to have reviewed the possibility of a second charge when studying the available documentation. If a decision to include an additional charge, for which there was no apparent hard evidence, had been taken, it would not only have been extremely difficult to prove, but it also might have opened up many awkward questions about the veracity of the prosecution case. Thus, proving the main murder charge might have been made significantly more difficult.

Although Beatrice's account of a shot aimed in her direction offered some enthusiastically accepted melodrama for the press, there was insufficient credible evidence to prove this took place. This leads us again to the complex issue of witness memory being affected by the stresses of the moment, especially when weapons were present.

We may, therefore, also consider a further very relevant piece of research into witness psychology. Two further American psychologists, John Yuille and Judith Cutshall, working in 1986 on the psychology of eyewitness testimony, identified a category

229

which they termed 'stress-induced arousal'. This suggested that the presence of a weapon at the scene of a crime can unwittingly cause the witness to imagine that the weapon had been used while they were present, even when it had not. Interesting.

I also found it of interest to learn that in 1972, and based on the interaction between language and memory, an eyewitness condition known as 'event schema' was identified by two American psychologists, Elizabeth Loftus and John Palmer.

Following tests, they established that a witness who considers that something *could* have happened often convinces him/herself that it has and can build up a false memory which can, with the retelling, remain in the brain to be reiterated at will as a 'script'. Perhaps a bit like hearing, yet again, your old man's never-altering exact memories of football matches played 70 or more years ago.

Based on all of this, you will understand that I am in no way suggesting that Beatrice deliberately invented the story and we must give due recognition to the horrors with which she had to contend. Seeing her blood-soaked husband expiring with a gaping chest wound, being herself covered in his blood, conversing with the killer, and then having to help the killer carry the corpse on to her parlour settee and stay with it until the doctor and police turned up would have shaken up anyone's mind.

Any contradictions or errors contained within her subsequent sequencing are, perhaps, easily explained, but in the cut and thrust of open court, Stagg's defence team at Stafford, and then London, certainly had good reason to challenge the veracity of her account.

The prosecution case rested heavily on Beatrice's credibility but, although it must have been discussed with counsel, I am surprised she did not withdraw the allegation from her deposition regarding a shot which no one else appeared to believe had happened. It was a high-risk strategy, but it may, ironically, have been considered a bigger risk for her to publicly withdraw what had been an already widely and sympathetically publicised version of events. Best to say nothing and move on, perhaps?

This doubtless made things rather difficult for the prosecuting counsel but, despite the defence team attacking Beatrice's overall testimony as largely fanciful, Mr Vachell held his nerve and at appeal emphasised how the consistency of Beatrice's testimony made her a reliable witness.

The ever-grounded *Scotsman* reporter at Stafford probably got it about right when he rather disparagingly said of her allegation, 'if that were so'.

It appears that George Stagg had quickly regained an element of composure which, given the practice he would have had in the army, is not a complete surprise. Reading his deposition, he and Beatrice come across as almost cordially formal, but I doubt the atmosphere was as civil as Stagg would have us believe.

Hiding the Evidence?

I think it likely that before Stagg left to find the doctor, he went back to his cottage to put on a greatcoat and to light a lantern. He would have spoken to his wife and, beyond my doubt, told her to say nothing to anyone. He might also have backtracked to the gate and picked up the remnants of the two fired cartridges expelled from his gun, but I think it more likely that Mary did this in between her subsequent visits to her neighbour's house.

What she thought could be gained from hiding them is unclear, but she was unlikely to be thinking clearly and I think it possible that she secreted them in the ash pan in panic. If so, it was not a helpful action as Stagg was to readily admit to firing two shots and the following day the family willingly handed over to the police a batch of unused cartridges while the weapon itself was standing on open display in their parlour.

Even though the existence of the 'ash pan' cartridges proved nothing other than two shots had been fired, attempting to hide the remnants was clumsy, especially when fragments of the cartridge were left on the ground outside for the police to find. The episode gave the impression of 'having something to hide' and does not sit well with George's attempts at 'coming clean' about things. As Mary did not take the witness stand, we will never know what lay behind it.

Explaining the Silence

Which brings us yet again to the curiosity of Mary Stagg's silence. Having weighed up all the possibilities, I think it is probably quite straightforward to explain. Mary suffered from diabetes and one of the symptoms of untreated diabetes is failing eyesight, characterised by blurred vision.

I have previously suggested that because of poor light she was at a disadvantage in not being able to clearly see what was going on, even though she probably would have heard part of the altercation perfectly well. Add failing eyesight to that and we could probably safely say that although Mary looked on at the row between the two men, she did not see it clearly.

There may, therefore, have been things she partly saw or thought she saw which may not have tallied with her husband's version of events. Any suggestion to emerge under cross-questioning that he was spinning such a yarn that 'even his wife would not stick up for him' would have gone down badly for him.

The easiest thing was to take advantage of the law and keep her away from police investigation and subsequent open-court testimony. And there was nothing the prosecution could do about it.

Going for the Doctor

There can be no doubting that it was Stagg's idea to search out a doctor and that he left the Ball house with little idea of where he should go once he reached the Walsall Road. Whether that was a man facing up to his responsibilities or a man exhibiting genuine contrition, or both, is up to the reader to decide but the episode certainly does him no discredit. Readers may lack sympathy with George Stagg but he could simply have run off and would not have been the first or last person in such a predicament to do so. Instead, he faced the music.

We should now return to Arthur Pitchford, the local man Stagg spoke to in the lane after he had left the house. Pitchford gave clear witness to the meeting in his deposition, confirming that the two had never spoken before. It serves as a useful piece of evidence to support Stagg's good intentions post-shooting and raises the question as to why Pitchford was never called to give evidence for the defence in court.

Stagg would have known that by rousing Garman and accompanying him back to the cottages the night would end for him in a prison cell. Nevertheless, he walked to the doctor's house, was quite open in telling him that he had shot a man and, travelling back with the doctor in the latter's car had, apparently willingly, hailed a 'beat bobby' to direct him to the cottages. Although I believe key parts of Stagg's story to be cleverly edited, I do not doubt his good intentions in this regard and Garman's deposition certainly does not paint him in a bad light.

Part 10

Fate Intervenes

The Court of Appeal and Review

At the request of the defence team, who cited irregularities in the Stafford hearing, the case was referred to the Court of Appeal and Review, or, as we now know it, the Court of Criminal Appeal, situated within the Royal Courts of Justice on the Strand, London. The case was heard on 18 March 1924.

As it had been established only in 1907, the court was still a relatively untried legal instrument. You will not mind me reiterating that part of the rationale in establishing the appeal system was the perception that some judges during the 19th century had been in the habit of sharing the jury's role as a trier of fact.

Nevertheless, the court's statutory function was to review only the verdict and the sentencing of a given case. Despite any perceived historical need to balance suspicions that assize judges might negate their own neutrality, the Court of Appeal's right to review the conduct of a case, including any appearance of bias on the part of an assize judge, was discretionary and was not the appellant's right to demand.

Thus, Coventry could not directly cite, for example, Rowlatt's intervention with the gun, though the appeal justices would have been aware of it and could have taken it into account should they have so chosen. Their Lordship's final choice of words in making judgement on this case leads one to suspect that, above and beyond deliberating the facts of the case, Rowlatt's handling of it had been closely examined.

The court had a bench of three senior judges and in this case they were Lord Chief Justice Sir Gordon Hewart, Mr Justice Sir Horace Avory and Mr Justice John Sankey.

Hewart, 1870–1943, who was later created First Viscount Hewart, was by seniority the presiding judge. He was a political and legal heavyweight who had been a former Liberal MP and Attorney General under Lloyd George. Unfortunately for Stagg, he was well known for never having reversed an assize jury decision and one might surmise that he retained a fraternal obligation to support fellow judges whose actions might be under the microscope.

Wikipedia records Hewart as being considered 'one of the most vigorous and vociferous believers in the impeccability of the English jury system', and was thus, one imagines, rather unlikely to make any decision that appeared to contradict his reputation as a defender of the legal status quo. It was something of a sensation in 1931 when, in connection with another case, Hewart finally did reverse an original assize sentence, saying that a jury had got a guilty verdict wrong in a murder trial.

It would not have helped Coventry's confidence in obtaining a favourable result when he learned that the second senior judge at appeal was to be Sir Horace Avory, 1851–1935. As an assize judge, Avory had passed a controversial death sentence for 'high treason' in 1916 against the Irish nationalist Sir Roger Casement, a ruling which today still causes hackles to rise. The apparent balance of the presence of John Sankey on the panel will be examined shortly.

It is worth pointing out that most of the country's senior judges were known to one another either professionally or socially, which inevitably raises questions about conflicts of interest amongst those sitting in appeal. It will not, therefore, be a surprise for the reader to know that each of the appeal judges knew Judge Rowlatt personally. Whether this made it easier for them to form an opinion on how the Stafford trial had been handled or whether it made any admonition of his handling of the trial more difficult is an open question.

It may be helpful to quote in full the report of the hearing as printed in *The Westminster Gazette* of 18 March 1924:

'Sir Reginald Coventry KC, for Stagg, said he had been a policeman, was of good character and had been a landlord and neighbour of Ball. The shooting of November 11, he suggested, occurred in circumstances which made the proper verdict one of manslaughter only. Counsel said that the jury after two hours' consultation came into court with a verdict of murder but with a strong recommendation to mercy. That recommendation showed, he submitted, that they had the greatest difficulty making up their minds whether it was murder or not. There was no motive, no evidence of dislike and no reason why Stagg should murder Ball.'

The Lord Chief Justice, in giving judgement, said 'unless it could be shown that the verdict of the jury was unreasonable, or that it could not be supported by the evidence, the court could not interfere ... The jury made a strong recommendation to mercy, and, no doubt, those responsible for dealing with it, when they came to consider it in the light of the evidence, would attach to it the weight it deserved. The appeal must be dismissed.'

The Belfast Telegraph of the same date added the following detail:

'Evidence for the prosecution [at Stafford] had been given by Mrs Ball who, said counsel [Coventry], was very hysterical and her evidence in his opinion was very unreliable. In fact, her story was inconsistent with three other witnesses. Immediately after the tragedy he [Stagg] went to Ball's assistance. He carried Ball into his own house and ran for all he was worth to the doctor. He told the doctor all that had happened. Mr Vachell said there was nothing hysterical about Mrs Ball and Stagg had dropped the defence that Ball was drunk. If it was a fact that Ball was sober, why did Stagg introduce the gun?'

As with all newspaper reports, the dictates of available space makes these accounts somewhat abbreviated. Paul Lester, writing in 1996, offered a little more 'meat' with the following unattributed account:

'Coventry focussed on discrediting Mrs Ball's testimony which ... was "very difficult to believe". She was, he claimed, "unreliable" and "very hysterical in her evidence ... and was in no condition to realise what was going on ... she was going up and down shouting she should go mad". Despite suffering from consumption Stagg ran for a doctor, and his subsequent conduct suggested an innocent man caught up in an unfortunate accident.'

Returning to *The Belfast Telegraph*, Vachell, for the Crown, said he felt he must put paid to any suggestion Mrs Ball was an unreliable witness. Quite the contrary, 'she was in the witness box on three different occasions and never faltered except when speaking of her husband's death. Her statements about the exchange between Stagg and herself after the shooting were quite at variance with those of the accused and could only incline the impartial to the opinion that Stagg's attributions to Mrs Ball were an invention. Mrs Ball made a strong character witness on her husband's behalf and had repeatedly denied that her husband had been a drinker … She had been consistent in denying that Ball ever kicked her and in asserting the shooting was no accident … There was good evidence from other witnesses than Mrs Ball that Ball was quite sober that evening.'

Mrs Ball's 'faltering' when speaking of her husband's death must have been a reference to her succumbing to emotion rather than her altering her account of things.

It is also worth adding that Vachell claimed Beatrice had asserted 'the shooting was no accident', conveniently omitting the fact that Beatrice, in her depositions, had implied she was not witness to it.

The Crown was also able to point to the absence of Mrs Stagg from the witness box, 'a woman who, according to Stagg's own statement, had seen the whole occurrence from the bedroom window'. Paul Lester adds the personal view that Mrs Stagg's absence as a witness 'strongly suggested Stagg's story amounted to a fabrication'. Although readers will know my conclusions on why Mary Stagg might not have seen the action clearly, Paul's view was quite probably what most contemporary observers had felt.

Paul also added that the Stafford jury's recommendation for mercy was seen by the appeal bench as due to 'Stagg's past character and the service he had been deemed to have done his country', and thus not because some members of the jury might have accepted the defence case. If that really was their Lordship's view, one would imagine they would have rejected the plea out of hand; after all, it had been within their gift to deny it but they purposely let it stand for higher authority to judge.

As they chose to retain the mercy plea and forward this to the Home Office for further consideration, there must have surely been better reason than Stagg's military service. Once again, *The Scotsman* helps us by pointing out that their Lordships' ruling said the 'other parties' to which the judgement was to be forwarded (i.e. the Home Secretary) might 'in the light of the evidence, attach to it [the mercy plea] all the weight it appeared to deserve'. That reads more like an endorsement of the plea than a dismissal of it.

Whatever the reasoning, the dented can was now being kicked a little further down the road and the matter of sentencing was now to be conveniently referred to the Home Office. By this time, and for the first time, this was headed by a Labour Party Home Secretary. The decision, therefore, to further refer the case gives much food for thought because their Lordships would have known full well which way the wind might blow when a Labour minister was brought into the equation, especially as within the previous month the gentleman in question had already reversed two capital decisions.

The retention of 'mercy' still left a chink of light for George Stagg as their Justices on the bench, and Judge Rowlatt before them, knew full well it would. I would suspect that the appeal justices were often faced with the tricky balancing act of ensuring that any debatable court decision might be corrected while at the same time maintaining public confidence in the efficacy of the legal system and avoiding giving offence to their brother judges who had passed sentence.

I believe, therefore, the Stafford jury's plea was forwarded on to the Home Secretary in the reasonable certainty that he would commute the death sentence without the need for them to publicly take issue with a senior assize judge. Everyone wins – perhaps.

If I am correct, the retention of the mercy plea would have flagged up to the Home Secretary a lingering concern that Stagg had somehow been hard done by; perhaps one of the appeal judges had spoken in favour. In musing over this I am led to the man who was arguably the most interesting, and certainly the most influential in historic terms, of the justices involved in the appeal and whose approach to justice may have been critical to the retention of the plea.

This was John Sankey, 1866–1948, who was in 1929 to become Lord Chancellor in Ramsay McDonald's ill-fated second Labour government and who was later given the title Viscount Sankey. His place in legal history was cemented by his judgement in the 1935 case Woolmington vs DPP, whereby he emphasised that it was, and always had been, an 'inherent duty' of the prosecution to prove a prisoner's guilt 'beyond reasonable doubt'. The force of his words resulted in the 'beyond reasonable doubt' requirement to become known as the 'golden thread' rigidly observed thereafter, one hopes, in criminal cases.

I am given to wonder idly whether Sankey's experiences of working with other, less liberal, judges, some of which may have been uncomfortable, in any way influenced his later thinking. In 1940 he was to lead the Sankey Commission, which drafted the Sankey Declaration of the Rights of Man, which surfaced internationally after the Second World War as the basis for the still current Universal Declaration of Human Rights. Of all the people involved in this story, John Sankey has had the most lasting influence.

Commutation

If the case itself had caused a sensation, it soon became a political cause celebre. As the instant justice practised in medieval times was long gone, Stagg was not immediately executed at Stafford, nor even when his taxi eventually arrived at Winson Green, but from 16 February he had effectively been on 'death row'. An execution date, probably towards the end of March, would have been set. Whether he returned to the care of Mr Hamblin Smith is not known.

At almost the last minute, on 27 March, he was fortuitously saved from the noose by the personal intervention of a former iron-foundry worker named Arthur Henderson who, on 24 January, had become Home Secretary in the country's first Labour government.

It is worth spending a few moments to consider Arthur Henderson. He was not an avowed abolitionist, nor was the then Labour government in the process of framing legislation to do away with the death penalty. Many Labour MPs would have liked to do so, being strongly of the opinion that the lower down the social order you were, the more likely it was that, if accused of murder, you would be hanged. Especially as you probably lacked the funds to employ a defence lawyer.

Henderson shared these concerns and into the bargain was seemingly troubled by the apparent ease and frequency with which the courts passed death sentences. It is difficult for us to comprehend nowadays, but from January 1900 to February 1923 there had been 376 hangings, which was at a rate of one each month, and many Labour Party figures were determined that, given time, the number of capital punishments the courts were passing would be lowered.

A working-class man born into poverty in Glasgow in 1863, and afterwards raised in Newcastle, Henderson was, like many of the thrusting new Labour Party politicians reaching the top of their party, formally educated only to primary school standard. Moving through trade union and local party ranks, he became the Labour Party's political heavyweight of the first part of the 20th century. He was secretary, thus principal power broker, of the party from 1912 to 1935 and treasurer from 1930 to 1935.

In 1918, alongside Sidney Webb, one of the party's founding fathers, he had laid the foundations for the modern party by restructuring local organisation and introducing an annual national conference. He eventually had two stints as party leader in the House of Commons, was twice Labour chief whip and into the bargain had held positions in Lloyd George's coalition cabinet during the war. He knew everyone who was anyone and was not a man to be meddled with.

Altogether, Henderson was an MP from 1903 to 1935, representing five different constituencies. As fate would have it, not only was he brought up in Newcastle, but he was representing Newcastle East as an MP at the time of Ball's shooting. Well before the file landed on his desk, he would have been attuned to a case involving the death of a prominent local footballer and, when the case went to appeal, he would have anticipated the decision their Lordships would pass on to him. And he almost certainly knew which way he was going to jump.

Until late in 1923, the prospect of a Labour government had appeared unlikely but on 16 November the Conservative government had called a December general election, which returned a 'hung' parliament. Although the conservative leader Stanley Baldwin, as sitting prime minister, was given the opportunity to form a minority government, it soon became apparent that with 258 MPs in a fractured party within a House of 615 the Parliamentary arithmetic was against him. It meant they would not last long, but there was little appetite in the country for another general election and the Conservatives might have struggled even more badly should he have called one. Baldwin was therefore prepared to cut his losses.

Following extensive manoeuvring, he eventually stepped down and was succeeded on 8 January, and for the first time by a Labour government. With merely 119 MPs, the party leader Ramsay McDonald could not believe his luck, but by cobbling together some grudging support from the now declining Liberal Party and taking advantage of a divided Tory party, he had been able to assure King George V that he could form a new government without the need for another general election. If Baldwin had found minority government difficult, McDonald was soon to find it impossible.

The mathematics were all against the new government lasting long. Ministers lived on their wits from one day to the next, which meant that an experienced 'fixer' like Henderson was an essential choice for one of the so-called 'great offices of state'. Despite being a self-proclaimed expert on foreign affairs, he was surprised, and apparently not a little put out, to be offered the Home Office, then, as ever, regarded as something of a poisoned chalice.

It was going to be difficult enough for the Labour Party to get legislation of any kind through Parliament and, even had Henderson been an abolitionist, any fundamental restructuring of an emotive area like the penal system was a non-starter. When a non–government-sponsored private members' bill to that effect was introduced in 1924 by a junior Labour MP to 'test the waters', it was easily defeated.

Henderson's opportunity to have influence over capital punishment came instead from his being responsible for dealing with any appeals made following the inevitable death sentences the courts would pass down. Three of these were duly presented to him in quick succession and he was prepared to take what chance he had to indicate which way things might go should Labour ever attain a majority government.

Before the Stagg case came up for discussion, Henderson had commuted the death sentences of two other convicted murderers. George Wood, who had been found guilty of murdering his wife and her lover, and Dora Sadler, a private nurse who had killed two children belonging to a former employer, were the fortunate pair. The decisions, in part, may have been galvanised, and made more publicly acceptable, by the execution of one Edith Thompson in 1923 for complicity in the murder of her husband by her lover and where there was significant public doubt surrounding the strength of the evidence against her.

For Stagg, the issues over scant evidence in the Thompson case may well have been the key to his survival. Given that the presiding judge at Stafford had admitted there was no clarity of evidence in the case and the appeal justices had been clearly reluctant to reject the Stafford jury's plea for mercy, Stagg's case probably presented Henderson with a relatively safe choice. In addition, the high profile of a case involving a wounded war veteran and a famous footballer offered Henderson the guarantee of his views on capital punishment being given plenty of newspaper space. It was also a useful signal to the public that the Labour Party in office was prepared to make difficult decisions.

Given the circumstances under which Stagg left the police force, I would not be inclined to agree with Simon Burnton's interesting point that 'cynics' might say Stagg was reprieved because he was a former policeman.

You may consider that Henderson had made a humane decision, or you may say that Stagg had been extremely lucky. Had the Conservative Party lasted another two months in government, Stagg's appeal would have been forwarded to Henderson's Conservative predecessor, William Bridgeman. As *Wikipedia* informs us, Bridgeman was noted for his 'harshness and resolve' in dealing with capital cases, so to that extent Stagg was particularly fortunate in the timing of his trial.

Stagg's sentence was duly commuted to life imprisonment and before the end of March he was directed to Parkhurst prison on the Isle of Wight, often throughout its existence a natural home for the country's most high-profile and dangerous criminals. I am not sure that Stagg would have ordinarily qualified to join such company, but the choice of a notoriously disciplined prison environment was perhaps a sop to those who might have accused Henderson of being 'soft' on crime.

The Labour government was able to last only until the following October when another general election, popularly known as the 'reds under the beds' election, returned the Conservatives to power with a huge landslide majority. This was helped in no small part by allegations of Russian Bolshevik collusion with the Labour Party: Russians meddling in western elections – whatever next? The Conservatives gained 228 seats, while Labour lost 40 and their erstwhile Liberal bedfellows were rewarded for their grudging support by losing 119.

Henderson was to obtain his coveted post of Foreign Secretary in McDonald's ill-fated second Labour government in 1929 and took over leadership of the party in 1931 when, to survive as Prime Minister, McDonald threw in his lot with Baldwin and the Conservatives to form the so-called 'national government'. Henderson's star waned domestically in the 1930s as Attlee, Morrison and Bevin came to the fore within the Labour Party, but he remained influential abroad, chairing the Geneva Disarmament Conference in 1934 for which rather short-lived service he was awarded the Nobel Peace Prize.

Part 11

When Life Meant Life

Parkhurst, March 1924-June 1926

As I suggested, Stagg's incarceration in a notably tough environment was probably to offset any public opinion that was critical of the commutation of his sentence.

Remembering that Stagg's 1923 assessment under Hamblin Smith rated him as being of 'sound mind and good intelligence', one can only assume that he deteriorated rapidly while in prison before being transferred to a mental hospital.

I have drawn attention to the current public domain unavailability of his Broadmoor case file, which is presumably quite specific in detailing his symptoms and clinical assessment; thus, what it was in his behaviour at Parkhurst that prompted the judgement to transfer him will remain a mystery until the file is made public. Perhaps some interested younger reader could make a note that the file is due to come into the public domain in March 2066, 100 years on from his death. It is always possible that some keen badgering from family members may persuade the authorities to make it accessible to them at an earlier date.

With naturally aggravating worries about his wife and children, some level of mental health deterioration during

Stagg's time in Parkhurst is probably not a surprise, though he would not have been alone amongst the prison population in experiencing such problems. Paul Lester makes much of how difficult that environment might have been for a former policeman, who might always be looked on with suspicion by his fellow inmates as a 'plant'. Prisoners of Stagg's media notoriety might also be easy targets for prison toughs who fancied showing who was top dog.

It should also be borne in mind that Stagg had been under severe emotional pressure before he arrived at Parkhurst, having spent six weeks effectively on 'death row' in Winson Green. For anyone, this would not have been a period of light relief and Paul Lester strongly and convincingly argues that the primitive conditions in which Stagg would have been held in the period between court case and planned execution were likely to make anyone go mad. Perhaps spirits were raised by the prospect of an appeal hearing but any high hopes would have been quickly dashed.

Between 7 and 11 September 1926, Stagg went on hunger strike, a tactic then often used for political effect by imprisoned suffragettes and Irish republicans. The record shows that when he began to refuse food on 7 September his stated reason was as 'a protest against the unjustness of his sentence'. Put kindly, it suggests that he must have held on to a fervent belief in his innocence; put less kindly, you may consider he was suffering from delusion and, having in fortuitous circumstances avoided the noose, had little reason for complaint.

As a response to the hunger strike, George Stagg was force-fed on 11 September. This was done by oesophageal tube; whether this was introduced orally or nasally is not recorded, but either way, involving as it did physical restraint, it would have been a highly unpleasant experience. Perhaps unsurprisingly, there is no record of him having repeated his protest.

The hunger strike might suggest that Stagg was becoming difficult to handle and we can imagine his behaviour perhaps becoming more verbally aggressive, but in truth such behaviour at Parkhurst was probably routinely expected and dealt with. Probably to the relief of all parties, his sojourn there was soon to end as eight months later, on 16 June 1927, he was transferred to Broadmoor. Whether the hunger strike and any associated delusion did contribute to this move remains, for the present, unclear.

Broadmoor, June 1927–June 1963

Opened in 1863, Broadmoor Criminal Lunatic Asylum was a mixed-gender, high-security psychiatric hospital situated in Crowthorne, Berkshire. It existed to offer medical and therapeutic treatment to criminals with mental-health issues or personality disorders severe enough to make them a likely danger to themselves and/or to others.

A high proportion of Broadmoor patients were men or women who had not stood trial because they were classified as mentally incapable of instructing counsel, understanding evidence, challenging witnesses or understanding the nature of their actions. Had Stagg been deemed mentally unfit to stand trial in 1924 it is likely that, in lieu of a criminal decision, Broadmoor, or a similar institution, would have been his first port of call and hanging would not have been an option. In the event, he was one of a minority sent to Broadmoor after serving part of a sentence at a 'normal' prison.

Built for 500 inmates, Broadmoor received up to 140 'new' men, and up to 20 women, each year and was invariably overcrowded; with beds sometimes in corridors, living conditions could be challenging. It sat, however, in a generous 40 acres and its activities included choir, drama, woodwork, gardening, table tennis, snooker, musical instrument tuition, football, cricket and athletics.

There is no doubt that the hospital has housed some extremely dangerous individuals. The ongoing media fascination with a dozen or so 20th-century serial killers and former gangsters does, however, tend to deflect from the reality that it has catered for a wide range of patients, associated with a wide range of crimes, most of whom remain unknown to the wider world and not all of whom have gone on to reoffend.

Nevertheless, being sent to Broadmoor gave the clear message that George Stagg was considered a danger to the public. This is not as straightforward as it might appear as he was not a serial killer, nor (though some readers may disagree) had he killed Ball in gratuitous circumstances, nor in 1924 did he appear, as far as we know, to present a threat to Ball's surviving family members or to the public in general. The possibility of him being a danger to himself might be plausible, but, as I have continually said, without an illness diagnosis we cannot know.

Whatever the circumstances of his deterioration, Stagg's move to Broadmoor was probably widely quoted as proof that he murdered Ball, along the lines of 'he must have done it – they later found out that he was mad', but this would have been a flawed view. The onset of serious mental incapacity almost four years after an event proves nothing, nor does simply referring to someone as 'mad' or 'insane' would. 'Insanity' exists as a non-specific verbal convention used, for the most part, as shorthand convenience to describe behaviour that is not socially normal. It is not a descriptor of a diagnosed medical condition, still less a personality disorder. As a one-word explanation of why Stagg shot Ball, neither 'mad' nor 'insane' would show evidence or logic.

Psychiatric treatments up until the 1950s read like something from *One Flew Over The Cuckoo's Nest* and included intravenous pharmacological drugs, electro-convulsive therapy, insulin coma therapy and surgical leucotomies (lobotomies). Again, with reference to Stagg's case file, it would be fascinating to know which therapies and medical treatments he experienced, with what level of frequency and with what levels of assessed success.

It is not just Stagg's medical records at Broadmoor that remain subject to closure rules. Also included are visitor records, which might prove interesting, and any records of him having conversed with staff about the Tommy Ball affair.

There has always been a general acceptance that, once in, a high proportion of Broadmoor's inmates would remain there for their lifetimes. For a man to spend 36 years incarcerated in Broadmoor suggests either he was a case needing serious ongoing treatment or there was an unavailability of alternative appropriate accommodation. Mental health review tribunals to which patients could appeal against their continued hospitalisation were only introduced after the 1959 Mental Health Act was passed. It is quite possible that making such an appeal is precisely what Stagg did in 1963 and that an appeal board may have accepted an alternative regime might have been appropriate to meet Stagg's ongoing needs.

Despite my bemoaning the lack of available evidence on Stagg's time in Broadmoor, there is, tantalisingly, one document that exists within the public domain. It is his entry on the 1939 Register, which was a census by another name. It did, in fact, take the place of the proposed 1941 census which was never undertaken and was, to the joy of ancestry detectives, not subject to the usual 100-year closure rule which has, excepting an early release of the 1911 record, been applied to each ten-yearly census.

The document lists Stagg's occupation as a 'fruit and poultry farmer', and given the 'chicken's angle' which has featured widely in the handed-down story you may think this somewhat ironic. I have found no reference elsewhere that Stagg himself kept chickens while in Somerville Cottage, nor that he had run some sort of a market-gardening sideline.

My excitement in believing I had unearthed hitherto unknown information became quickly dimmed by the reality that the 1939 Register often ignored a person's pre-war occupation and referred only to any wartime work. It is almost certain that the fruit and poultry 'occupation' referred to is simply a summary of the daily routines and interests Stagg followed within Broadmoor and nothing to do with anything he did before he was imprisoned. As with much connected with George Stagg, things are not straightforward.

Highcroft, June 1963-February 1966

Highcroft Hospital was built in 1899 into extensive grounds in the Reservoir Road/Slade Road area of Erdington in north-east Birmingham, only minutes away from the modern Spaghetti Junction. It was initially the infirmary and maternity home of the Aston Union workhouse and stood in large grounds.

As readers will doubtless know, the workhouse system was a form of poor relief administered by local authorities and which allowed local unemployed and/or destitute individuals and their families access to rudimentary lodgings and food in return for a day's work. Many workhouses also became de facto 'care homes' for the elderly and mentally ill.

The unpleasant nature of the workhouse system is well enough documented but despite its grim reputation, the system was initially developed with the best of intentions in supporting needy local folk through times of poverty and ill health. For example, many residents living in rural areas returned on a seasonal basis when harvest employment ended.

The more punitive side of the system was designed to encourage the unemployed idle to find work, though the prison-like regimes put in place to encourage this tended, in many institutions, to be indiscriminately applied to the general resident population. The existence of what was a substantial infirmary near to the urban challenges of Aston, doubtless erected and staffed at considerable expense, probably illustrates the better intentions behind the system.

My initial view of Stagg's transfer to Highcroft was that it was likely to have taken place following the foundation of the National Health Service in July 1948 when national arrangements for custodial mental health were reorganised. The Aston Union Infirmary was then redesignated as a psychiatric and geriatric hospital within the new Birmingham Hospital Board until administration was transferred to the Northern Birmingham Mental Health NHS Trust in 1994. Most of the original estate has now been given over to residential housing, while much of the surviving and imposing central block, a minor Victorian architectural masterpiece, has undergone modernisation as luxury flats.

Many of the folk memories of the hospital, recorded online by relatives of residents and by local residents, give evidence that it seemed a grim place even into the 1960s, with stories of windows almost permanently closed to mask the shouts and screams from within.

Following a degree of perseverance in persuading the 'parent' West London NHS Trust that not all the information I was seeking from the Broadmoor archives was case-sensitive, I was eventually informed that Stagg was transferred to Highcroft much later than I had thought, on 14 June 1963. That is to within two days of 36 years spent in Broadmoor.

The date and reason are probably both easy to explain. Stagg's wife, Mary, had died in the preceding February and by the spring of 1963 both of his daughters were critically ill. As, at that point, he was most probably no longer classified as being of danger to the public or to himself, his transfer may have been made on compassionate grounds. It may still have taken a tribunal appeal under the new Mental Health Act, but until his records are officially released we cannot know for sure. The perennially overcrowded Broadmoor was probably relieved to be able to move on any of its less severely ill patients who might be appropriately cared for elsewhere.

It was a humane gesture, whether made under appeal, by common sense or a mixture of the two, and it is likely that the Birmingham police would have been party to any consultation process that might have taken place. Nowadays, it may prove difficult to expedite such a move without due notice being taken of the views of a victim's surviving family, but I doubt that such niceties were observed in 1964.

George Stagg eventually died in Highcroft of bronchopneumonia on 1 February 1966, aged 87. When he was born, the average length of life for a British working-class male was around 42 years. Given that he had survived action in two major military conflicts, being once severely wounded, and that in 1923 he was represented by the press as a physically frail and prematurely aged man, his life represents an unexpected, indeed staggering, longevity. Despite any misgivings about the facilities and treatments in his various incarcerations, it does say something positive about the levels of care and food he received, and probably about his own constitution.

His death certificate, with information given to the registrar by his then surviving son, rather coyly records George's occupation as 'Police Constable (retired)' and the place at which he died to be simply '18 Highcroft Road, Erdington'. The address was very much a softening of fact, but one dictated by the government as, after 1918, registering a death as having occurred in a workhouse, a prison or a mental asylum was forbidden. Into the bargain, each of these institutions had to be represented 'in code' by a normal-sounding street address and '18 Highcroft Road' was the one used in this instance for all deaths at the hospital.

With great irony, the conversion of the hospital's surviving building into luxury flats now, one imagines, gives a Highcroft Road address a rather more desirable cachet.

It may surprise some readers to learn that despite his conviction Stagg would have continued to receive his police pension, quite possibly his war pension and eventually a state pension, minus an agreed amount sent regularly, before her death, to his wife. He could not, of course, personally access his money whilst incarcerated, but savings held by convicted criminals may remain extant and untouched by officialdom as long as the monies held are not the proceeds of crime.

You will forgive me for not divulging the exact probate value of George Stagg's estate, but let me say it was comfortable for a man who had earned no wage for the best part of 46 years. This is probably explained by the incremental accumulation of his pensions over that time and, had he been a beneficiary of the sale of his cottage, from any lingering share of the profits, all with bank interest added.

Part 12

Moving On

Brick Kiln Lane

Once Perry Barr had been incorporated into Birmingham, the city's council made the decision to build housing over much of the old Perry Hall estate. To do this, the council contracted as developers Henry Boot, a Sheffield-based building company and now a major international player within the construction sector. As stated earlier, once the development was habitable it was rebranded and extended over former Perry Hall fields as 'Perry Beeches', becoming a long-standing design and build flagship development for Boot's company, pictorially featuring in advertising literature for many years.

All properties were initially rented out and a Boot subsidiary, the First National Housing Trust, was installed as landlord with the local managers occupying a property in Beeches Road known as the 'White House'. In the late 1920s and the 1930s, a great many families were attracted to renting newly built property in the area and one can imagine that the change of Brick Kiln Lane's name, with its industrial overtones, to Beeches Road, with its hints of country living, was made for good commercial reason. It is said that in naming the roads on his estates Henry Boot carefully used names with rural connotations, such as trees and Pennine villages, as a marketing tool. In the early 1950s, the Beeches Road leasehold houses began to be offered for sale to sitting tenants.

The ageing properties owned by the Staggs and Laurences would have initially stood out visually against the modern designs introduced by Boot and were probably not seen as helpful in attracting tenants to the new stock, hence my assumption that they were probably purchased from Mrs Stagg and from Mr Laurence on a compulsory basis. My guess is that the old cottages were demolished around 1934 and 1935 and subsequently built over. I am open to guidance on this.

The Ball and the Richards Families

Euphemia Ball died in Gateshead in June 1926 aged 67. She was never, as many chroniclers have incorrectly stated, a single parent. Despite being invariably cited as a man who had 'died young', Tommy's father later lived in the New Washington area of Durham for several years with his married daughter Elizabeth and died in May 1937 in hospital in Chester-le-Street.

As Ball was a common surname name in the North-east, and Joseph a popular given name, I found Joseph Ball's death initially difficult to pinpoint. If other researchers had this challenge, then combined with the absence of any surviving record of his attendance at either Tommy's marriage or funeral, it may have been inferred that he was no longer alive by 1923.

As further detailed research lies outside the scope of this work, as best I can tell, each of Tommy's surviving brothers appeared to have died in the Northumberland and Durham areas in the decade up to the late-1960s. Doubtless there are many descendants.

Far from being 'lost to history' as Paul Lester surmised in 1996, Beatrice Ball was then still very much alive. Courtesy of the crowd collection made for her at Villa Park, she unexpectedly became a wealthy young lady and throughout the time of the various court cases was briefly quite famous. Although she initially moved into the accommodation above the family shop in Aston Road, she was able, perhaps with her matchday collection windfall, to obtain a property in the newly developing outer-circle dormitory area of Stechford.

This was then becoming a desirable suburb of semi-detached houses carved out of farmland on the eastern edge of Birmingham and, like Perry Beeches, the area was subject between the two world wars to rapid, estate-style development. The substantial middle-class 'semis' of the 1920s and 1930s are still there and, by and large, they retain the look of the desirable period residences I recall from my younger years.

At some point in the 1920s, Beatrice took work as a butcher's assistant, almost certainly in her father's shop. It would have been a relatively straightforward journey, though not especially speedy, on the number 10 tram from its Stechford terminus opposite the Fox and Goose, changing to the number 8 at the road junction known as 'the Gate' in Saltley, thence up into Aston along the later bus route I took to Villa Park on a Saturday afternoon in poor weather. Who knows, she may have met her second husband on one of those trips, as in 1929 she wed a railwayman who lived in the vicinity of the Saltley–Aston route and the couple began a family.

The story is briefly picked up when Beatrice is to be found on the 1939 Register keeping house for a family in Worcestershire. She eventually settled back into a different house in the Stechford area and passed away in 1998. The number of times I have unknowingly passed the end of her later road by foot, cycle, bus or car must run into the high hundreds.

The William Richards butchery business continued into the early 1950s before becoming 'Farr and Smith'. Harold Edward 'Teddy' Farr had been, according to an entry on *Birmingham History Forum*, 'boss' of the Richards' shop before the name change. We might assume 'boss' to mean the in-shop manager, a position to which, had things turned out differently, Tommy Ball might have aspired on retirement from football.

I must admit to abject failure in trying to pin down William Richards's date of death, but somewhere around 1950 and 1951 may not be too far out. Whether Farr and his associate had bought him out or purchased the business from his estate I do not know, but as my research makes it appear unlikely that Farr married into the family, I would rule out any inheritance ownership on Richards's death.

It is not unusual for a long-established commercial name to remain in local currency until well after the founder has moved on and, in this case, the photographic evidence within *Birmingham History Forum* suggests the retention of the 'Richards' sign above the shop into the 1950s. This might indicate that the subsequent owners had felt the original name represented a quality mark not to be lightly disposed of. Teddy Farr emigrated to Canada in the late-1950s and moved on the business. It later had a brief life as a mini-mart but is now long gone.

The Stagg Family

Mary Ellen Stagg may have had her husband taken away from her, but she still had a roof over her head and, with three children to support, was able to go on living at Somerville Cottages into the 1930s. How she was able to pay off any remaining loan is open to question, but it is not impossible that she continued to rent out the Balls' old cottage and may even have taken lodgers into her own home, as remained common practice throughout the country for many years afterwards.

As we have seen, by 1930 Brick Kiln Lane had, as Beeches Road, become a central artery of the Perry Beeches estate. In the 1930 electoral register Mary was registered as living in 'the Cottage', also identified as a now numbered address in the road. A house bearing the cottage's new number exists today and a pair of 'semis' was probably built on the site of Somerville Cottages once they had been demolished.

Of the old families, in 1930 only Mary and the Laurences, then shown in records under their modern guise as the Lawrences, were still living in the road. As they had remained in their original houses, they were probably the only freeholders in what had by then been laid down as a road of leasehold properties. It is unclear whether George Stagg had remained legal owner and so become a beneficiary of any eventual sale or whether title and any outstanding financial commitments had been transferred to Mary.

Of interest, the 1930 electoral roll shows Mary as 'OW', the contemporary shorthand which indicated that a woman had occupied a dwelling for more than six months and was thus eligible under the 1928 Equal Franchise Act to vote in local and parliamentary elections. As a freeholder and a voter, Mary was one of a newly emancipated generation of women, as was Beatrice Ball in her Stechford home.

We know for certain that by the outbreak of the Second World War Mary had moved out of Beeches Road and was living around a mile away on the other side of the Walsall Road. Her new road was, I believe, developed by the company that built the

Perry Beeches estate as the properties bear the company's visual hallmarks. With its resonance of fresh-air Yorkshire country living, the road also has the type of name favoured by builder Henry Boot.

There is a strong chance that the move may have been part and parcel of an arrangement made with the builder at the time Somerville Cottages were demolished. Mary's eventual probate record suggests that, like her husband before her, she had scraped and saved over the years before her death. The 1939 Register has Mary living with her youngest son and gives her occupation as 'cook', the first indication I had of her taking paid employment since she had left the press pin trade over 30 years beforehand.

Mary's daughters had probably stayed with her until both married in the mid-1930s and thereafter continued to live in Birmingham with growing families until their early deaths in 1963 and in 1964 respectively.

As we already know, Mary's eldest son had emigrated in 1923 to Australia, aged 16 years. At first, I took this as a natural enough knee-jerk move to escape the family's sudden notoriety. I was surprised, therefore, to discover that he had embarked from London on 30 October, 11 days before the shooting. He did not arrive in Brisbane until 17 December, so it is quite likely he may have known nothing about events at home until he saw newspaper reports in Australia.

The difficulties in communicating with his mum can only be imagined, but they did manage to stay in touch until his death. The lad settled in Queensland, eventually marrying and raising a now-extended family. Being too old for military service during the Second World War, he was called up by the Queensland government in September 1942 under what was known as 'military impressment'. Despite the terminology, this was apparently a voluntary act, and George Junior became a member of the Australian Civil Construction Corps which carried out defence-related public works, such as building aerodrome runways. When he passed away in November 1962, he pre-deceased his dad by four years.

George's elder brother Tom died in March 1935 in Birmingham and Simon, the younger, died in September 1949 in Solihull.

Mary Stagg died on 9 February 1963, aged 78, from cancer of the cervix as well as from the diabetes mellitus that had plagued her for almost a lifetime and it is a fair assumption that her later years were characterised by painful and debilitating symptoms. Thus, the once apparently extremely sick George Stagg was surprisingly pre-deceased by his wife and by three of his four children.

Mary Stagg illustrated her strength by rebuilding her life in Somerville Cottage and staying in the area thereafter. I find it interesting that her death certificate proudly shows her occupation not as 'cook' or 'housewife' but as 'wife of George John Allen Stagg, Police Constable' – note the misspelling of 'Alan'! This description is despite her husband having left the police service 49 years earlier and I feel it highly unlikely that son Cyril, as informant, would have offered this precise identification to the registrar unless he had known that his mother would have wished it.

Cyril passed away in the Midlands in 1999, the final survivor of the events of 1923.

Aston Villa FC

As Aston Villa FC is unwittingly the origin of the tragedy, I think it appropriate to offer a few words to suggest how things progressed for the club and for some of the individuals we have mentioned in the years following the tragedy. My apologies to supporters who know the stories well enough, but there may be readers who do not!

There had always been a wistful belief held by the old-time Villa faithful that Tommy Ball and his team-mates, at the end of the 1923/24 season, may well have earned themselves the first Football League and FA Cup 'double' of the 20th century. As the team lay in third place in the league on the day Tommy was shot, and current form was strong, it was not unreasonable to think that the league championship might return to Aston for a seventh time.

Under the circumstances, however, a dip in form was understandable and only three of the remaining 11 matches to be played before the end of December were won. On the plus side, only two matches in this run were defeats but, frustratingly, four were drawn and ground was lost to the leading teams, Huddersfield Town and Cardiff City. December was, as it often has been, a particularly difficult month for the team with only one victory in seven games. In later years, several of Ball's old Villa team-mates cited the emotional impact of his death as being the primary reason for a sudden loss of form. I doubt whether this was simply a convenient excuse.

Tommy's place in the Villa team was, as expected, taken by the redoubtable Dr Victor Milne, and once he had settled into the side the defence tightened up again. Despite the considerable feat of conceding only 37 goals in a 42-match league season, the title was beyond them, being won by Huddersfield Town on goal difference from Cardiff City. Both teams amassed 57 points, while Villa finished in a disappointing sixth place, eight points adrift, largely courtesy of winning their final three games. They would rue the 11 drawn games during the campaign and, despite the presence of usually reliable hot shots Walker and Capewell, the lack of goals from an attack which failed to score in six of the 17 fixtures played in 1924.

To no one's surprise, full-backs Smart and Mort were selected to play together for England, so, had he maintained his form, a call-up for Tommy might have been on the cards. It is interesting to note that the team's good defensive work did not persuade the Scottish selectors to call up Milne, who had already been on their radar, and it is equally interesting to speculate again on whether the Scots would have come knocking on Tommy's door.

What really excited the Villa crowd was a long run in the FA Cup. All looked good as they defeated Ashington, Swansea Town, Leeds United, West Bromwich Albion and Burnley, making it to the final to play none other than Newcastle United. A week before the match was played, Villa entertained the Toon at Villa Park and romped home 6-1, so the final appeared, at least to people outside the game, to be a foregone conclusion.

Sadly, as all Villa supporters know only too well, there has never been any such thing in B6 as a foregone conclusion, and so it transpired. Although things looked set fair for a seventh cup triumph, and their first at the final tie's new Wembley Stadium venue, Villa had to contend with the inconvenient fact that in the league fixture Newcastle had put out what was virtually a reserve side. They had also done so in several other matches leading up to the final.

Nowadays, we would call it squad rotation, but this was in the days before the squad system and when clubs were required by league rules to make a decent game of all fixtures by putting out their strongest available pick. The league was not slow in fining clubs for breach of this rule and Newcastle were eventually made to pay the then massive sum of £7,500 or just over £464,000 in 2022 money.

This was no comfort to Villa fans when their team lost 0-2 against Newcastle's well-rested, first-choice team. It was perhaps still a match Villa could have won with reportedly 'open goals' going begging. As the great Billy Walker was quoted as saying afterwards, 'we had 20 chances, they had two. They accepted theirs, we missed ours.' In football 'twas ever thus!

Villa supporters had to wait until 1957 for their next, and to date last, FA Cup victory. It was a match won a week after I had first seen them play so I watched the final on TV with great enthusiasm. Several hundred in that Wembley crowd would have remembered seeing Tommy Ball play, but his name was slipping from the collective memory, and it was to be at least another ten years before I first heard of him. Such is the march of time.

1923/24 had, unsurprisingly, appeared to be a good season for income with an average home crowd of 29,732. This is small beer today, perhaps, but in those days, and for decades afterwards, that was a regular attendance to be reckoned with. The visits of both Newcastle and Sunderland pulled in over 40,000 and there was the bumper 'royal' crowd of 56,000 against Bolton. 52,000 turned up to watch West Bromwich in the league and 43,000 to watch the same opposition in the cup, while the match against Leeds in the cup attracted 51,000.

The offset was the cost of building the Trinity Stand and, as the season's financial balance was to show, the club, and not for the last time, was operating on the proverbial shoestring.

Villa supporters taking a broad and dispassionate historical view may, with some justification, see the missed opportunities of 1924 as the turning point season which ended the club's 'golden age'. To stretch a point, some may even feel the lack of success led indirectly to the club's first relegation into the Second Division 12 years later.

By Villa's established standards, they were then to enter a long and, saving the 1957 FA Cup win and being inaugural winners in 1961 of the newly invented Football League Cup, almost barren period until a 1970s and early-1980s renaissance. Under Vic Crowe, and then Ron Saunders and Tony Barton, the club arose from the desert of the Third Division to a First Division title and a European Cup victory in successive years.

The well-established patrician style of governance headed by 'Villa men' was to last until 1969 when a shareholders' revolt overturned the 'antiquated Dickensian board', as Colin Abbott, perhaps not unfairly, described them. You may not be surprised to learn that the club chairman at this historic moment, Chris Buckley, was a man who had played under George Ramsay before the Great War.

Many of my father's generation who followed the side throughout the 1920s and 1930s saw a different picture. To them, the near misses of 1924 were the natural continuation of the established order of inevitable greatness. In the decade following Ball's death, and despite no trophies having been won, regular fans saw some of the most exhilarating football the club had ever played.

It featured some of the club's greatest stars and the names Walker, Waring, Houghton, Gibson, Talbot and Tate, for instance, were always uttered by elderly supporters with almost cap-doffing reverence. There were record-breaking numbers of goals and an almost assured top-six finish until the slump, which saw them diminish eventually to be relegated in 1936. This run included a league-record 128 goals in the 1930/31 season, in which they finished only in second place and during which centre-forward Tom Waring scored a staggering 49 league goals. My father worshipped those players.

Having first been appointed to the position in 1884, Scottish former club captain George Ramsay remained with Villa as club secretary until 1926 when he was appointed 'honorary advisor' and became a vice-president. During his time as secretary, he had recruited, trained, selected and managed the senior team, winning six First Division championships and finishing second on another six occasions. He had also won six FA Cups.

In any era this would have been some going and, despite the term 'manager' not having been coined in his day, he remained the most successful person in charge of an English team until the era of Alex Ferguson and Arsène Wenger. In 1927, in recognition of his service to the game and to the Villa club, Ramsay received a second 'service medal' from the Football League, his first having come in 1909. He died, aged 80, in October 1935.

Liverpudlian Frederick Rinder had become a committee member in 1881, and while Ramsay built the team, Rinder developed the infrastructure. He was chairman from 1898 to 1925 and, following an enforced time away from the board, returned as vice-president in 1930. Like Ramsay he did not suffer fools and was quite happy to 'take on' players who he felt were over-reaching their position or letting down the club in some way, on or off the field. Punctuality, sobriety and obedience were three of the qualities he demanded and one unpleasant semi-public incident at New Street Station with latecomer Tommy Smart became particularly infamous. His assertive manner meant that he often fell out with fellow directors, some of whom took full advantage of his Trinity Stand overspend to force his temporary banishment.

A surveyor by profession, Rinder was a man with big ideas and grandiose schemes and had been a prime mover behind Villa's relocation from Perry Barr into the Aston Lower Grounds. But for the outbreak of war in 1914, he would probably have gone ahead with the planned construction of the largest sports stadium in the world with a projected capacity of 120,000, mainly standing of course. Thwarted in that enterprise by the outbreak of war, Rinder was persistent in his desire to enhance the ground and, by dipping into the 1914 plans, he built the new grandstand in Trinity Road.

He later bounced back from his period in enforced exile to have another look at his 1914 drawings and plan the construction behind one of the goals of the massive 'Aston End' or 'Church End' terrace as it was then variously known by fans to differentiate it from the established 'Witton End' opposite. Later generations came to know the terrace as the 'Holte End' after the hotel, and now public house, which lay just beyond and which itself took the name of the family which had built and lived in Aston Hall, the Tudor mansion which overlooks the ground. Unlike the experience in 1914, the eventual construction of the Aston End continued to its completion some months after the declaration of the 1939–45 war. Fans were left to wonder how Villa managed that.

It is said that Rinder was twice urged to allow his name to be used on one or other of Villa's two main stands in Trinity Road and Witton Lane, but he refused on the grounds that it would not be appropriate for him to be so recognised when so many other men had done great things for the club. Not that everyone subsequently in charge has taken that grounded view of their place in history.

Until 1939, it was usual for the England team to be selected by an 'International Select Committee' of 14 worthies drawn from the leading clubs and, inevitably, Frederick Rinder was a selector for several years; he was also made a life member of the Football League. He died in 1938 after being taken ill while attending a match; given the choice, he would probably not have had the inevitable happen in any other way.

What of some of the players we have mentioned in passing?

Tommy Smart held down a first-team place until 1933, winning five England caps, while his full-back partner, Tommy Mort, won three caps and played until 1935, by which time he was 37 years of age. Mort died in 1967 and Smart in 1968. Between them they had played for Villa in 820 games and, over a ten-year period, had partnered each other in the majority of those.

Aberdonian Dr Milne was to make 175 appearances between 1923 and 1929. As a player and as a person he was held in great respect by my father who, when reminiscing, always referred to him using the honorific 'Doctor', never the more familiar 'Vic'. On retirement, Milne became club doctor for a time before concentrating on developing a medical practice in nearby Aldridge where he was to spend many years as the area's Medical Officer of Health. He died in 1971.

Frank Moss, an Aston man, was a commanding presence on the field and a forceful character off it – in short, an ideal team captain. Following 281 appearances and five England caps, he moved on to Cardiff City in 1928. Setting an unusual family record, both of his sons, Frank Junior and Amos, played for Villa and Frank Junior's record of 314 appearances was to better his father's. Frank Senior passed away in 1965.

Tommy Weston, the man whose position in the team Tommy Ball may have coveted, had won FA Cup winner's medals either side of the Great War. After 178 appearances for Villa, and with Mort having taken over his position in the team, he left for newly promoted Stoke in the summer of 1922. Having been selected by his new club to play on just a handful of occasions during

Stoke's 1922/23 relegation season he hung up his boots. Weston died in 1952.

Frank Barson's time at Manchester United, once he had left Villa, was notable for the frequent injuries he suffered, most probably through over-robust play. A brief move to Watford in the Third Division South followed where he constantly found himself on the wrong side of referees and was often suspended. He then wound things down by joining Hartlepool as a player-coach, followed by brief stints at Wigan Athletic, at Rhyl and then as manager at Stourbridge before taking a coaching post back at Villa Park.

In classic 'poacher-turned-gamekeeper' style, he stayed until the end of wartime fixtures and so must have become rather less 'assertive' when faced with higher authority than he had been previously. A coaching job at Swansea followed and he later managed Lye Town. Barson died in 1968 in Winson Green, that is the district, not the prison.

Billy Walker also stayed in football, achieving the unique distinction of adding to his 1920 winner's medal as a player by winning the FA Cup as a manager either side of the Second World War. He managed Sheffield Wednesday to success in 1935 and Nottingham Forest in 1959.

His playing record of 531 games for the club has only been surpassed by left-back Charlie Aitken, who recorded 660 appearances between 1961 and 1976. I doubt if any other player will come close to those numbers. In addition, Walker scored a club-record 244 goals and earned 18 England caps, scoring nine goals. He died in 1963 and in December 1973 his widow came on to the pitch before a match to present Aitken with a memento to mark his breaking of her late husband's appearance record.

Freddie Miles, the Aston-born man whose testimony probably sank Stagg's story about Tommy Ball's drinking habits, continued as Villa 'trainer' and led them into the 1924 FA Cup Final. Ill health got the better of him and he died prematurely at the age of 42. His playing career with Villa had been distinguished and it is quite possible he would have developed into an equally outstanding coach. The bearers at his funeral in February 1926 included Harry Hampton, Charlie Wallace and Dr Milne.

Postscript 1

Roy Jenkins

In 1927, the Labour Party published its abolitionist 'Manifesto on Capital Punishment', but there was little real progress made until 1957 when Parliament watered down the numbers being executed by passing the Homicide Act. This was a precursor of abolition, which created a distinction between capital and non-capital murder and allowed for the defence of diminished responsibility.

In 1965, the Murder (Abolition of the Death Penalty) Act, suspended the death sentence for murder, initially for a period of five years. In December 1969 this was ratified in perpetuity. This development would have been unimaginable in Arthur Henderson's time.

Shortly after the Murder Act was passed, the Welsh-born social reformer Roy Jenkins became Home Secretary in Harold Wilson's Labour government. His first action was reputedly to have taken down from his office wall the updated list of condemned prisoners that had hung there by long tradition, presumably as a sign that the Home Secretary was doing his job. Jenkins was said to have filled the space with a refrigerator.

Together with the earlier abolition, this act of iconoclasm signalled a cultural shift in the attitude of the Home Office and fittingly Jenkins was in office when the 1969 abolition was ratified by Parliament.

As this work is dedicated to my father, I feel it appropriate to conclude 'in full circle'. Many readers will recall that from 1950 to 1977 Jenkins was MP for the then newly created, and now dismembered, Parliamentary constituency of Birmingham Stechford. Stechford, which stretched into Saltley and Alum Rock, was my home constituency and my father, a lifelong socialist, was one of Jenkins's local agents, helping fight four successful elections for him in the 1950s. 'Uncle Roy', as he was known to me, was a family friend and regular visitor to our house.

Postscript 2

Dalian Atkinson

I have taken several opportunities to comment on the speed at which George Stagg's case was taken through the court system, and especially the shoehorning of hearing, jury deliberations and sentencing into one day at the Stafford Assize.

I am certain, therefore, that many readers will have drawn comparison with the case of PC Benjamin Monk who on 23 June 2021 was found guilty of the manslaughter of former Aston Villa player, Dalian Atkinson.

The incident in question took place on 15 August 2016 and, including police investigations and procedural delay owing to Covid issues, the case took four years and nine months to reach court. In an ironic reflection of the Stagg case, Monk's defence was predicated on the belief that Atkinson presented him and a fellow defendant with a physical threat. Jurors were directed by the judge to find Monk guilty of murder only if they were sure he intended to cause really serious injury. The jury was also clearly instructed to find an alternative charge of manslaughter if they were not certain Monk or his fellow defendant intended to cause serious harm.

The trial at Birmingham Crown Court lasted just under two months, from 26 April to 23 June 2021; jurors deliberated for a total of 18 hours 48 minutes and the other accused person was referred for retrial following the jury's failure to reach a majority verdict. Monk's sentencing took place five days after this guilty verdict was delivered.

Appendices

A1: Tommy Ball's Playing Record

This is produced with acknowledgements to the works of David Goodyear and Tony Matthews, and of Rob Bishop and Frank Holt.

All appearances are in the Football League First Division unless shown by asterisk *, which denotes Football Association Cup, or 'English Cup' as it was sometimes referred to in contemporary accounts. You will note the peculiarity of the immediate post-1918 model of playing most opponents, home and away, on consecutive weeks and the suspiciously common practice of estimating the number of paying spectators present to somewhere approaching the nearest thousand.

Note also that the club referred to as 'Stoke' was renamed Stoke City in 1925 and the club referred to as 'Birmingham' was renamed Birmingham City in 1943.

Season 1919/20

Opposition	Date	Venue	Position	Result	Attendance
Bolton Wanderers	7 Apr	Home	Right-half	Lost 3-6	26,000

Season 1920/21

Bolton Wanderers	15 Sep	Away	Centre-half	Lost 0-5	45,000
Tottenham Hotspur	18 Sep	Away	Centre-half	Won 2-1	45,000
Oldham Athletic	25 Sep	Home	Centre-half	Won 3-0	40,000
Bradford	20 Nov	Home	Centre-half	Won 4-1	30,000
Bradford	27 Nov	Away	Centre-half	Lost 0-4	12,000
Newcastle United	4 Dec	Away	Centre-half	Lost 1-2	25,000
Everton	25 Jan	Away	Left-back	Drawn 1-1	35,000
Burnley	5 Feb	Away	Left-back	Lost 1-7	40,000
Sunderland	23 Feb	Away	Centre-half	Won 1-0	40,000
Bradford City	26 Feb	Home	Left-half	Lost 1-2	31,000
Huddersfield	19 Mar	Away	Left-half	Lost 0-1	20,000
Middlesbrough	26 Mar	Away	Left-half	Won 4-1	25,000
Derby County	2 Apr	Away	Centre-half	Won 3-2	14,000

Season 1921/22

Preston North End	17 Sep	Home	Centre-half	Won 2-0	28,000
Bradford City	12 Nov	Home	Centre-half	Won 7-1	28,000
Liverpool	3 Dec	Home	Left-half	Drawn 1-1	30,000
Liverpool	10 Dec	Away	Left-half	Lost 0-2	40,000
Newcastle United	17 Dec	Away	Left-half	Won 2-1	30,000
Newcastle United	24 Dec	Home	Left-half	Won 1-0	34,000
Sheffield United	26 Dec	Away	Left-half	Won 3-2	40,000
Sheffield United	27 Dec	Home	Left-half	Won 5-3	38,000
Burnley	31 Dec	Away	Left-half	Lost 1-2	20,000
Derby County	7 Jan	Home	Left-half	Won 6-2	41,000*
Luton Town	28 Jan	Home	Centre-half	Won 1-0	53,832*
Bolton Wanderers	22 Apr	Away	Centre-half	Lost 0-1	20,000
Oldham Athletic	6 May	Away	Centre-half	Lost 1-3	12,527

Season 1922/23

West Bromwich Albion	9 Sep	Home	Centre-half	Won 2-0	40,000
West Bromwich Albion	16 Sep	Away	Centre-half	Lost 0-3	39,576
Middlesbrough	23 Sep	Home	Centre-half	Drawn 2-2	27,000

Middlesbrough	30 Sep	Away	Centre-half	Drawn 2-2	25,000
Tottenham Hotspur	7 Oct	Home	Centre-half	Won 2-0	40,000
Tottenham Hotspur	14 Oct	Away	Centre-half	Won 2-1	50,000
Bolton Wanderers	21 Oct	Home	Centre-half	Won 2-0	27,000
Bolton Wanderers	28 Oct	Away	Centre-half	Lost 0-3	25,000
Oldham Athletic	4 Nov	Away	Centre-half	Won 2-0	12,464
Oldham Athletic	11 Nov	Home	Centre-half	Won 3-0	28,000
Liverpool	18 Nov	Away	Centre-half	Lost 0-3	30,000
Liverpool	25 Nov	Home	Centre-half	Lost 0-1	42,000
Sheffield United	2 Dec	Away	Centre-half	Drawn 1-1	18,000
Sheffield United	9 Dec	Home	Centre-half	Lost 0-1	20,000
Newcastle United	16 Dec	Home	Centre-half	Drawn 1-1	17,000
Newcastle United	23 Dec	Away	Centre-half	Drawn 0-0	30,000
Burnley	25 Dec	Away	Centre-half	Drawn 1-1	25,000
Burnley	26 Dec	Home	Centre-half	Won 3-1	50,000
Preston North End	30 Dec	Home	Centre-half	Won 1-0	30,000
Preston North End	6 Jan	Away	Centre-half	Lost 2-3	20,000
Blackburn Rovers	13 Jan	Home	Centre-half	Lost 0-1	47,000*
Nottingham Forest	20 Jan	Away	Centre-half	Lost 1-3	20,000
Manchester City	10 Feb	Away	Centre-half	Drawn 1-1	18,000
Stoke	17 Feb	Home	Centre-half	Won 6-0	30,000
Stoke	24 Feb	Away	Centre-half	Drawn 1-1	20,000
Huddersfield Town	10 Mar	Away	Centre-half	Won 5-3	15,000
Birmingham	17 Mar	Away	Centre-half	Lost 0-1	50,000
Birmingham	24 Mar	Home	Centre-half	Won 3-0	40,000
Chelsea	30 Mar	Home	Centre-half	Drawn 1-1	30,000
Arsenal	31 Mar	Away	Centre-half	Lost 0-2	45,000
Chelsea	2 Apr	Away	Centre-half	Drawn 1-1	30,000
Arsenal	7 Apr	Home	Centre-half	Drawn 1-1	18,000
Everton	14 Apr	Away	Centre-half	Lost 1-2	40,000
Everton	21 Apr	Home	Centre-half	Won 3-0	18,000
Sunderland	28 Apr	Away	Centre-half	Lost 0-2	10,000
Sunderland	5 May	Home	Centre-half	Won 1-0	20,000

Season 1923/24

Birmingham	5 Aug	Away	Centre-half	Lost 0-3	41,300
Manchester City	29 Aug	Home	Centre-half	Won 2-0	12,000
Birmingham	1 Sep	Home	Centre-half	Drawn 0-0	59,147
Manchester City	5 Sep	Away	Centre-half	Won 2-1	33,000
Chelsea	8 Sep	Away	Centre-half	Drawn 0-0	46,000
Everton	12 Sep	Home	Centre-half	Drawn 1-1	14,000

Preston North End	22 Sep	Away	Centre-half	Drawn 2-2	21,000
Preston North End	29 Sep	Home	Centre-half	Won 5-1	23,000
Burnley	6 Oct	Away	Centre-half	Won 2-1	17,000
Burnley	13 Oct	Home	Centre-half	Drawn 1-1	20,000
West Bromwich Albion	20 Oct	Away	Centre-half	Lost 0-1	42,096
West Bromwich Albion	27 Oct	Home	Centre-half	Won 4-0	52,550
Notts County	3 Nov	Home	Centre-half	Drawn 0-0	17,000
Notts County	10 Nov	Away	Centre-half	Won 1-0	12,000

A2: Court Exhibits List, Rex Vs Stagg

With thanks to National Archives.

1. Notice to quit
2. Neck tie
3. Box containing wads, shot, part of neck tie and shirt button
4. Gun
5. Part of cartridge case
6. Card
7. Card
8. Card
9. Card
10. Card
11. Bases of cartridge cases
12. Stoneware jar containing bag and cartridges
13. Sergeant Davenport's notebook
14. Gate
15. Photograph
16. Photograph
17. Photograph
18. Photograph
19. Plan of cottage
20. Plan of vicinity

Notes:

1. Each of these items was submitted by the prosecution. It is not known whether items are extant, item 1 being arguably the most important.
2. Items 2 and 3 would have been handed to the police by Dr Garman following post-mortem.
3. Item 5 would have been retrieved from the scene during subsequent investigation.
4. Items 6–9 were the 'distance' cards used by John Fearn during ballistic testing.
5. Item 11 was presumably retrieved from Stagg's parlour ash pan.
6. Item 12 was the spare cartridge store kept in Stagg's cottage.
7. The subjects of items 15–18 are unknown.

A3 North-Eastern-Born Aston Villa Players

The North-east has traditionally been an area from which Aston Villa has recruited heavily. Figures in parentheses indicate each player's total Football League and Football Association Cup first-team appearances for the club, including, where appropriate, any appearances as a substitute. My apologies if I have inadvertently omitted anyone. The list does not include wartime 'guest' players.

William Armstrong, Born High Spennymoor 1914. Signed from Darlington, 1939 [0].

Tommy Ball. Born Usworth, 1900. Signed from Felling Colliery, 1920 [77].

Tommy Barber. Born West Stanley, 1886. Signed from Bolton Wanderers, 1912 [68].

George Brown. Born Mickley, 1903. Signed from Huddersfield Town, 1929 [126].

Archie Campbell. Born Crook, 1904. Signed from Spennymoor United, 1922 [4].

Bob Chatt. Born Barnard Castle, 1870. Signed from Middlesbrough Ironopolis, 1893 [96].

James Clayton. Born Sunderland, 1910. Signed from Wolverhampton Wanderers, 1937 [11].

Roland Codling. Born Durham, 1979. Signed from Clapton Orient, 1906 [82].

George Cook. Born Evenwood, 1895. Signed from Huddersfield Town, 1927 [61].

Gordon Cowans. Born Durham City, 1958. Signed as an apprentice, 1974 [501].

Johnny Dixon. Born Hebburn-on-Tyne, 1923. Signed from Spennymoor United, 1946 [430].

Thomas Dodds. Born South Shields, 1918. Signed from North Shields, 1939 [1].

Albert Evans. Born Barnard Castle, 1874. Unattached when signed, 1896 [203].

Graham Fenton. Born Wallsend, 1974. Signed as a trainee, 1992 [34].

George Garratt. Born Byker, 1884. Signed from Crewe Alexandra, 1904 [17].

Colin H. Gibson. Born Normanby-on-Tees, 1923. Signed from Newcastle United, 1948 [167].

George Harkus MBE. Born Newcastle, 1898. Signed from Scotswood, 1921 [4].

John Hickman. Born Durham, 1901. Signed from Hartlepool United, 1927 [2].

Raymond Hogg. Born Lowick, 1929. Signed from Berwick Rangers, 1955 [21].

Tommy Jackson. Born Benwell, 1897. Signed from Durham University, 1919 [186].

Tommy Johnson. Born Newcastle upon Tyne 1971. Signed from Derby County, 1995 [47].

Albert Kerr. Born Lanchester, 1917. Signed from Medomsley Juniors, 1936. [29].

Billy Kirton. Born Newcastle upon Tyne, 1896. Signed from Leeds City, 1919 [261].

James Leach. Born Spennymoor, 1890. Signed from Spen Black and White, 1912 [76].

Alan Little. Born Horden, 1955. Signed as an apprentice, 1971 [3].

Brian Little. Born Hordern, 1953. Signed as an apprentice, 1969 [301].

John Neal. Born Silksworth, 1932. Signed from Swindon Town, 1959 [114].

Jim McConnon, Born Burnopfield, 1922. Signed from Rowlands Gill, 1939 [2].

John McLaverty. Born South Shields, 1892. Signed from Birtley Colliery, 1913 [2].

John Martin. Born Ashington, 1946. Signed as an apprentice, 1962 [1].

Tommy Mitchinson. Born Sunderland, 1943. Signed from Mansfield Town, 1967 [52].

Kevin Richardson. Born Newcastle, 1962. Signed from Real Sociedad, 1991 [180].

John Robson. Born Consett, 1950. Signed from Derby County, 1972 [176].

Joe Rutherford. Born Fatfield, 1914. Signed from Southport, 1939 [156].

Tommy Southren. Born Southwick, 1927. Signed from West Ham United, 1954 [72].

Ronnie Starling. Born Pelaw, 1909. Signed from Sheffield Wednesday, 1937 [99].

Clem' Stephenson. Born Seaton Delaval, 1891. Signed from Durham City, 1910 [216].

George T. Stephenson. Born Horton, 1900. Signed from Leeds City, 1919 [95].

George H. Stephenson. Born Stillington, 1908. Signed from Durham City, 1931 [4].

Jimmy Stephenson. Born Seaton Delaval, 1895. Signed from New Delaval Villa, 1913 [32].

Steve Stone. Born Gateshead, 1971. Signed from Nottingham Forest, 1999 [122].

Albert Surtees. Born Willington Quay, 1902. Signed from Preston Colliery, 1924 [11].

Martin Taylor. Born Annfield Plain, 1899. Signed from unknown club, 1920 [1].

Alan Thompson. Born Newcastle upon Tyne, 1973. Signed from Bolton Wanderers, 1998 [58].

Jack Thompson. Born Cramlington, 1900. Signed from Ashington, 1919 [28].

Tommy Thompson. Born Fencehouses, 1928. Signed from Newcastle United, 1950 [165].

Fred Turnbull. Born Wallsend-on-Tyne, 1946. Signed as a trialist, 1966 [183].

Ray Walker. Born North Shields, 1963. Signed as an apprentice, 1979 [19].

Charlie Wallace. Born Southwick, 1885. Signed from Crystal Palace, 1907 [349].

Steve Watson. Born North Shields, 1974. Signed from Newcastle United, 1998 [54].

James Welford. Born Barnard Castle, 1869. Signed from Birmingham St George, 1893 [83].

Andy Young. Born Darlington, 1896. Signed from Blyth Spartans, 1919 [26].

In addition, Joe Grierson ('Trainer', 1893–1914) was born in Leadgate in 1855 and joined Villa from Middlesbrough Ironopolis in 1893, while Tommy Cummings (manager, 1967–68] was born in Sunderland in 1928, joining from Mansfield Town in 1967.

References

I am indebted to a number of people who have kindly and enthusiastically carried out research on my behalf.

Newcastle United club historian Paul Joannou searched that club's archive to establish whether there was any record of Tommy Ball having worn black and white. Facsimile copies of *The Villa News and Record* published on 7 February 1920, 17 November 1923, 24 November 1923 and 24 January 1924 were forwarded by the former *News and Record* programme editor, and now Villa club historian, Rob Bishop. Information relating to working conditions in the Durham coal-mining industry was offered by Frank Nutter, volunteer at the Durham Mining Museum within Spennymoor Town Hall.

George Stagg's medal record while in the Warwickshire Regiment was provided courtesy of David Baynham, research assistant at the Warwickshire Fusiliers Museum, assisted by volunteer Ian Binnie. Stagg's Birmingham City Police employment record was researched by Corinne Brazier, subject matter expert at the West Midland Police Heritage Project. His Great War enlistment details and service record were provided by Ernie Pope, research and volunteer co-ordinator at the Highlanders Museum in Perth and his Army Pension Records were obtained via Fold3 at ancestry.co.uk.

Although I was unable to obtain closed records on Stagg's sojourn in Broadmoor, efforts to do so, which eventually resulted in information relating to his dates of admission and transfer, were vigorously undertaken on my behalf by Rosie Everitt, archivist at the Berkshire Record Office. Rebecca Jackson of the Staffordshire Record Office and Rory Powell of Sandwell Archive Service kindly offered advice on court locations. Court Deposition Papers and other key documents, including Ball's post-mortem and Hamblin Smith's judgement on Stagg, were provided courtesy of Paul Johnson, library manager at National Archives under Reference TNA: ASSI 6/59/1, while Oliver House, Superintendent of Special Collections at the Bodleian Library, University of Oxford, enthusiastically located John Sankey's personal diary for 1924.

My copy of M. Hamblin Smith's seminal work *The Psychology of the Criminal* was published by Jarrold and Sons in 1923, shortly before George Stagg came under his supervision.

References to research into witness behaviour were obtained via my completion of the Open University's Forensic Psychology module at futurelearn.com, July–August 2019.

Copies of original documents relating to Births, Deaths and Marriages (BDM) were provided by the General Record Office's ordering service at Gro.gov.uk.

Other BDM information, voluntarily recorded family history, electoral registers, trade directories, probate records, obituary notices, census returns, extracts from the 1939 Register, records of Stagg's hunger strike and ships passenger records, all of which are readily available within the public domain, were obtained variously at Ancestry.co.uk; Find My Past.co.uk; Genes Reunited.co.uk; My Heritage.com; Curiousfox.com and flickr.com.

Press reports were taken from online facsimile copies of newspapers via Britishnewspaperarchive.co.uk. These were, primarily:

The Aberdeen Press and Journal 13.11.1923/18.03.1924
The Belfast Telegraph 18.03.1924
The Birmingham Daily Gazette 7.4.1920 / 12, 14, 17, 19, 21, 22, 29.11.1923; 20.02.1924; 18.03.1924; 29.03.1924; 13.02.26.
The Coventry Evening Telegraph 13.11.1923
The Derby Daily Telegraph 21.11.1923
The Exeter and Plymouth Gazette 20.02.1924
The Illustrated Police News 22.11.1923
The Nottingham Evening Post 20.02.1924
The Portsmouth Evening News 20.12.1924
The Sheffield Daily Telegraph 13.11.1923/20.02.1924
The Staffordshire Advertiser 14, 22.11.1923/16, 23.02.1924
The Scotsman 19.02.1924/18.03.1924
The Westminster Gazette 19.03.1924

Books, periodicals, and online and newspaper articles consulted were:

Anon., *Move From Wardley to Aston Villa* (*The Northern Echo*, 08.02.2008)

Baxter. M., *Stechford, Ward End and Washwood Heath* (Stroud: Tempus Publishing Ltd, 2004)

Bishop. R., Holt. F., *Aston Villa. The Complete Record* (Derby: Derby Books Publishing Company, 2010)

Brunton. S., *The Forgotten Story of The Life and Death of Tommy Ball* (*The Guardian*, 17.12.2014)

Butler. B., *The Football League 1888–1988* (London: Macdonald Queen Anne Press, 1988)

Butler, D., Freeman. J., *British Political Facts* (London: McMillan & Co, 1963)

Cowan. M., *The Star Villa Player Shot Dead by Neighbour* (*The Birmingham Mail*, 06.05.2010)

Farrelly. J., Abbott. C., Russell. J., *Aston Villa. The First One Hundred and Fifty Years* (Sunbury: Legends Publishing, 2020)

Giles. J., *The Western Front Then and Now* (London: Then and Now Publishing, 1991)

Goodyear, D., Matthews, T., *Aston Villa. A Complete Record* (Derby: Breedon Books, 1988)

Harrison. D., *Salute to Snow Hill* (Birmingham: Barbryn Press Ltd, 1983)

Harvey, D., *Birmingham in the Age of the Tram* (Kettering: Silver Link, 2004)

Holmes. R., *Tommy: The British Soldier on the Western Front 1914–1918* (London: Harper Perennial, 2004)

Inglis. S., *Last Rites for the Holy Trinity* (*The Observer*, 14.05.2000)

Inglis. S., *Villa Park, 100 Years* (Warley: Sports Projects, 1997)

Jeeves. K., *Grizzly Tale of Tommy Ball* (The Football Adventurer, 25.05.2011)

Joslin, E.C., *British Orders, Decorations and Medals* (London: Spink and Son Limited, 1972)

Lester. P., *The Murder of Tommy Ball: An Aston Villa Tragedy* (Rubery: Protean Publications, 1996)

Matthews, T., *Aston Villa Who's Who 1874–1989* (Edinburgh: Mainstream Publishing Company, 1989)

Morris. P., *Aston Villa. The First Hundred Years* (Birmingham: Studio Press, 1960)

Page. S., *Pinnacle of The Perry Barr Pets* (Sheffield: Juma, 1997)

Pickford, W.M., *A Murder Mystery Interlude* (blogspot.com. The Goalmaker, 24.08.2007)

Price, V.J., *Aston Remembered* (Studley: Brewin Books, 1991)

Russell. J., More Tales From The Magnificent Meadow (*Heroes and Villains* Issue 241, Exact Editions, May 2019)

Spinks. D., *Aston Villa. A Portrait in Old Picture Postcards* (Market Drayton: SB Publications, 1991)

Spinks. D., *Aston Villa on Cigarette and Trade Cards* (Redditch: Supaprint, 1993)

Spinks. D., Murder Most Foul (*Heroes and Villains*, Exact Editions, August 1990)

Tisdale. H., Tate. M., *Aston Villa 2000* (London: SportsDays, 1999)

Todd, Selina., *Snakes and Ladders: The Great British Social Mobility Myth* (London: Chatto and Windus, 2021)

Twist. M., *Saltley, Duddeston and Nechells* (Stroud: Tempus Publishing Ltd, 2001)

Warner. P., *Army Life in the Nineties* (London: Country Life/ Hamlyn, 1975)

Wolfiewiseguy, *Tommy Ball – Death of a Footballer* (Blogspot. com, 5.10.2015)

The Villa News and Record of 31.10.2021 offered thumbnail sketches of the Great War service of former players.

The following online resources were essential reference points variously providing evidence in the forms of facsimiles of original documents, contemporary photographs, videos, extracts from printed works, informed comment based on contemporary evidence and folk memory:

a2psychologyedexcel.blogspot.com (for criminal behaviour)

Astonbrook-through-astonmanor.co.uk / bildargue.jimbo.com / Birminghamhistory.co.uk /Facebook.com / midland-ancestors. co.uk / visionofbritain.org.uk (for Birmingham folk memory and locality information)

Astonvillaplayerdatabase.com

avfchistory.co.uk

Bookdepository.com / Chessgames.com / chesshistory.com (for F R Gittins)

Capitalpunishmentuk.com /Cps.gov.uk / Oldbaileyonline. org / The free dictionary.com / Justice.gov.uk / Vcp.eubn. org / Genguide.co.uk / scholarlycommons.law.northwestern. edu / historyextra.com/Revolvy.com/parliament.uk/ capitalpunishment.uk.org/genguide.co.uk/Staffordshire.police. uk (variously for legal definitions, personalities, procedures, capital punishment and legal history)

Countrygunshop.co.uk / enfield-rifles.com / gunshot-eb.com / gunstar.co.uk /We Love Bolt Action at You Tube.com / Webley and Scott.com (for guns and ammunition)

deepdyve.com (for W Hamblin Smith obituary)

dmm.org.uk (for Ball family and pit villages]

englandfootballonline.com (for general football background)

Geni.com/ livesofthefirstworldwar.org.uk / gracesguide.co.uk / nicholsonmemorial.org.uk / Wikipedia.org (for Stafford jurors) henryboot.co.uk / Visitoruk.com (for First National Housing Trust and Perry Beeches estate)

legislation.gov /Westernfrontassociation.com (for military pension)

Longlongtrail.co.uk (for casualty clearance)

Mace archive.org (for an interview with Dr Milne shown on ATV Today, 26.02.1971)

Maps.nls.uk/os

MilitaryHistorySociety.com/Spartacus-educational.com (for military campaigns)

Nonleaguematters.co.uk / northernfootballalliance.co.uk (for Felling football)

Nursekey.com (for force feeding)

Taylorfrancis.com (for police pension)

The peerage.com (for Reginald Coventry)

Thepsychologist.bps.org.uk (for Broadmoor Hospital)

thisismoney.co.uk (for historical price comparisons)

The Football Adventurer.blogspot.com / Playupliverpool.com / Londonhearts.com / wmpickford.blogspot.co (for court hearing information)

Taxadvisers.org.uk / SweetandMaxwell.co.uk/British - Tax – Review / Howold.com / commercialcourt.London / Everipedia.org / prabook.com / worldcat.org (for Sir Sydney Rowlatt)

Time and date.com (for historical weather records)

Unlock.org.uk (for prisoner's bank accounts)

Wartimememoriesproject.com (for Seaforth Highlanders deployment)

wrighthassall.co.uk/api.parliament.uk (for tied cottages)

YouTube.com (for the video, The Murder of Tommy Ball, prepared and presented by Rob Bishop and Mat Kendrick, dated 11.11.2018)

About us

Acorns Children's Hospice provides care, support, fun and laughter for life limited and life threatened babies, children and young people and support for their families.

We provide care in our three hospices in Birmingham, the Black Country and the Three Counties, as well as in the family home and community. Our hospices provide a home from home environment where children can take part in a variety of fun and therapeutic activities, from arts and crafts sessions to hydrotherapy. Children visit Acorns for short breaks, end of life and emergency care, whilst providing families with a much needed break from caring round the clock.

We understand that family time is precious when a child's life is limited, and we support families in any way we can to create lasting memories. Acorns is here to help families feel equipped to cope at every stage of their child's life with our dedicated team offering psychological, emotional and practical support. In the past year we have cared for over 700 children and more than 9400 families, including those who are bereaved*. It costs around £10 million* every year to provide our services and we rely on the generosity of the public for the majority of this amount.

*All figures based on the year 1 April 2020 to 31 March 2021